The Social World of Batavia

In the seventeenth century, the Dutch established a trading base at the Indonesian site of Jacatra. What began as a minor colonial outpost under the name Batavia would become, over the next three centuries, the flourishing economic and political nucleus of the Dutch Asian Empire. In this study, Jean Gelman Taylor offers a comprehensive analysis of Batavia's extraordinary social world. With an emphasis on the Dutch-Eurasian ruling elite, she describes the marriage patterns, religious and social organizations, economic interests, and sexual roles that defined a distinctive colonial culture. Her original work—at once a vivid re-creation of a culture and a people, a case study in colonial society, and a telling look at the European experience in Asia—offers remarkable reading.

THE SOCIAL WORLD OF BATAVIA

European and Eurasian in Dutch Asia

Jean Gelman Taylor

THE UNIVERSITY OF WISCONSIN PRESS

Published 1983

The University of Wisconsin Press
114 North Murray Street
Madison, Wisconsin 53715

The University of Wisconsin Press, Ltd.
1 Gower Street
London WC1E 6HA, England

First printing

Printed in the United States of America

For LC CIP information see the colophon

ISBN 0–299–09470–7

For my Father

who cherished a love for learning

Contents

Illustrations

Maps

Acknowledgments

This study could not have been made without help from many quarters. No one can write on Indonesia's colonial history without acknowledging an immense debt to the Dutch archivists and historians, and in particular to the late Drs. F. de Haan and J. A. van der Chijs. Nor can I begin without acknowledging the help of Dr. John R. W. Smail of the University of Wisconsin–Madison, who guided me over a long period of research and writing. He was a most careful critic, and his stimulating perspective and relish for the English language cannot be forgotten. I owe him the special debt of student to mentor.

During my student days at Wisconsin, Mr. John Little and Mr. Mathew Charles elucidated many Dutch terms for me, while Dr. Bana Kartasasmita and Mr. Toenggoel Siagian guided me in Indonesian and encouraged my interest in "Old Batavia." My thanks go to Dr. Bana also for assistance in preparing the photographs which accompany the text. I would like to thank Ms. Dorothée Buur, Reference Librarian of the Koninklijk Instituut voor Taal-, Land- en Volkenkunde in Leiden, for her many kindnesses during my stay in the Netherlands. The staff of the Instituut library were particularly helpful to me. I thank, too, Professor Rob Nieuwenhuys and Dr. M. A. P. Meilink-Roelofsz, who set aside time to advise me in my studies; also Professors Paul W. Van der Veur and William Frederick of Ohio University, Professor Robert Frykenberg of the University of Wisconsin, and Mr. Giok-Po Oey of Cornell University Libraries. I wish particularly to acknowledge Dr. Robert Clodius, Ms. Janet Franke, and the late Mrs. Liesl Tarkow of the University of Wisconsin Indonesian Higher Education Projects, for whom it was a privilege to work.

The University of Wisconsin Graduate School awarded me a fellowship and travel grant that allowed me to study in the Netherlands, for which I am properly grateful. I wish to thank also the staff of the University of Wisconsin Press, and particularly Ms. Mary Maraniss, for encouraging me to bring this text to print.

And finally to my family: to my late father, the Reverend George Stewart Taylor, to my mother, Louisa Jean Taylor, and to my husband, Howard Gelman, my gratitude and sense of obligation.

Guide to the Text

For ease of reading, common English variants are used in the text for some place names in Europe and in Asia. Thus the English form The Hague is employed, rather than the Dutch 's-Gravenhage, and the Celebes rather than the Indonesian Sulawesi. Other place names in the Indonesian archipelago appear in standard Indonesian spelling. Sri Langka is referred to in the text by the name the Dutch knew, Ceylon. The capital of Indonesia, Jakarta, is represented as Batavia when it was a Dutch city and as Jacatra for the Sundanese town of the pre-1619 period. Place names cited in the text are located on maps grouped together following the text.

The spelling of personal names has not been altered. An asterisk beside a surname indicates that the family tree is given in appendix 1. Abbreviations are few: *Mr.* preceding a name represents the Dutch abbreviation of *Meester in de Rechten* and is the lawyer's title; *Drs.* represents *Doctorandus* and is an academic title; *VOC* stands for *Verenigde Oost-Indische Compagnie* or United East Indies Company. Foreign terms are translated into English when they first appear in the text. Those used several times are listed in the glossary.

Introduction

This study describes a colonial society that was formed in Dutch settlements on the coasts of Asia and that evolved for a brief period into a ruling caste in the Indonesian archipelago. It surveys aspects of colonial life that are seldom treated in the general histories of Indonesia, where greater attention is given the political and economic relations between Dutch and Indonesian. The aim is to complement these histories by showing a further dimension of Dutch colonial experience in Asia. Colonial society is viewed here as an autonomous entity between the Muslim Indonesian world and Netherlands society, which at the beginning of our period was Calvinist and newly independent of Roman Catholic Spain. The book therefore does not discuss Netherlands society, the economic history of the East Indies Company, or relations between Dutch and Asian rulers; nor does it treat the histories of those Asian states that lay outside the reach of the Dutch, or give ethnographic data on Indonesian peoples and cultures. Rather, it concentrates on the interaction between special groups of Asians and Europeans from which a distinctive culture evolved.

At first glance, the book may seem like an old-fashioned history of Dutch colonial society in the East, for the names of governors-general and of senior merchants of the Netherlands East Indies Company are sprinkled through its pages. Such characters as these have yielded place in recent histories to local peoples, the peasantry and elites who were often depicted by earlier historians as foils to the heroes of a European history staged in Asia. Since publication of essays by J. C. van Leur and J. R. W. Smail,[1] Western historians of Indonesia have concerned themselves with questions of perspective, and now write more than formerly from the point of view of Indonesian peoples. This reorientation in historical thinking has opened up new subjects of study and thereby expanded our knowledge of Indonesia. It has led to a revision of the former characterization of the colonial past as ''three hundred and fifty years of Dutch rule in Indonesia'' by looking for evidence of the extent and nature of that rule in the local histories of Indonesia's ethnic groups. Still, the nature of Dutch society in Indonesia remains somewhat obscure. In studying that society as it developed principally in the colonial capital, Batavia, my book returns to an old subject but from a contemporary point of view, tempered by the perspectives of van Leur and Smail. Using such an approach, the history of Europeans in Indonesia sheds light not on conquest but on Dutch social relations with Asians and on the influence of Asia-born women on the colonial ruling elite.

In the older histories but passing mention was made of the social characteristics of the Dutch administrative and trading centers established on the fringes of Asian states in the seventeenth century. Nepotism was allegedly rampant in the seventeenth and eighteenth centuries, but actual family relationships were neither detailed nor explained. More recently, Holden Furber and M. A. P. Meilink-Roelofsz have pointed to the need for studying Company personnel in order to enlarge our understanding of the Dutch overseas, and F. Lequin, writing in 1979, signalled the "importance and possible influence of family-relations" as an interesting variable to be anticipated from his analysis of data on Company employees in Bengal in the eighteenth century.[2] In this book I have taken these family relationships as an organizing center for study of Dutch colonial society. Whilst this is a preliminary study based on published sources, it can be shown that there developed an Indies clan system, one in which descent may be traced through locally born women of mixed Asian and European ancestry, and through which Dutch male immigrants forged alliances among themselves for control of positions of power and wealth in the Company. My return to the governors-general, then, serves to inject into the story of the Dutch overseas the role of Asians in shaping colonial culture.

The presence or absence of Europe-born women in the Dutch Asian settlements is one measure of the nature of Dutch social life overseas; yet to date, the subject of women has scarcely been examined in the general histories, and information on Dutch female emigrants rarely appears in published documents. There are, furthermore, few reliable figures for the number of women having European status in many places of Dutch settlement before this century. Late-nineteenth- and twentieth-century heirs to Dutch colonial culture have left ample record of it in memoirs, novels, newspapers, paintings, and photographic collections, but Asian, European, and Eurasian women of East Indies Company times have left scanty evidence of their contribution to the society of the settlements. The sources I have used for such information are genealogical data, legal decrees, inscriptions on tombstone and memorial plate, travelers' narratives, and albums of old paintings, those available in the United States and those which I could consult during a brief visit to the Netherlands. During my period of study, the Batavian church registers of baptisms, marriages, and deaths that have been acquired by the Genealogical Society of Utah were not catalogued and available to the general public for research. When they are available and combined with study of the personnel records stored in the Royal Netherlands Archives in The Hague, these church registers, which date from 1619, should provide valuable insight into the composition at all social levels of households in the chief Dutch settlement in Asia. The nature of the material that I could consult necessarily limited my study to the Dutch elite, and the treatment of elite women, whether European, Eurasian, or Asian, is episodic and selective here; but my findings should give an indication of the possibilities for further research in this field.

The duration and intensity of contact between Europeans and Asians varied considerably in the colonies of the former Western imperial powers. The Dutch case permits study of that interaction over a long period of time. Throughout this history, colonial culture evolved in response to two key related conditions: the changing perception of the settlements' distance from Europe and the growing proportion, over time, of women among the immigrants from Europe. When the political authority of the Netherlands seemed most remote and Asia-born women dominated the female population of the settlements, there grew up a society with interests of its own and a singular family system and network of clans whose development is a major theme of the first part of my study. In the second half of the nineteenth century, colonial society grew away from these roots in the East Indies Company settlements. Now there developed a greater distinction between the European and Eurasian components of colonial society. The Europeans, who monopolized the senior levels of government, did not see themselves as the elite of an autonomous society, but tended to retain their identity as immigrants and their dependence on Europe, whilst the Eurasians were divorced from the symbols of status of the colonial elite.

Indonesian societies were affected by the colonial culture of the Dutch in the nineteenth century, too, for it spread with the expansion of Dutch territorial power in the archipelago. Colonial culture, which combined parts of the cultural legacies of European and Asian, was the medium through which Dutch and Indonesian came to know each other. The epilogue to this book suggests directions for further research into relations between the two in the period before Indonesian nationalism brought an end to Netherlands rule and before remnants of the old colonial society were absorbed within a new Indonesian order.

In this book I have used the word *Mestizo* throughout for persons of mixed Asian and European ancestry and for the culture that grew up in the Dutch settlements in Asia from the meeting of the two. *Mestizo* (feminine *Mestiza*) was one of the terms employed by the Dutch in the seventeenth and eighteenth centuries to describe people of mixed birth. As used here, it signifies Eurasian, but without the old Dutch distinction as to degree of proximity to a white male. The term *Mestizo* characterizes a culture made up of many influences, extending beyond the Dutch and Indonesian. It underlines the fact that the migrants on Dutch ships represented many states in Europe and that the local peoples amongst whom they lived included Indians, Japanese, Indonesians of all sorts, and people descended from an earlier meeting of East and West, from unions between Asians and the Portuguese.

For the purposes of my work, I use *Indonesia* and *Indonesian* in the geographic sense, for there existed, in the period under examination, no nation-state and no archipelago-wide concept of Indonesian identity. *India* and *Indian* are similarly geographic expressions in this text and period. I use *Netherlands East Indies* for those parts of today's nation-state of Indonesia then under direct Dutch rule. *Indiesman* denotes a European who partook of Mestizo culture in marriage practice, habit, and loyalty. *European* here refers to a person born in Europe. The term *European community* is used in the legal sense and could include, as will be explained, persons born in Europe or Asia and certain persons of mixed, Eurasian ancestry. *Creole* is used to mean a person born in Asia of Europe-born mother and father.

The focus for my study of Mestizo culture is Batavia, the chief city of the Dutch, one that within years of its founding dominated the Asia trade and the Indonesian archipelago. In order to explain the nature of colonial society, however, it is necessary from time to time to move out of Batavia and even the archipelago, for Company officials and their families moved between the settlements subsidiary to Holland's Asian capital. The framework for the study of Dutch colonial society is greater than Indonesia, then, but it is also less than Indonesia, for Mestizo culture had not spread into all parts of the archipelago before war and revolution in the twentieth century ended Dutch rule. The redefinition of the Netherlands Asian Empire early in the nineteenth century itself made its mark on the development of colonial culture, since the actors were now exclusively Indonesian and European, and since it coincided with a change in the type of authority exercised by Holland and in the composition of the immigrant group from Europe.

The principal trading settlements outside the archipelago that provide this broad framework for the first part of the study were on the Malabar and Coromandel Coasts of India, at Bengal and Surat, at Malacca, on Taiwan, and on Ceylon, with the chief settlement at Colombo after Dutch conquest of the Portuguese in 1656. Dutch merchants and soldiers numbered in the hundreds in some of these trading posts, whereas other settlements, such as Hirado and later Deshima in Japan, had at any one time only tens of East Indies Company employees. Most of these trading posts were planted between the years 1638 and 1663, when the Dutch were engaged in expelling the Portuguese from the Asian trade. Within the archipelago itself the same process of establishing Dutch power began with attacks on the Portuguese at Ambon (1605) and on the Spanish in the Ternate-Tidore islands.

The Indonesian world which the Dutch came to know in the seventeenth century was the zone that comprehended the port cities on Java's north coast, the southern arm of the Celebes, and the spice islands further to the east, with highly mobile traders living in wards in the ports according to their areas of origin. The Dutch made contact, too, with the agriculture-based kingdom of Mataram, whose court was in Central Java. Traders from many parts of Asia exchanged

Indonesian luxury goods for textiles, porcelain, coins, and medicinal products from China, India, and the Arab world, and for the rice which Mataram's rulers collected from a settled, homogeneous peasantry controlled through a bureaucracy of appointed officials and fiefholders. Rulers of the ports were Muslim, as were rulers of Mataram, but the court life of the latter was deeply influenced by the Hindu-Buddhist culture of earlier generations of Brahmanic religious specialists. In the early seventeenth century when the Dutch first arrived in Indonesian waters, Mataram was attempting to enforce actual rather than nominal suzerainty over sultanates on the north coast of Java and beyond.

In the course of establishing trading settlements, the Dutch became the dominant naval power in the Indonesian archipelago. Their Asian trade was organized through the United East Indies Company (Verenigde Oost-Indische Compagnie, referred to frequently here by the Dutch initials VOC). It had received from the Netherlands States-General in 1602 an exclusive charter for trade and enforcement of Dutch interests against competitors. Since the East Indies Company was a commercial as well as a governing agent in Asia, its business was conducted by a hierarchy of officials called merchants, with headquarters in Batavia after 1619.

The Company ended in bankruptcy late in the eighteenth century. By that time, however, its Asian empire had ceased to consist of the network of trading settlements, and its navy had yielded control of the inter-Asian trade to the English East India Company. The Dutch company, instead, had acquired territorial power through a long process of intervention in local dynastic disputes and wars between Indonesian states. Increasingly, trade goods for the Company's European markets were acquired as tribute from the Indonesian peoples under its rule, rather than through commerce.

At the time of the VOC's financial collapse, its territorial power was limited largely to Java, but under rule from the Netherlands through the ministry of colonies in the nineteenth century, Dutch territorial power slowly expanded into the hinterlands of the coast settlements in the archipelago. In the nineteenth century, the agent of Dutch power was the civil servant rather than the VOC merchant, but the colonial capital remained Batavia.

The origins of Dutch colonial society and culture in Indonesia lie, then, in the Asian trading settlements of the East Indies Company. Colonial society's development can be traced with greatest continuity in the chief of these settlements, Batavia, which was built over the sixteenth-century port, Jacatra, in whose memory the capital of today's Republic of Indonesia is named. In addition to continuity of settlement, there are three other reasons for focusing on Batavia for a study of the development of colonial society: Batavia's population, Asian as well as European, was imported; this population developed in a degree of isolation from the homelands of its original, imported peoples, cut off from the rest of Java by high city walls and by jungle; and Batavia was to its European community a world in itself, with interests quite distinct from those of the VOC in Holland. Concentration on the capital of Dutch Asia allows comprehension of the Dutch in Indonesia on their own terms rather than as the corrupt despots and smugglers of some Dutch texts, or the imperialists of the Indonesian. It is to the early history of this settlement that we now turn to study the formation of Dutch society and culture in Asia.

The Social World of Batavia

1

Origins of the City of Batavia

POPULATION

WHEN THE DUTCH NAVIGATOR Cornelis Houtman first put in at Jacatra on 13 November 1596, the town was a minor port lying across the mouth of the Ciliwung River on the northwest coast of Java. Its inhabitants, principally members of the Sundanese ethnic group and numbering several thousands, lived within a bamboo enclosure; there was a small settlement of Chinese traders and arrack brewers outside the wall on the north side. Jacatra was a vassal of Bantam, which was at the time a major port in the pepper trade and one of the sultanates defying claims by the Central Javanese kingdom of Mataram to suzerainty over the entire island.

The Dutch were the first Europeans to stop at Jacatra. Portuguese traders never settled there. The town's chief harbor master spoke Portuguese, however, which illustrates how that tongue had established itself as a major language of international commerce in the markets of Asia. From 1596 to 1610 Dutch ships called at Jacatra for provisions. In the latter year a contract was signed between the town's ruler, Wijaya Krama, and Jacques l'Hermite, agent for the Netherlands East Indies Company, giving the Dutch land in the Chinese quarter and permission to build a stone house within a walled compound.[1]

The first years at Jacatra passed peaceably enough. Towards the end of 1618, however, agents of England's East India Trading Company were also assigned land and privileges in Jacatra, and Jan Pieterszoon Coen, then second-in-command for the Dutch Company in Asia, determined to establish supremacy over the town. He would make it a rendezvous for shipping, the chief entrepôt for Dutch warehouses, and the seat of Dutch government in the East. The Company's directors had been urging this course since their first appointment of a governor-general nine years earlier. Late in 1618, then, Coen withdrew to the Moluccas to assemble a fleet that was to destroy the Jacatrans and Bantammers and their English allies.

On 23 December 1618, while the Dutch compound at Jacatra was under siege from the groups leagued against the VOC, a roll call had been taken by senior merchant Pieter van den Broeck of all residing within its walls. Already

3

the Dutch were showing characteristics that were to be enduring features of their settlements in Asia and for which they had no precedent in their native city-states in the Netherlands: they were owners of slaves and took concubines from among the local women. Thus those answering to the roll call, some 350 in all, were found to include both free and slave Asians, as well as European merchants, settlers, women, and soldiers.[2] These were the key elements of colonial society throughout Company times. They will be reviewed here in the categories originally assigned to them within the Company's system of governance.

Principal among the inhabitants of the beleaguered Jacatra settlement and in all the Dutch settlements in Asia was the group known as merchants. They derived their authority from the central board of directors of the VOC, whose policy decisions, taken at their twice-yearly meetings in Holland, were binding on all their representatives in the East. The six commercial chambers which composed the East Indies Company outfitted their own ships and recruited their own personnel for service in Asia. But appointment of the chief of these, the governor-general, his second-in-command the director-general of trade, and the councillors of the Indies—who together made up the supreme government of the Dutch in Asia—was made by the directors.

The governor-general and his Council were required to report annually to the Company's directors and to submit for their approval all appointments, regulations, and edicts enacted locally. In the East, however, in the VOC centuries, when the interval between reporting decisions taken and receipt of confirmation or disallowance could be as long as thirty months, the governor-general and his colleagues on the Council held near-absolute powers over the inhabitants of Dutch settlements.

In the first years of settlement the most senior officials were sent out directly from Holland to conduct the Company's business. But soon they were chosen also from among men with years of experience in Asia who were promoted locally, although such promotion always required confirmation from the Europe-based directors. Just below this group of senior officials were the merchants in three descending ranks: senior merchant, merchant, and junior merchant. A trading post might be headed by a man with rank of senior merchant or governor, according to its size and importance in the Company's Asian empire. Governors were named councillors extraordinary of the Indies.

All Company officials in the East were subordinate to the hierarchy at Batavia, as Jacatra was renamed following Coen's destruction of the town. It was from Batavia that appointments to the subsidiary settlements were made and general orders issued, and it was to Batavia that officials looked for transfer and promotion. All senior boards of the VOC in Asia were located in Batavia:

4

the governing Council of the Indies, the supreme court, the chief bookkeeper's office, and warehouses.

If we now look at the civilian arm of the Dutch East Indies Company in Asia from the bottom up, we find at the lowest level copyists and clerks. In the early years of Batavia they were quartered at the Castle that replaced the original Dutch compound. They ate at a common table, for it was as a bachelors' society that the settlement was first run. Their hours were long and exacting, taking no more account of the climate than of the food they ate or of the heavy woollen clothing they clung to.

In theory, a clerk possessed of diligence and wit could move up the ranks of the Company to assistant and then bookkeeper, and by degrees to junior merchant and then merchant. He could next expect to act as administrator of one of the Company's warehouses or be sent to head one of the other settlements. Later he could be raised to governor of one of the more important settlements such as Ambon or Malacca. With good health and luck the former clerk could then be transferred back to Batavia as councillor and eventually even become governor-general. In fact some did. Governors-General Hendrik Zwaardecroon, Jacob Mossel, Johannes Thedens, Abraham Patras, and Reynier de Klerk, in the eighteenth century, started as either ship's boy or soldier, switching to the civilian, clerical service when they arrived in Batavia. Governor-General Antonio van Diemen took this route in the first half of the seventeenth century, closer to the period we are discussing.

Those so succeeding were few in number. Death took a great many men within years of their leaving Holland, and patronage and connections also played their part in a man's rise. Mattheus de Haan, for instance, who became governor-general in 1725, spent twenty-four years in climbing from assistant to senior merchant and fifty-three years altogether in reaching highest office. Gustaaf Willem van Imhoff, on the other hand, rose through the ranks of junior to merchant and then senior merchant in only four years, and was installed as governor-general after just fifteen years of service. His promotions were accelerated by his powerful connections with the Company's directors in Amsterdam.

Also influencing a man's climb in the hierarchy was his nationality. Many states in Europe were represented among the Company's employees, but it was only the Dutch who held the highest posts. Exceptions to this rule were few: a couple of Germans, in Thedens and van Imhoff; a descendant of French Huguenots, in Patras; a Eurasian, in Dirk van Cloon, for instance. A man's religion also influenced his career. Civilians were required to be of the Reformed faith, although even in the seventeenth century a man like Governor-General Joan Maetsuyker, who was rumored to be a Roman Catholic, could reach the top. It was not until the middle of the following century, however, that a governor-general could afford openly to display allegiance to a Protestant denomination other than the Dutch Reformed.

Civilians signed renewable contracts committing them to five years of service. Coen, when governor-general, constantly complained to the directors of incompetence in men sent out and on occasion returned them to the Netherlands in disgrace, but others who signed contracts renewed them again and again, and some chose to remain as free townsmen and settle permanently in Indonesia. As time went on, the consequence which senior officials had enjoyed while in office compelled recognition after their retirement, and they continued to take precedence over lesser men in public ceremonies.

For some, the confines of Batavia were the confines of the world. Others had more varied careers, moving between the secondary settlements, accompanying embassies to China and Japan, journeying into the interior of Java to the Mataram court, or following VOC armies. In whatever position, the merchant group stood at the apex of European communities in the Asian settlements, and they remained, throughout the VOC era, superior in rank, authority, and social distinction to the captains of the Company's army and navy. A few among this merchant group were also men of learning, and recorded in prose or verse the momentous events in which they took part, or dedicated themselves to translating the Bible into Asian tongues. The history of their intellectual pursuits and growing knowledge of the world in which they found themselves will unfold with the narration of the growth of colonial settlement. Throughout the VOC era, however, while dominating colonial life in the East politically and setting social standards for all the Company's subjects, the merchant group constituted but a fraction of the populations of Batavia and the subsidiary settlements. More numerous among the European group were the soldiers of the VOC army.

Approximately seventy of those responding to senior merchant van den Broeck's 1618 roll call in the Jacatra compound were in fact soldiers. They were not all Dutch, if we are to judge from figures C. R. Boxer gives for the year 1622.[3] The Batavia garrison was then 143 strong and 77, or half, were Germans, French, Scots, English, Danes, Flemings, and Walloons. The presence of other nationalities than Dutch was to be a constant feature of the Indies army. The Norwegian Frederik Andersen Bolling, who signed up with the Dutch Company's army in 1669, for instance, explains daily brawls among soldiers as arising because "there were so many different nationals," and another foreigner in the VOC army, Johann Gottlieb Worms, says that in 1710 there were only ten Dutchmen in all Batavia's militia.[4] Clearly it was not a distinctively Dutch culture that was transmitted in contacts with local people. This fact partly explains why Dutch was not naturally used as the language of Company settlements.

Seventeenth-century Europe was a battleground for politics and religion.

6

Many of those signing the five-year bond of service as Company soldiers were displaced persons and the destitute. They were often in poor health before they undertook the sea journey to Batavia. In the seventeenth century the voyage could last as long as ten months. Confined quarters and spoiling food further undermined the soldiers' health.

We have descriptions of conditions aboard the East Indiamen from Nicolaus de Graaff, who in the course of his long life and many years at sea made five journeys to Indonesia. As ship's surgeon he was in an excellent position to observe the fevers that struck passengers and crew as they neared the equator. De Graaff first saw Batavia on 10 September, 1640 after a voyage lasting eight months and four days. Eighty of the 300 leaving Holland had died. "It was as if the plague was in the very Ship," de Graaff later recalled, "and the men were tormented and half-crazed. Some of them had to be tied to their Bunks. . . . Teeth simply fell out of the mouths of many because of Scurvy, and their gums were so swollen, blackened and rotted that we had to cut and wash away the flesh every day. Many of our Crew also had serious, cancerous ulcerations."[5] Many died within months of setting foot on shore.

It has been common to suppose that the Company's soldiers were men of low character in addition to being poorly educated and without resources. Such a view starts principally with Coen. Writing to the directors in 1628, he complained of the soldiers' laziness, stupidity, and smutty language.[6] Some recruits were orphaned boys, sent by the charity houses of Dutch towns on ten-year bonds and at a few guilders a month. But others were men of education and standing in their communities. These, however, were soon transferred to the civilian arm of the Company's service and rose through the ranks as bookkeepers and merchants.

Of the ordinary soldier we catch only glimpses, and then from sentences passed by the supreme court that was established in Batavia in 1617. The most common crimes were insubordination, blasphemy, brawling, and drunkenness, and punishments included branding, labor on the chain gang, and execution. More than a century passes before a soldier's voice is heard, and then it is through letters begging release from the contract and repatriation.[7]

The common soldier also makes his appearance in records the Batavia church kept of baptisms, communicant membership, and weddings. In pages of the Marriage Register reproduced in E. C. Godée Molsbergen's illustrated history of the Dutch East Indies Company, one can still read the entry for 10 February 1630. On that day Claes Jacobsz. of Gouda, soldier, married Wybrecht Jansd. of Amsterdam, widow of one Jan IJsbrantsz. Another entry states that in 1622 Abraham Strycker, "captain of this place," married Aeltjen Lubberts of Amsterdam, who had reached Batavia on the ship *Heusden*.[8]

It will be noted that both Strycker and Jacobsz. married women who had emigrated from Holland, though that is not the usual image we have of Batav-

7

ian life in the early seventeenth century. Few Dutchwomen migrated before the opening of the Suez Canal (in 1869), with the result that ordinary soldiers usually took local women as their partners. It became common in ballads to celebrate the pleasures of wine, "black women," and the walks of Batavia. The hostility and contempt for Asian women that are such striking features of some ballads, however, may also reflect the ordinary soldier's point of view. Take, for instance, these verses from "Farewell to Batavia":

> I give to you Batavia
> As I depart for my Fatherland.
> There lives my soul, my joy, my heart and life
> On Netherlands' sweet strand.
> India, you may parade your harlots.
> Those black, lewd cattle never shall
> Lead me from out the citadel of virtue
> However beguilingly they eye me.[9]

Soldiers were always the largest European component in Dutch settlements in Indonesia. From sheer numbers, theirs was the group to have most contact with local peoples, and this mainly through their liaisons with Asian women. But since there were few among them possessed of an education, there is none to tell us of the exact nature of relations struck between soldiers of the Honorable Company and Asians. One can only conjecture that little in the way of European civilization was transmitted. Bereft of formal education, stemming from the deprived of Europe, soldiers could not pass on a typically Dutch bourgeois culture to their wives, mistresses, or children.

Few of these children grew to adulthood counting themselves as part of the European group. A handful might find their way to the Company's poorhouse or orphanage. The majority, it must be assumed, were abandoned by the father through either his death, his desertion of the mother, or his escape to the Netherlands.[10] Such children grew up in the mother's ethnic ward of the city or perhaps eked out an existence in one of the Christian Indonesian quarters. There the boys became candidates for companies of militia formed as early as 1622 for night watch duty and fire prevention and as auxiliaries in the Company's campaigns. The girls were brides for new generations of soldiers and men of that mixed group designated variously by the Dutch as *Mardijkers* (free[d]men) and Christian Natives (to be introduced in the next chapter).

It is unlikely that changes in living patterns—in food, entertainment, vocabulary, and so forth—which European soldiers acquired through their Asian wives and mistresses had much influence beyond the barracks. The social gap between them and civilians stretched wide, particularly after 1650 when the governor-general no longer felt beholden to call army officers to his table. Until that time it had been customary for governors-general to give dinners to officers departing for battle, captains of the return fleet, and envoys to the courts of Asia.

Few soldiers can have achieved the promise held out in F. G. Drieduym's song, written around 1670, that "if everything works out right / You can become a lord there."[11] But some men did make fortunes in Asia, causing a number of their fellow soldiers and merchants to stay on in Indonesia as "free townspeople" after their contracts had expired.

We first hear of townspeople in 1616 stationed in the eastern part of the archipelago, and two years later as part of the group under siege in the Jacatra settlement. The terms under which they settled are described in a report Coen sent the VOC's directors in 1616: "To promote the Company's business and acting upon Your Excellencies' resolution, we have approved the request for a discharge from the Company's service of various persons who have served their time, provided they make their residence in the Moluccas, Ambon, or Banda, and we have granted them permission to sail yachts, junks or other small craft between these islands with cargoes of rice and other provisions and confections, but they may not trade in clothing, silk or silken garments."[12]

Settlement in Indonesia upon expiration of one's bond, or as a migrant, required written permission. In Holland this was sought from one of the member chambers of the VOC, but in Indonesia application had to be made to the highest-ranking merchant. The new burgher had to swear an oath of loyalty and obedience to the Company's laws before the aldermen's council.[13] Burghers also vowed to engage only in such business as the directors pleased. In time the list of places in which free townspeople might lawfully reside was expanded, with most choosing Batavia or settlements in Ceylon. They were liable to military duty in defense of the Company's possessions, and they might not marry or repatriate without written permission. Furthermore, for actions judged troublesome, burghers could be forcibly repatriated, reduced to soldiers' ranks, or placed before the mast.

Coen often complained of the behavior of free citizens. Governor-General Cornelis van der Lijn was another. His complaint, made in a letter to the VOC directors, affords us a glimpse of Batavia at mid-century: "While Batavia is progressing daily in trade within its walls, as well as in agriculture outside them, due to the assembly of many nations within and to the Chinese who cultivate the fields round about, the Dutch burghers apparently have little interest in any of it. All they want is to grab riches in the easiest possible manner so they can fritter them away in the Netherlands, instead of committing themselves for a while to stabilize Batavia."[14]

The circumstances were these. Free townspeople found little scope to earn a livelihood. Most land around Batavia was already owned by senior Company

9

officials and leased to Chinese sugar cultivators,[15] while in commerce few legitimate areas were open to private trade and "Heathens and Moors" were favored over free settlers. These complaints and others the burghers set out in a letter to the Company's directors on 10 January 1650. This was one of the rare occasions when they spoke out as a group. The directors were not sympathetic, but renewed the obligation of free townspeople to submit to Company rules and authorized the governor-general to dispatch back to the Netherlands any "disturbers of the general order in the East Indies, without having to give any reason other than maintaining the well-being and authority of the Indies government."[16]

Some burghers profited nevertheless. They might be appointed vice-president of the city aldermen or captain of the militia, the two highest offices to which a burgher could aspire in all the long history of Company rule. The aldermen's council, composed of leading free townsmen, had been formed in Batavia as early as 1620, signaling the city's rapid growth and the need for an authority to collect taxes, maintain the canals, organize fire prevention, and the like. Unlike the case in Holland's municipalities, the town hall where aldermen convened was never the center of Batavia's civic life. Power lay always in the Castle, which housed the governor-general and councillors of the Indies. A councillor of the Indies always acted as president of the aldermen and attended their meetings. All decisions of the town council had to be approved by the governor-general. Aldermen usually held their post for two years, and new members were sworn in each year on May 30, the anniversary of Coen's victory at Jacatra in 1619 and most important of the public holidays celebrated in Batavia.

Militia officers were chosen in the week following the May 30 festivities. The companies they commanded were composed of adult males with the status of free townsmen. In the earliest days of settlement, companies of European burghers were called to join in the defense of VOC possessions and their very lives—for example, during the siege of Batavia by Mataram troops in 1628. Dipping into instructions from that year one reads that "Bartholomeus Cunst, burgher of this town, shall take several musketeers to the new town ramparts near the Gelderlandt redoubt in order to defend the bulwarks and bridges."[17] Later, when the Dutch were well entrenched, burghers' military duties became largely ceremonial and the numbers under arms shrank.

Population estimates are extraordinarily difficult to make for the entire Company period, as there were no regular head counts of municipal residents. Coen says there were 2,000 in Batavia in 1620, and another source has it that the city's inhabitants totalled 8,000 just four years later.[18] Throughout the VOC period the proportion of burghers to Company employees was small, and they were always few in number. Figures from 1673, for instance, give 340 of the total population of 7,286 living outside the walls of Batavia as adult Dutch burghers.[19] In part, the small numbers can be explained by the high mortality rates and by the failure of the Company to retain burghers who at first applied to stay. However, the size of the free community in the seventeenth century depended primarily on the colonization policies favored by the Company's directors.

Their scheme was simple, if ambitious. An absolute monopoly on trade in the Indonesian archipelago was to be enforced by Dutch naval might. Spices and other goods would be delivered to the Company warehouses at fixed prices under agreements with local rulers or arrangements with Dutch lessors of land, as in Banda. All goods would be exported on Company ships to Europe or to other ports and factories in Asia and the Middle East. To avoid private trading, strict controls would be placed on the number of persons sent from Holland, while the baggage of those repatriating would be regulated for amount and contents. It was soon found, however, that clerks, merchants, soldiers, and seamen needed the services of other specialists, and already on Governor-General Pieter Both's fleet, which reached Indonesia in 1610, there were shipwrights, carpenters, sailmakers, and other artisans.

The directors had no vision of planting colonies of Dutch settlers around the world. In their earliest instructions they spoke only of the need for a central "rendez-vous" in Indonesia's islands. Among their employees were men whose more expansive views had been shaped by actual service in the East. Coen was one. In dispatch after dispatch he called for types of migrants needed to build a permanent settlement and a civilization as he knew it: farmers, craftsmen of all sorts, clergy, and schoolteachers. Not that it was to be an authentically Dutch colony, for slave labor held an important part in his schemes.

Pitching his appeal to the legendary niggardliness of the directors, Coen explained how colonies would save money. Migrant settlers would provide generations of men for the VOC's armies and for clerical jobs. And he advocated that colonists be drawn from the orphanages of the Netherlands, which had control of parentless minors living on municipal charity. Coen was confident that orphans, having no relatives, fortune, or ties of sentiment to draw them back to Holland, would become permanent residents of the Indies. He also hoped that as products of strict Calvinist upbringing, they would be less vicious elements in the Dutch settlements than the adult immigrants.

While Coen was always the most astringent in his judgments of the character of the Dutch settler, he understood that certain conditions were needed before rough settlers could be transformed into peaceable citizens. One was a secure means of livelihood, and he therefore urged on the directors a more liberal policy on private trade. At times the directors acted on this advice, but in 1676 they banned nearly all private commerce as "a pestilence and cancer in the Company's body" that was to be stamped out "with all vigor."[20] Burghers, they opined, should become farmers or small shopkeepers.

11

There was another inducement needed to build up a settlers' colony. Coen, who was never a man to mince words, put it this way: "Everyone knows that the male sex cannot survive without women. And yet it seems that Your Excellencies have planted a colony without wishing to. To make up for this lack we have looked for funds and have had to buy many women at high prices. Just as you, Sirs, would only send us the scum of the land, so people here will sell us none but scum either. . . . Should we expect to get good [citizens] from rejects, as you apparently expect? Shall we have to die out to the last man? We therefore request Your Excellencies, that if you cannot get honest married folk, then send us young girls, and we shall hope that things will go better than our experience with older women to date."[21] This letter raises another issue in the debates of the seventeenth century on burghers and colonization, and brings to the fore the category "women" listed in the roll call of 1618.

Thirty-six women had sailed with Both's fleet in 1609. Two of them did not survive the journey, which lasted more than ten months. These women pioneers were wives to soldiers and sailors in the VOC's employ. Most were sent to Ambon, the oldest of the Company's permanent settlements. Perhaps some also found their way to Jacatra and are among those identified only as "some women and children" by senior merchant van den Broeck. Of the surviving thirty-four we know nothing. The women were probably illiterate and have left no record of their own. Although selected to be progenitors of the Dutch settlements in Asia, they rarely obtrude in the records of Company business, which deal with the weighty matters of commerce,[22] and so it is only through the unsympathetic eyes of men that we catch an occasional glimpse of them, and primarily through Coen. "As far as domestic matters are concerned," he writes the directors, "you will have heard from the Governor-General [Both] how ill your good intentions have turned out, that is, with the arrival here [Ambon] of the married couples. Our reputation has suffered badly and the Indians are absolutely scandalized by them, because of their bestial living, their constant drunkenness and lewdness."[23]

It seems that Coen was convincing in his arguments advanced in behalf of colonization by "decent, married folk." By 1621 the directors had decided to further his vision of recreating Holland in Asia. They wrote Coen that same year with the encouraging news that three families would sail for Batavia on the *Mauritius* bringing several young girls with them.

Girls so transported received a set of clothing from the Company, and it later became customary to give each a dowry upon marriage. They received no wage, but signed a contract in the ordinary way of VOC employees binding them to five years in the East. If they were already married upon emigrating they were bound to stay fifteen years, and the Company made special allowances to such wives in clothing and extra rations.[24] The Batavian government was obliged to provide suitable housing and other assistance to these pioneer families.

The first six girls so provided for arrived in 1622. They were called "Company daughters," a name which stuck and which never shed its pejorative overtones, despite the great social jump many of them made through marrying into the merchant group. That same year a letter from the Amsterdam chamber announced the departure of a large party of women, most of them single. This is one of the earliest records of its type, and unlike most entries in the Dagh-Register or Daily Register which was kept at Batavia, it lists the women by name, age, and place of birth where known. "Various persons, married and single, are being sent on the *Leyden*," the letter reads: "Maritjen Jacobs from Briel, wife of Claesz. Pietersz. Verslepen, visitor of the sick, who has already gone out on the 'Gouden Leeuw'. . . . The aforementioned Maritjen Jacobs has agreed to act as midwife if necessary, and for that the Company has granted her a chemise and other articles of clothing. . . . Gilles van Mol, master bricklayer, has been engaged at 12 guilders a month, and his wife Madaleen at 8 guilders a month. . . . Hans van der Voorde has been engaged as an authority on silks, porcelain and other rare objects at f.18 a month; and his wife has been hired for f.12 a month as mother and supervisor of all the young girls. . . . " The list of the unmarried girls began: "Anneken Meynerts from Jeveren, about 20 years old; Angnietje Coninck from Antwerp, aged about 12; Maritjen Jans from Munster; Elsjen Barents from Husum, 13; Trijntjen Jans from Embden, 11; Anneken Claes from Bergen in Norway, 16. . . . "[25]

The girls must have been orphans or members of extremely poor families. It is not to be expected that daughters of the prosperous would be allowed to head for the Indies. Even if they survived the sea voyage and diseases of Batavia, life was full of dangers for the young and unattached. Letters of the Company's senior officials afford an occasional glimpse of the conditions female immigrants had to expect in the settlements early in the seventeenth century, and these included prostitution and the denial of rights to repatriation.[26]

A few women of good family did travel to Indonesia, the dangers notwithstanding, even in the earliest days of settlement. They came as wives of senior officials. Margaretha Nicquet was one of the very first.[27] She accompanied her husband, Gerard Reynst, to Indonesia in 1614 when he succeeded Both as Governor-General. She lived for the most part on board ship, sailing between fortified factories in the Moluccas and Bantam. Governor-General Reynst died in December 1615. The date of Margaretha's death is not known; we know only that it was before 1619 and occurred in the factory at Jacatra.

Living on board ship and constantly moving, Margaretha Reynst-Nicquet could not promote a Dutch style of life in Indonesia. Coen had something quite different in mind when he wrote urging the directors to include several socially prominent families among the migrants.[28] From the first experiments with colonization, he knew the Company daughters were not likely to recreate the God-fearing, sober circles of Holland's bourgeoisie amidst the drunkenness and displays of wealth that were a part of settlement life from the beginning. He himself insisted that he be given permission to take a wife out East before he would accept a second term as governor-general. His choice was Eva Ment. In 1627 she sailed to the Indies, accompanied by her brother and sister, to take up the task of "civilizer." She was then just twenty-one.

Not every official in the Company's Indies service was of the same mind as Coen. Hendrik Brouwer, although he returned to Indonesia as governor-general in 1632 bringing his wife, her sister, and two maids, yet opposed female immigration. He felt Coen had been too liberal "from blind obsession with Batavia's growth." Burghers worked to make money and repatriate rather than to settle permanently overseas. "Many believe," he continued in a letter to the directors, "that it is the Dutch women who are most responsible for this turn of events. They come here poor and, having prospered, never stop complaining until they can return home and appear before old acquaintances in their new riches. . . . There are good households here where the men are married to Indian women, their children are healthier, the women have fewer demands, and our soldiers are much better off married to them."[29]

Earlier that same year, 1632, the directors had decided to cease sponsoring women as migrants to Dutch settlements east of Africa.[30] Small numbers of women did continue to migrate to Indonesia and other settlements throughout the seventeenth century, as entries in the Batavian Daily Register and church records show, but their numbers were always tiny. The largest party sent out at one time totalled eighty-two, and that was in 1623. If we are to believe Nicolaus de Graaff, the small number of Dutchwomen in Indonesia was due entirely to the Company policy of strictly controlling their admission.[31] This remark is set in a context of vilifying women migrants as "riffraff," come out from Europe to get rich and parade as nobly born. His contention that some emigrated disguised as soldiers and sailors is corroborated occasionally in VOC records. The record-keeper at Batavia made this entry for 6 June 1675, for instance: "This morning the ship 't Eylant Mauritius berthed here, sent out by the Delft Chamber via the Cape, leaving the fatherland on 2 September of last year with 289 souls, to wit: 156 sailors, 119 soldiers, 6 women, 7 children and 1 free emigrant. . . . During the voyage 6 sailors, 13 soldiers, 2 women and 3 children died; and on the other side a child was born and a woman was found among the soldiers."[32]

The men heading the VOC continued to debate the question of female migration from the Netherlands. By 1652, however, the directors had adopted a policy which with modifications was to remain the Company's position: restriction of immigration by Dutchwomen, preference for bachelorhood in European recruits, and limitations to marriage with Asia-born women. Their position was spelled out in a directive to the Batavian government, banning the carrying of Dutchwomen on Company ships except for wives of "senior merchants, clergymen, visitors of the sick, sergeants, and only those others who (having offered good reasons for it) get special leave from the Seventeen [Directors] in session."[33]

In 1669 the policy of promoting limited female migration seems to have been revived briefly, and new contracts for unmarried women were lengthened to fifteen years. By and large, however, the question of female migration was settled for the next two hundred years. Some of the Indies clans that grew up derive in the female line from Dutchwomen who emigrated in the first half of the seventeenth century, but the overwhelming majority of families were quite different, built as they were around male immigrants from Europe and the Asian or part-Asian women who were their slaves or wives.

From the beginning there was the freest intercourse with slave women. Most were household servants, and there were already upwards of eighty slaves of both sexes in the Jacatra fort recorded in the 1618 roll call. One man who survived the long siege has left a journal noting nightly orgies within the Dutch compound and marriages rowdily celebrated between Company servants and "black women," the Reverend Evert Hermans conveniently being one of the company.[34] From Both's official correspondence we know, too, that senior merchants of the Company took local women and imported slaves as concubines.[35]

At first little could be done to control the situation. Soldiers and sailors had been uprooted from their homeland, bereft of female society, and deposited in beleaguered factories on the fringes of strange civilizations. They heard sketchy rumors of harems from the first encounters between the Company's merchants and Asian princes; their own senior officers acquired slaves for personal service. In such peculiar circumstances the moral constraints learned from their homeland no longer seemed to apply.

Coen, therefore, on being appointed to his first term as governor-general, set about transforming the "scandalous living" of the Indonesian factories into civilized society. One measure, binding on all who "reside within this our republic of Jacatra or come under its jurisdiction," was a prohibition on maintaining "one or more women slaves, concubine or concubines, in one's house or in any other place, on whatever pretext."[36] One reason for this ban is worth quoting here because it is a very early expression of views held of Asian women, views which, two hundred and fifty years later, were still being repeated in the novels of Françoise Junius and P. A. Daum. In Coen's words, there were "all too many lamentable and well-known cases of abortion, and of a concubine attempting to murder [her master] with phenyl or some other poison." The ban was not effective and had to be renewed before two years had passed,[37] this time with a clause specifying that it applied to all ranks of men. And not to men only; no Christian woman, so ran the text, might have sexual relations with "Heathens or Moors."

At the same time as it proscribed extramarital relations, the Batavian government promoted lawful unions between its low-ranking employees and the slave women imported into its settlements. It required that such marriages be licensed in writing by the local authority and that the banns be posted three weeks before the ceremony. Furthermore, the prospective groom was obliged to purchase his bride's freedom and have her baptized with a new, Christian name. In time, a knowledge of Dutch was also made a formal requirement before marriage could take place.[38]

Not only did the government give its blessing to such unions; it also purchased women in the markets of Asia for transport to Batavia, where they were advertised for sale as brides. At first they were housed in a building which was also used as a school, but later special lodgings were acquired for the purpose. Occasionally, and in uncharacteristic generosity, the Batavian government would make over such women to men eager to marry but lacking ready cash, and deduct the bride's price in monthly installments from their salaries.

Two other decisions of the Batavian government touching on marriage must be related at this point. Customarily, a portion of each bachelor's wages was held back for deposit in the Netherlands. Whenever a man married overseas, however, his salary was paid him there in full. The other regulation, whose object was also to discourage Dutchmen from returning to the Netherlands, forbade wives and children of Asian heritage from going to Holland. In this way it was hoped that the pull of Europe on low-ranking Company employees would be slight and that a stable community of settlers would grow up around the Company's factories.

Promoters of settlement based on Eurasian rather than immigrant burgher families advanced several reasons in support of their preference. One already mentioned proclaimed that Asian women had fewer material wants than their European counterparts. The Company, so ran this argument, would save both from dropping the expensive, sponsored female migration and because wives with presumed simpler tastes would not encourage low-paid employees to increase their income through illegal trade. Nor would the Company lose the services of immigrants, for Asian wives would dissuade their husbands from repatriating. Another justification advanced was that children of mixed parentage thrived in the tropics, whereas children born in the tropics to immigrant mothers and fathers (and called Creoles by the Dutch) had a far lower chance of survival. Governor-General Pieter de Carpentier, who was of this opinion, attributed the differing mortality rates to race, although he also believed that in time, Europeans would acclimatize to tropical conditions.[39]

The supporters of colonies based on mixed marriage sought to ensure the

16

descendants' loyalty to the Netherlands by granting European status to the bride and her offspring. This is why Asian women had to be freed from slavery and christened before their marriages to European men could be solemnized. At baptism they took European names, usually Dutch, but sometimes Portuguese. A convention grew up whereby the new Christian would take the name of her sponsor. If baptism immediately preceded marriage, the woman convert's name was often composed of some part of the groom's. In illustration of this practice is an entry in the marriage register for 27 December 1629. Here a woman appears under the Christian name of Magdalena *Goossens*, widow of *Goossens* Thomasz.[40]

Thus through marriage Asian women joined the European community, bearing Dutch names and assuming their husbands' nationality. But it was not according to Dutch practice that they raised their children. The dominant cultural influence in the household was Asian. It has already been noted that marriage to a woman of Asian background cut off a man's right to repatriate, and eventually the Company also denied him the privilege of sending his Eurasian sons and daughters to Europe. Men of rank and wealth always had their way, sending their boys to the Netherlands for schooling, taking a part-Asian wife home, but they were the minority. For most married men, the settlement overseas became home and the only homeland their children knew.

In the early years of Dutch settlement, then, progression from slavery to mistress of a household could be rapid for some Asian women. Later, the preferred marriage was with Eurasian girls, although most female slaves were kept as maids and concubines anyway. Laws had to be framed to meet this situation, regulating the status of the woman and the children she had by her European owner. No such legislation needed to be devised for male slaves. They had no avenue for escaping life servitude other than their skill in some craft or the arbitrary circumstance of emancipation by their owners.

Slaves constituted a large element in the population of Company settlements. Many of the men were household slaves or were engaged in crafts and retailing on their owners' account. Others were employed as valets, honor guards, and musicians. The Company purchased slaves for its own purposes, too, having them sink canals, lay roads, and erect the new buildings that marked the prosperous early years of Batavia. Many a slave labored in forges and carpenters' shops in the artisans' quarter of the Castle under supervision of European master craftsmen.

Some slaves were paid a small wage in addition to their rations, and a few salaried slaves were able to purchase their manumission. Others were released as acts of piety by their owners, either following the slave's conversion to Christianity or to conform to a provision of the owner's will. Freed slaves then fell under the Company's jurisdiction in the same way as burghers, requiring a license to reside in VOC settlements and to marry and being obligated to serve in the citizens' militia.

Most slaves died in servitude, undernourished, ill-housed, and ill-clothed. Punishments were harsh, the most ferocious reserved for striking an owner or overseer. Company documents often note that slaves ran amuck, and at times measures were taken which reflect the fear Europeans felt before the slave populations of their settlements. One restricted the import of certain categories of adult males as slaves. Makassarese and Balinese were deemed particularly vicious; after 1685 none above the age of twelve might be brought to Batavia.[41] Slaves came from many other parts of the archipelago too, and also from the coasts of India and from Arakan in northwest Burma. They were also acquired through capture in land and naval engagements. The following is a typical entry in Company documents:

> "Captured in September 1616 with the frigate *Ceylon*: Pasquael Denis, Francisco Fernando, Domingo Parang, Francisco Rodrigo, all married; Rodrigo Rodrigo, Deremia Grande, Gregorie de Sine, Ysmael, Salvador Fernando, all single."[42]

This diversity of origin is worth stressing because of its consequences for the history of the Dutch in Indonesia. First of all, daily Dutch intercourse was with Asians of widely assorted backgrounds and generally representing the economically and socially deprived of their home territories. The Netherlanders did not enter an orderly society with a civilization of great antiquity, such as the Javanese. Indeed, the Company banned Javanese people from living within Batavia's walls and did not use them as slaves. The culture that evolved with the growth of Batavia and other Asian settlements fused manners from a great many pårts, assumed by individuals all displaced from their points of origin whether by choice, social and economic rejection (the case for many Europeans), capture, or sale.

From the first, the Malay language was used by the Dutch to communicate with the many peoples they encountered, although Portuguese was often spoken in the seventeenth century. Official correspondence between Indonesian rulers and Company officials was often conducted in Portuguese, and Portuguese could also be heard on the streets, in the markets, in church, and in the households where European men kept Asian mistresses. Its dominance in those early decades has been explained by the fact that many slaves were bought on the Coromandel and Malabar coasts of India, where they had become familiar with the Portuguese language. Some, as shown in the examples above, had Portuguese names and were Christian. At the time, however, different explanations for the prevalence of Portuguese were given. Governor-General Maetsuyker, for one, discounted the extent of contact with the Portuguese and attributed adoption of their language as a lingua franca to certain peculiarities of the Dutch national character. "We are constantly encouraging the spread of the

Netherlands tongue," he wrote to the Directors in 1674, "both here and in other places within the Company's possessions, conscious that the security of the state is bound up in it, but apparently in vain so far, as [use of] the Portuguese language is growing and it easily holds the upper hand, mostly through the idiocy of our own Netherlanders, who hold it for a great honor to be able to speak a foreign language, however badly and corrupted. . . . They speak no other language but Portuguese with their slaves, although most of them come from the East [eastern Indonesia] and have never heard that tongue."[43]

We shall return to this matter of language later. For now it need only be stressed that, outside the Company's offices, neither the culture nor the language was Dutch. Moreover, most inhabitants in the settlements were not Dutch by birth. The servant, underling, and guardian of children with European status were all Indians or Indonesians, and their presence was a fundamental influence on colonial life.

The cast of characters as it appeared in the 1618 roll call is now complete: soldiers and civilians from many parts of Europe; free citizens; Asians, all lumped together as "blacks"; and women, whether Dutch, inhabitants of the archipelago, or from India. These were important elements of the urban population throughout Company times. Three groups are missing. One is the Chinese who settled in Batavia in great numbers only after it had become the hub of VOC power in Asia. The other two are still invisible; they spring from groups named above. The first of these are the Eurasians, or Mestizos, who derive from unions between European and Asian. The other, the Indonesians, are more difficult to identify. They emerged as a cultural category from among the peoples of Batavia: imported slaves; Eurasians deserted as children by white fathers; and peoples from all parts of the archipelago drawn to the city by the prospect of new opportunities. At the time, this group classified as "Natives" was by no means homogeneous, for it included Christian and Muslim, and later, people for a while identified separately as Mardijkers.

All these groups came together in Batavia and grew from it. In conquering Jacatra, Coen had destroyed the town's original twin centers, the *kabupaten,* or official residence of the local Sundanese ruler, and the mosque. On Jacatra's ruins he had built a walled fortress, the Castle of Batavia, replacing the Indonesian kabupaten and the Islamic mosque as the new center of authority and prestige. Within the city itself there grew up this special society in isolation from other peoples of Indonesia.

Another wall contributing to the society's isolation was that formed by the surrounding jungle. Wild animals were bold enough to come right to the city's outer walls and snatch laborers from the sugar fields. Premiums for captured tigers were discontinued only in 1762. Runaway slaves and hostile Bantammers also made the environs of Batavia dangerous to Europeans. In 1642, women were expressly forbidden to pass beyond the city's limits, under penalty of a fine, because of the risk of attack from "people lurking in the jungle, ruffians, Javanese, and others of our enemies."[44] For a long time, then, the city's chief outlet was by sea, which the Dutch dominated and which linked Batavia to Holland and its other Asian settlements.

Culturally, Batavia was isolated too. Many of the original Sundanese inhabitants had fled in 1619. All Javanese, the major ethnic group on the island (principally in the center and east), were excluded from the city, and a new population was brought in from many parts of Asia and Europe. Later, when peace treaties had been signed with Bantam and Mataram, the suburbs immediately outside Batavia expanded, and wealthy people began moving further from the city, laying out pleasure gardens for themselves and taking trips upriver. Gradually the web of society that was forming within the settlement moved beyond it also. In the first half of the seventeenth century, however, attention was turned towards Holland.

This immediate and rapid growth of Batavia compelled senior Dutch officials in Asia to devise laws and institutions that could control the city's inhabitants. Quite naturally, the model they chose was that of the Dutch municipality, just as in the design of the earliest buildings and layout of the city they strove to recreate the appearance of a Dutch town. The circumstance of a polyglot citizenry, however, demanded laws and institutions for which there was no precedent in Holland, and from the first, local practice took on a unique character and molded Batavia's residents in ways uncharted at home. Laws and institutions created in this early period were to govern Batavia and its subsidiary settlements with little real change for the next two hundred years. It is to a review of these that we now turn.

INSTITUTIONS AND LAWS

The mid-century visitor to Batavia would have noted stone churches rising amidst the Dutch-style houses of the city. All were intended for worship in the manner of the Reformed Church, the only denomination permitted by the Company's directors in their overseas possessions.[45] At first, public worship had been conducted in the town hall, and the official character thus lent this Calvinist church was further strengthened by the custom of morning and evening prayers in the Castle which all had to attend. Sunday rest, decreed as early as January 1620, stamped Batavia with the externals of a godly city. Furthermore, it was habitual for the governor-general to mark events such as the departure of the fleet for Holland by special days of prayer and fasting. Prayer days might also be called to celebrate a military victory, abate an epidemic, or avert heavenly wrath from the citizenry. Pious declarations are scattered through official correspondence of the Company and other records such as the Batavian Daily Register; policy was often couched in terms of religious aspirations or imperatives.

The Indies church represented both the lofty and sordid elements of Dutch rule overseas. In organization it was modelled on the Netherlands church, but it acquired other characteristics that reflected its subordinate position, in the Asian settlements, to a commercial company. In Holland the church, while supporting the state, maintained a certain independence in matters of faith, internal organization, and the social institutions it sponsored. In the Indies, however, the church was made subservient to local government from the beginning.

A political commissioner of Batavia's government sat in at the first session of the Batavia synod, on 21 January 1621 and at every meeting thereafter in Company times. No spiritual regulation could be decided upon without written approval of the temporal powers. Even such matters as the number of sermons a week and their hours were established by decree of the governor-general in Council. Nor might clergy correspond with their counterparts in Holland without first submitting all documents for the political commissioner's inspection. For the government's convenience, Batavia's synod was made supreme in the Company possessions; its decisions and practices became the rule for all matters of church life. In this, church and secular organization were inspired with the one hierarchical and autocratic spirit, although the Dutch models—provincial synods and city-states—sprang from quite other convictions.

Clerics were salaried employees of the VOC, fitting into the Company hierarchy below junior merchants and above sergeants. No parish had the right to "call" its own minister, although that privilege was an article of faith of the Protestant movement in Europe. Instead, Batavia's church council assigned clergy to parishes throughout the Company's territories, and its appointments had to be confirmed by the government. The government did not hold its powers of confirmation lightly, and on occasion it assigned clergy without consulting the synod, or it overrode the synod's decisions.

Not unexpectedly, high officials abused their power over the clergy. Governor-General Jacques Specx was able, for instance, to dictate to Batavia's synod whom it must exclude from the celebration of communion. In the closed society of the seventeenth century, exclusion from the sacraments cast sinners into social obloquy as well as denying them the means of grace according to church doctrine. Specx, however, enforced exclusion on three councillors of the Indies in a private feud over the honor of his illegitimate part-Japanese daughter Sara. A few ministers of the church did pursue matters of faith with rigor. The Reverend Georgius Candidius was one, and his opposition to concubinage cost him his post in the Moluccas in 1627. But most clergy trod safely, and their sermons caused the VOC's representatives no alarm.

21

Few ministers found service in the tropics alluring. In all, about nine hundred were engaged during the two centuries of Company rule, to serve Dutch settlements from southern Africa to Indonesia.[46] Some served Christian communities for terms far exceeding the five and ten years they had contracted for, but most worked their contracts and repatriated, or stayed in Asia in some other capacity than minister. Andreas Lambertus Loderus, for instance, exchanged pulpit for government printing house in 1701 and continued as town printer until his death in 1719. Many engaged in illegal commerce, including trade in slaves, to expand their incomes. They grew wealthy, buying up pleasure gardens beyond the city walls when it became fashionable in the second half of the seventeenth century. Joost Tielen, a native of Rotterdam, was one dominie who was caught and his fortune confiscated. Other clergy fell foul of the law because of the conduct of their private lives. Forced repatriation might follow, or the miscreant might, like the Reverend J. L. Scotanus, be jailed in cells deep within the walls of the Batavia Castle.[47]

Because of the limited number of clerics and because of Company policy, which was to keep peace and save "unnecessary" expense, Holland's Reformed Church never regarded Indonesia as a mission field. Pastors were appointed to serve Dutch settlements and to convert those Asians who had turned to Roman Catholicism as a result of contact with the Portuguese. Batavia always had the largest number of resident clergy in all Dutch Asia. In 1683 the capital's quota was set at ten. Elsewhere there were few, and beyond permanent posts such as in Ceylon and Ambon, Dutch settlements might be visited by a touring minister only once in several years. Semarang, on Central Java's north coast, for instance, did not have a pastor until 1753.

When there were no men of the cloth in colonial settlements, Europeans were obliged to live without such "technical" services of the church as the solemnizing of marriages, burial of the dead, and invocation of blessings on state occasions. There were other consequences of this lack of clergy too. In Europe, ministers were the inheritors of a tradition of learning; in their communities they sponsored a veneration of the intellect and an ideal of civilization. Their absence from Dutch settlements in Indonesia before the nineteenth century explains in part the slowness of European culture to root itself and the dominance of the Asian contribution to the manners and ways of colonial society.

It would be a mistake to consider the role of church and cleric without mentioning the lay worker. Variously called visitor or comforter of the sick, these officers of the Company were hired to lead prayers in the absence of ordained clergy, to minister to the condemned criminal, and to superintend the charitable institutions of the Indies church. Most were emigrants from the Netherlands, men of little formal education, who would sign a five-year contract for employ in Dutch Asia. Public opinion of sick-visitors was never high, and they, too, might be repatriated as morally unfit, or degraded to serve the Company as soldiers.

For a time the Company attempted to solve the problem of staffing the Asian churches by financing the religious studies of Dutch students who in return had to sign for double the usual term in the East. A training school had been opened by the Company in Leiden in 1622 with twelve candidates. One, Nicolaus Molinaeus, was to minister to Batavia's Portuguese parish. The experiment was discontinued in 1634, however, at the same time that the Company renounced sponsored female emigration.

As a group, ordained and lay servants of the Asian churches were poorly educated men, often prejudiced against the lower socioeconomic classes of the settlements, against those of other faiths, and against Asians generally. A few were men with scientific interests and commitment to intellectual pursuits. It is primarily through them that knowledge of Asian languages and civilizations was first acquired and scientific study of tropical environs fostered.

From the first, churchmen in the Indonesian archipelago had to resolve the problem of which language to use. Very early on they settled on two: Malay, which was widely used as a language of commerce, and Portuguese, which was used as a lingua franca between Asians and Europeans along many stages of the Asian trade routes. Use of these two languages also reflects the fact that the Asian peoples with whom the Dutch had most contact in these early years were residents of the port cities, not subjects of the inland, agriculture-based kingdoms such as Mataram, where Javanese was spoken.

Services were conducted in Malay in the fort church on Ambon in 1614, and the first in Batavia's Malay church was led on 30 January 1633 by Drs. Sebastiaen Danckaerts. One of the earliest word lists, *Nederduitsch en Maleisch Woordenboek (Dutch and Malay Dictionary)*, comes from Drs. Caspar Wiltens, who was the first ordained minister of the Dutch Reformed Church in Asia. It was published in 1623. Another Batavian minister, Justus Heurnius, compiled a dictionary and translated the Gospels, the Acts of the Apostles, and some of the Psalms into Malay. In 1653 Johannes Roman translated the catechism into Malay, the Ten Commandments, and a number of prayers. His Malay grammar was printed at the Company's expense in 1674.

Beyond these very practical contributions there were also the linguistic studies of Herbert de Jager, a former minister engaged as a merchant by the Company. He devoted his enquiries to the relationship between the Old Javanese, Sanskrit, and Tamil languages. Melchior Leydekker's Malay translation of the Bible was printed in both the Latin and Arabic scripts. And one of the major sources for seventeenth-century colonial history and social life, the five-volume *Oud en Nieuw Oost-Indiën (Old and New East Indies)* was the work of yet another minister, François Valentijn, who was stationed in Ambon from 1685 to 1695 and again during the years 1707 to 1713.

23

Such scholars were not typical of the average clergyman or sick-visitor. They had been highly educated at home, and in the Indies they were well connected with the ruling class; Leydekker, for instance, married a sister of Governor-General Abraham van Riebeeck. Nor did the scholar-ministers leave a deep impression on the seventeenth-century settlement. Their endeavors attracted interest in a restricted circle only. Yet their study of Malay and promotion of it as a lingua franca were in themselves to be lasting contributions to Indonesian life. It was to their lesser colleagues that the church's more immediate tasks were left: care of the poor and sick, oversight of community morals, and education of the youth.

The first Dutch school in Indonesia was opened in Ambon by the VOC admiral Cornelis Matelief, one of those early adventurers of expansive vision who dreamed of a Netherlands Asian empire. Assimilation of Dutch cultural heritage and religious credo was a necessary part of his plan, and to give it form he appointed as teacher one Johannes Wogma at eighteen guilders a month. Wogma's duties were to teach Ambonese children reading, writing, arithmetic, and prayers of the Reformed Church in the Dutch tongue for four hours daily.

Use of Dutch as the medium of instruction was quickly found to be impracticable. Nevertheless, it was also the language of instruction in Jan van den Broecke's little school in the Jacatra factory in 1617, although his pupils included "Native Christians" as well as Dutch children. This school, predating the founding of Batavia by some two years, had been called into existence by the directors. Article 34 of their instructions to Governor-General Reynst had stipulated, "The Governor-General and Councillors of the Indies shall issue all appropriate orders for the planting of the Christian religion, establishment of good schools and other germane matters."[48]

In order to appreciate this policy, one should remember that in the Netherlands schools were foundations of local churches. In viewing promotion of schools as a duty of government, the directors adopted a policy radical in its time and implications. It was a course consistent with their broader aim, which was to control all aspects of life in the Asian settlements. Precisely how schools fitted in with this conception may be perceived in the duties spelled out for schoolmasters in regulations of 1643: "The duty of the schoolmasters is primarily to sharpen in the young a fear of the Lord, to teach them to pray, sing, attend church and to catechize them; next, to teach them obedience to their parents, the authorities and their masters; thirdly, to teach them to read, write and do arithmetic; fourthly, to teach them good morals and manners, and finally to see to it that no tongue other than Dutch is used in the schools."[49]

In time the Company operated four schools in Batavia, two of them in its poorhouse and orphanage. Beyond making pious and loyal subjects, the Company had no greater educational plans for pupils. Male graduates could hope for nothing more than employment as soldiers, artisans, or copyists. Men ambitious for their sons had them educated in the Netherlands, since it was not VOC policy to employ the locally-schooled in positions of trust. In all the history of the Dutch in Asia, few men rose to positions of prominence in government without schooling in Europe.

Company schools always lacked qualified teachers and teaching materials, especially texts in Malay. Not that the VOC entirely neglected the matter; by 1617 school books for the Indies were actually being printed in the Netherlands, some of them in Malay. Texts for Indies schools were also printed in Batavia by the Company's press. J. J. Steendam's "Songs of Morality for the Batavian Youth" appeared in Dutch in 1671, for instance, and explanations of the Gospels in Malay, translations of prayers, and the like were published there in the eighteenth century.[50]

Van Diemen's tenure as governor-general (1636–1645) signals a time of consolidation and of the strengthening of institutions of municipal life. When this ninth governor-general turned his attention to education, therefore, he was receptive to the Reverend Johannes Stertemius's proposal that a Latin school be established. Twelve orphans of both Dutch and Eurasian heritage commenced their studies in 1642. They were to converse in Latin alone, the language of Europe's educated elite, although beginners might also use the Dutch tongue "and none other." Costs were to be shared by the government, the orphanage treasury, and the church's charitable funds.

The identity of two of the pupils is known. They were sons of the Frisian minister Tiberius Ravesteyn, who set out for Java in 1652. Ravesteyn and his wife died during the voyage, but their three children reached Batavia safely. The daughter was placed in the household of a lay minister, while the boys were lodged in the orphanage and enrolled in the Latin school as wards of government. Their school career was not long, however, for in October 1656 the institution was closed on executive order, and the pupils, then numbering eleven, were taken into the Company's employ.

The closing of the Latin school had already been foreshadowed in a letter which Governor-General Maetsuyker wrote to the directors in 1654. The pupils, he reported, showed "slight inclination" to study, "so that we very much doubt if any good can be expected of this school to begin with, which would make the expense worthwhile, particularly since the youth of these lands do not have a decent upbringing as do their counterparts in the fatherland, because of their intercourse with men and women slaves who have vile, abject natures."[51] The directors blamed the school's failure on parents who preferred sending their sons to the Netherlands. This desire, they opined, was "in no way in harmony with service in the Company, since it displaced those born and bred to the climate and who should look on the country as their homeland.''[52] At the directors' urging the school was reopened in 1666, but it was shut down for good in 1671, when the number of pupils had dwindled to one.

The directors' response explains why pupils of the Latin school were exclusively orphans and sheds light on attitudes in the middle years of the seventeenth century. It would have been logical to build up the schools and seek future employees for all levels from their graduates. This the Company never did. It continued to send out Dutch males for offices of trust, in order to ensure loyalty to the Netherlands. At the same time, it aimed to keep the immigrants in Asia all their working lives by encouraging them to establish families with locally born women. To the immigrants' daughters the Company offered a secure and promising future as brides; to the sons very little. Consequently, throughout the VOC period schools were always to fail in terms of duration, quality of education, and cultural influence.

Throughout the Company period the condition of schools depended on the whim and interest of the governor-general of the day. Johannes Camphuys was one who paid more than passing attention to schools, but his regulations of 1684 still laid stress on religion and manners over general knowledge. The intellectual qualifications stipulated for teachers were limited to the ability to read "without stumbling, write in a good hand, sing the Psalms of David well, and be able to do arithmetic passably." Teachers were to see that there was no blasphemy and that boys and girls sat apart in the classroom to discourage "all improprieties." Finally, special provisions were appended for the school housed in the orphanage. Each Sunday following morning worship the unfortunate orphans were to answer questions from the catechism put to them by members of the congregations of the Dutch-language, Portuguese, and Malay churches of Batavia, churches which the orphans attended according to their origins.[53]

Orphans were one of the long-standing concerns of Batavia's government. Already in October 1624, just five years after the founding of Batavia, the first orphanage had been established. Its early date suggests the existence of grave social problems arising from high death rates that left children without parental care as well as from the presence of numerous abandoned children of mixed race. From the beginning, Batavia's orphanage cared for the fatherless among Indonesian Christians, Eurasians, and Dutch of the city. In creating the orphanage in 1624, the government stated that it was acting to promote an orderly society "in this Republic which is growing enormously every day" and to fashion it after Netherlands' usage "as far as possible."[54]

Supervision of the orphaned children and their property was entrusted to several townspeople chosen annually by the governor-general from a list, submitted by the town council, of the most pious, wealthy and distinguished burghers of the city. Theirs was the duty of registering property of all Christian orphans and of investing it on the orphans' behalf (the profits going to the orphanage treasury) or of supervising its management by an approved guardian. Orphans might be raised in the homes of their guardians or placed in foster care of "good, pious townswomen," who had to report regularly on their charges to the trustees. All major decisions, such as choice of spouse, had to win the trustees' consent.

Other children were reared in the orphanage itself. In general, propertyless orphans were a charge of the community until their early teens. Girls might be placed as servants with town families or earn their keep in the orphanage by sewing and housework. They were given a dowry upon marriage. Those still single at eighteen had to become self-supporting and were given their marriage portion in advance, if they were deemed deserving. Boys were apprenticed in some trade—saddle and sail-making, cobbling and tailoring were vocations thought particularly suitable—or were taken on as ships' boys at twelve.

By the time they left the orphanage, the children were expected to be grateful to society, respectful to their betters, and fluent in Dutch. This often-noted stress on fostering Dutch illustrates important aspects of social life in the seventeenth- and eighteenth-century settlement. Firstly, it records the obvious: the Dutch were not able to establish their tongue in Asia in the ordinary manner by passing it on to their children. Within two decades of settlement the Dutch language was being maintained and spoken only by male immigrants from Holland in the VOC office.

Now the significance of Dutch to the government was this: it was a stamp of political allegiance, as was profession of Christianity. This is the reason why senior officials tried to make it the language of daily intercourse, not only for the native Netherlander but for the Creole, Eurasian, and Asian Christian and for the slave retainers in their households. Maetsuyker put it this way: "We have wholeheartedly encouraged the spread of the Dutch tongue . . . knowing full well how much the stability of the state lies therein, but apparently in vain to date . . . so that we shall have to think up more efficacious means . . . and thus be able to assure ourselves more of the trustworthiness of the native subjects."[55]

It must be remembered that the settlements were frequently under attack in the first half of the seventeenth century. One can see in the early years an attempt by the Company to win populations to itself. Thus decrees and other documents refer to part-European children who had been found living with their Asian mothers in Indonesian residential quarters. Some were removed and placed in the orphanage, that they might be raised as Europeans.[56] The municipal orphanage, then, was not only a haven for the bereaved and expression of VOC beneficence. It was a means of making citizens, an instrument of state policy.

27

This is not to argue that Batavia's authorities made no distinction between European, Eurasian, and Indonesian. While religion was a unifying bond, Asian and part-Asian ranked lower socially. It is true that wealthy, highly placed men could promote their part-Asian sons and that Eurasian men in settlements subsidiary to Batavia, and in Batavia itself in the eighteenth century, did rise to positions of influence and authority. Many part-Asian women also achieved high social status through marriage. But as far as the majority were concerned, the principle of racial superiority was maintained by institutions as by individuals, and this can be seen in the clothing allowances for orphans.

According to orphanage regulations of 1752, clothing was allocated in the following manner. To European girls were given each year: 2 blouses of ordinary bleached cotton; 4 bodices of Chinese linen; 2 chintz skirts; 2 sailor-style *kebayas* (overblouses); 2 kebayas of Surat cloth; 1 Makassar sarong; 3 handkerchiefs; 3 pairs of stockings; 2 pairs of shoes; and 2 pairs of sandals. Every second year they were to receive 1 cotton floral frock and 1 pair of stays. The clothing rations for Mestiza girls consisted of: 2 fine blouses of guinea cloth; 1 coarse blouse of bleached cloth; 3 bodices of Chinese linen; 2 sailor-style kebayas; 4 fine Bengali head veils; 1 fine garment of Indian cloth; 2 handkerchiefs; 2 pairs of shoes; 2 pairs of sandals; and 3 pairs of stockings.[57] It will be noticed that the Mestizas' issue had no article of distinctively European dress, such as the corsets; instead, Mestizas received more items of Asian costume, such as the head veils.

No distinction was made in the regulation clothing for European and Mestizo boys. I believe the reason is this: in the eyes of the Company locally born boys of all races shared the same lowly status and could be used for the same ends, as manpower for the army and as scribes. Their way upward was barred; Dutch males were sent out from Europe to fill the posts with a future. Women were not directed to the Asian settlements after 1632. Those who migrated with husband or father occupied instantly, by virtue of origin, the uppermost rank in colonial society; hence the distinctions made between orphan girls on the basis of race.

A great many more institutions were devised in seventeenth-century Batavia than can be touched on here. There has been passing mention of the municipal council and court, which persisted also until the Company's dissolution, but none at all of such institutions as the hospitals, poorhouse, women's reformatory, and commissions established for smooth conduct of the city's affairs. Those selected for particular attention here have this in common, that they were created to serve multi-racial clienteles. Christian Asians, Eurasians, and immigrant Dutch came together in Batavia's orphanage, as in its schools and poorhouse.

It is now time to clarify colonization policy, and this will be done by reference to laws promulgated in seventeenth-century Batavia having to do with the city's expansion and administration. As this review of Batavia's laws proceeds, it will be found that they always stand for increase in the city's population and for binding European inhabitants to permanent residence. They might include denial of entry and settlement to certain categories of migrants from the Netherlands, and they were subject to alteration by successive boards of directors. But a general consistency of principle can be distilled from particular regulations issued as circumstance demanded, confirming that Company lawgivers settled on a society ruled by European males whose mates were selected from local population groups.[58]

From the beginning, women were not allowed to join husbands stationed in any VOC trading post without especial dispensation. This ban was of general application, but restated at times for specific categories of employees. In 1642, for instance, the spouses of sick-visitors were so singled out. After 1652, however, general practice was to allow men above the ranks of soldier and assistant in the civilian hierarchy to bring out their families, but they had to continue in the Company's service ten years above the usual term. A man marrying a Dutch immigrant in the East was bound to an additional five years' service upon expiration of his current bond.

All widowed female immigrants had to remain in the East a minimum of five years after remarriage, and no Dutchwoman might return to the Netherlands at her own inclination. In 1629 it was decreed that European women attempting to join a husband who had gone to the Netherlands on business or leave would be jailed until his return or news of his death arrived. Girls of immigrant families also fell under Company regulations, being obliged to continue on in the East a minimum of five years after contracting a marriage there. After 1632, assisted female migration from the Netherlands was cut off. When relaxed in 1669 the law required a fifteen-year residence in Asia of all women immigrants.

In view of the limited supply of European brides, Company employees and free citizens alike had to turn to the locally born for mates. Again Company law intervened, and again with the aim of establishing stable settlements. No married employee, for instance, might take a leave in Europe unless he had served a full five years from the date of marriage. Nor, after 1633, could he depart without first depositing funds sufficient for the wife's maintenance in his absence. No man, married or single, could repatriate without written permission from the governor-general. Burghers, furthermore, must have lived at least three years in a settlement and were required to deposit the price of passage in advance.

From 1639 on, no man married to an Asian or part-Asian woman might repatriate while his wife and their children still lived. Men discovered on ship were to be put off at the Cape and returned by the next outgoing vessel. In 1716 the ban on repatriation was extended to all men, married or bachelor, who had part-Asian children.

Nor could a locally born woman accompany her Dutch husband in retirement to the Netherlands without especial dispensation. This ban was enacted by Governor-General C. van der Lijn's government in 1649 and covered all women, "whether slave or free, Mestiza or other natives of these lands." Equally, it was forbidden them to travel to Europe aboard ships of any other nation. The precarious position of the Asia-born is illustrated in the case of the Eurasian Susanna Muller, who was married to the Creole Cornelis van Out-hoorn. Although the marriage made Susanna sister-in-law to Governor-General Willem van Outhoorn (1691–1704), and although she had European status, yet she still had to apply for citizenship for herself and her three children upon arrival in the Netherlands as a widow in 1709.[59]

The Company's administrators attempted to keep its Asian communities permanently settled, too. Free Asians had to gain permission to leave as well as to settle. No Asian might travel to Europe nor go aboard a VOC ship without permission. By the 1640s, however, it was already the practice of departing Europeans to take slaves with them. Van Diemen forbade slaves accompanying their owners to Europe, but within thirteen years his ban was relaxed to permit repatriating families an Asian wet nurse, provided the cost of her return journey was deposited in full.

The many modifications of this ban in subsequent years show how impossible it was to coerce the wealthy into reducing their suite, and indeed Batavia's government was sympathetic on this point. In 1734, retiring members of the supreme government were allowed four slave attendants for the voyage, lest they be like everyone else "to the decrease of the splendor and honor of the government." Nine years later all former employees from clerks up were permitted slaves aboard, the number varying according to the individual's rank and marital status.

The success of these laws meant the great and constant increase in the Company's Asian communities and the establishment of a locally rooted colonial society. According to population estimates, Batavia's population, for instance, increased tenfold in the century following Coen's 1620 figure of two thousand, with another ten to fifteen thousand people in the suburbs grouped about the city walls.[60] But while simple increases in totals demonstrate growth, they tell us nothing of the permanence of groups such as the European. For certainty on this point we have to turn to a different source.

Tombstone inscriptions from the graveyards of European communities fit this purpose. Often, in addition to the usual names and dates, they give the places of birth and some clues to the worldly importance of the deceased. Such epitaphs enable one to descry little settlements along the coasts of Asia whose members reared children, moved between settlements in the course of career and marriage, and came to die and so record their existence in one or other of them.

The epitaphs below demonstrate the effects of the laws just reviewed. They have been chosen from a compilation of inscriptions for the European community in VOC settlements on Ceylon dating from 1638, when the first trading post was established, until 1796, when the island passed under British control. They therefore illustrate the links between outlying settlements and Batavia, as well as the autonomous life of a subsidiary community:

> Hercules Lindeman of Drontem, free burgher and vice-president of Colombo civic council, died May 1664 at Colombo, aged 42.
>
> Juff. Adriana Alebos, born Tayouan [Taiwan] December 1656, died at Colombo Castle September 1684. Wife of Floris Blom, merchant and secretary of Ceylon's government.
>
> Juff. Johanna Margarita Schilhoorn, born Batavia, died Colombo October 1695, aged 17 years. Married to Gerrit van Toll, junior merchant.
>
> Cornelis van der Parra, born and died Ceylon, 1687–1719. Merchant and secretary of Ceylon's government.
>
> Anna Henrietta van Beaumont, born Cape of Good Hope 1716, died Colombo 1755. Married at Batavia to Joan Gideon Loten, Councillor of the Indies and Governor of Ceylon.
>
> Henrikus Philipsz., born and died Ceylon 1733–1790. Clergyman.
>
> Susanna Engelberta Schreuder, born Surat 1743, died Colombo 1760, with newborn daughter. Wife of Joan Schreuder, Councillor Extraordinary and Governor and Director of Ceylon.
>
> Mr. Imam Willem Falk, born Colombo 1736, died there 1785. Councillor, Governor and Director of Ceylon.
>
> Nicolaas Brasser van Heuvel, born 1701 at Triconamele [Ceylon], died Galle 1721. Assistant. Youngest son of Nicolaas van Heuvel, Commander.
>
> Ursula Theodora Petronela Mooyaart, died Jaffnapatnam 1847, aged 60. Granddaughter of Commander Anthony Mooyaart. Married to Capt. French Gray of the Ceylon Regiment.[61]

These inscriptions, selected from several hundreds, illustrate certain features of colonial society in the days of the Company. First, they establish the fact of female immigration from Holland. Second, they show that Dutchmen settled in Asia to raise families while in the VOC's service or as burghers; that they recognized their offspring, giving them Dutch names and guarding their place in European society. Third, they show that daughters of such men were sought as brides by new migrants and they often, through marriage, ranked high socially. Fourth, they illustrate that, despite laws to the contrary, men born in Asia of European fathers could and did find employment with the Company, as high as commander with the rank of councillor extraordinary. (In time, this pattern established itself in the very capital of Dutch Asia; in the seventeenth century, however, the exception to the rule was more commonly found in the subsidiary settlements.) The little list given above closes with the example of a woman tracing residence in Asia at least three generations back in the paternal line and who, through marriage, bridges the change in regime from Dutch to British.

In this manner was the character of colonial society laid down. The basic institutions that were to serve Batavia and its subsidiary settlements for the entire period of Company rule were already legislated for in the first four decades of the seventeenth century. Batavia's earliest lawgivers defined permissible relations across racial lines and brought certain groups together in the institutions they created for a multiracial colony. Laws on residence, marriage, and the like, appearing haphazardly, nevertheless succeeded in promoting stable and expanding communities. The European component soon developed Creole and Eurasian subgroups. The type of society that evolved from these conditions will be examined in the following chapter through biographical sketches of representative European immigrants, Eurasians, Creoles, and Christian Asians.

2

Growth of Settlement Society

FROM THE MATERIAL PRESENTED thus far, one can see that the categories of actors composing Dutch colonial society were already determined by the 1640s, and that the laws directing their lives and the institutions giving their lives shape were set by that time. Also determined by the middle years of the century was the economic system of monopoly and control. It is thus clear, from the first decades of settlement, that the only way for a European man to gain wealth and worldly success was through employment in the civilian arm of the Company.

Salaries paid to medium- and low-ranking VOC employees were always notoriously low, and it is well known that many men augmented their incomes through private trading, or "smuggling," as the VOC directors perceived it. Because trading on one's own account was illegal, only those in high positions could engage in it with some assurance of immunity, while their senior positions naturally offered the best opportunities for illegal commerce on a vast scale. The goal of the ambitious man was, therefore, to climb the VOC hierarchy.

The political structure of colonial society, too, was settled by the 1640s. The first governors-general were men sent out by the Company's directors for several years and then recalled to the Netherlands. In the very first stage of settlement, of course, all officials came directly from Holland. The third governor-general, Laurens Reael (1616–19), however, began a tradition in recommending his director-general of trade as his successor, a practice that was to be overturned only infrequently by the directors. Coen's death during his second term in office (1627–29) occasioned the development of another practice that shaped relations between Batavia and Amsterdam fundamentally: Indies councillors voted immediately upon a successor (usually the director-general as the most senior councillor and member of the inner group) and then notified Holland of their choice for confirmation.[1] By 1636, with the appointment of Antonio van Diemen as governor-general, all these lines of action were fused in an enduring pattern, the accession to highest office of men with years of experience in Asia. Beginning with Cornelis van der Lijn's appointment in

33

1645, moreover, one sees accession by men with years of service in Asia unbroken by leave in Europe. Not until H. W. Daendels's appointment in 1808 is an outsider selected. Consequently, there is a very long period when political control is locally determined, and when government is virtually immune from immediate direction from the Netherlands on account of the vast distances between Batavia and Amsterdam and the slowness of sea transport.

Given that power and fortune were only to be made through senior appointment with the Company and that control of promotions lay largely in Batavia, how was the colonial elite formed? The answer to that question goes to the heart of the making and development of colonial society. The seventeenth century is a period of search for connecting links between men of good health, longevity, and ability. Material presented in chapter 1 makes it clear that the connections between such men could not be based on birth into noble families in the Netherlands, nor on an "old school" network, nor even on common home city or region. The links between men were arbitrary, so that the Council of the Indies often divided into opposing cliques. This gave the distant directors a measure of power, as one group would lodge allegations of smuggling against the other and the directors would intervene, recalling one party or refusing to confirm the majority choice of the Council. By the second half of the eighteenth century, however, Batavia's ruling clique was virtually independent of direction from Holland; Governor-General Willem Arnold Alting (1780–97), for instance, could expressly oppose the directors in appointing his son-in-law Joannes Siberg as his director-general.

Over the course of time, the ties between men were increasingly based upon family: men promoted their relatives. The rules governing immigration and employment determined the peculiar characteristic of the family system and hence the distinctive nature of colonial society, for VOC policy had settled on marriage of its employees with local women and it denied full opportunities to their sons. Hence the important links between men were based, not on passing position (and access to wealth) from father to son, but on passing it to brothers-in-law and other kin by marriage. This family system is properly an eighteenth-century development and will be examined in chapter 3. But women were already important in the seventeenth century in linking powerful men to each other in a way that was secure from treachery. It is instructive, for understanding colonial society, to see who they were and how they, too, changed over time.

In the earliest days, women accompanied their husbands for their terms as governors-general. Like their husbands, these women had no prior connections with Asia, and they returned to Europe when their husbands were recalled. In Batavia they held a modest court, were attended by ladies-in-waiting, and performed the public rites of state such as laying foundation stones. With van

Diemen's appointment in 1636, however, there came a change in the type of first lady presiding over Batavia, too, for his wife, Maria van Aelst, had already spent at least fourteen years east of the Cape of Good Hope.

It is not clear when she first migrated nor under what circumstances. Possibly she was already married to her first husband, Johan Libener, who in 1622 appears in Company records as senior merchant at Batavia. Her second husband was Bartholomeus Cunst, whom we have already met defending the Gelderlandt redoubt. He had been chief of the Jambi factory and then a leading free burgher, holding many honorary posts, including that of orphanage trustee. Cunst was dismissed from that post following a scandal in the orphanage's financial management, and he died soon after. A year later, in 1630, his widow married again, this time van Diemen, who had been one of her husband's judges and who at that time held the rank of councillor of the Indies.

Maria van Aelst's career throws light on certain aspects of VOC society. The Company felt some responsibility towards widows, continuing to pay them their food allowances until the departure of the fleet for Holland or until they remarried. Van Aelst's decision to stay upon being widowed suggests that the Indies held a more promising future for her than did Holland. Widowed a third time, however, and being now the dowager van Diemen, she found the Netherlands sufficiently attractive to return. Clearly, marriage offered the few Dutchwomen who journeyed to the Company's settlements in the seventeenth century the possibility of social advancement and fortune.

By mid-century, the wives of senior officials came from among immigrants who had spent the greater part of their lives in Asia or who were born there. Governor-General Maetsuyker's first wife, Haasje Berkmans, for instance, accompanied him East at the start of his Indies career and spent twenty-nine years in Batavia, dying there in 1663. His second wife, Elisabeth Abbema, had emigrated at fifteen with her family and lived nineteen of her thirty-six years in eastern Indonesia and Batavia. Françoise de Wit, who was wife to the eleventh governor-general, Carel Reyniersz., had been born to Dutch migrants at Masulipatnam on India's Coromandel Coast in 1634. In 1648, when the marriage took place at Batavia, Reyniersz. was forty-four, once-widowed and director-general. Two years later he was governor-general, and the sixteen-year-old Françoise, who had never seen Europe, was first lady of all the Netherlands eastern possessions. Her father's promotion to governor of Coromandel occurred the following year.

This pattern of senior officials cementing alliances through family ties and supporting each other had already started with Governor-General Coen. His wife had brought a younger sister, Lysbet Ment, to the Indies with her in 1627. Within months the sister was wife to one of Coen's councillors. Thus during Coen's second term his Council consisted of three personal protégés and his brother-in-law, Pieter Vlack. "Dynastic" rule was a later development, discernible once Indies clans were established with a network of ties stretching across the VOC's Asian empire. Even in the early period, however, senior employees marrying in the East chose women with useful connections. In Elisabeth Abbema, for instance, Maetsuyker married the widow of the governor of Ambon and sister-in-law of Mr. Andries Boogaert, governor of Banda and later director of Surat. Governor-General Willem van Outhoorn married the daughter of a councillor extraordinary.

The first complaints about the character and style of living of Batavian ladies came from the VOC directors in the 1640s, precisely when all the determining circumstances of colonial society were flowing together. Maria van Aelst is the first to draw notice. Until she assumed residence in the governor-general's quarters in the Castle, first families lived soberly, with few attendants or other marks of worldly pomp. This simplicity reflected the personalities of early office-holders, but it also reflected daily living conditions—the dangers from without, rough life within the walls, the few persons of education and leisure in Batavia, and the absence of such centers of social life as theaters and coffee houses. By the 1640s, life was more settled and the governor-general could take his recreation with pomp, before the citizenry. The *Daily Register* contains references to the first official riding out with a suite composed of senior Company servants, their wives, and visiting dignitaries.

The grand style that begins with the van Diemen–van Aelst period is underlined by Valentijn. He says that on his deathbed van Diemen extracted promises of the councillors in attendance that Maria would be continued in the state she had come to expect, including use of the governor-general's residence, until the return fleet should lift anchor from Batavia. All this was granted, and Maria was allowed "out of pure liberality," in the words of the Company's biographer, J. P. I. du Bois, to take to the Netherlands all the furnishings and effects she had accumulated "in extraordinary quantity."[2] She had apparently indulged a taste for outings, too. The directors responded by forbidding her successors to use the state carriage.[3]

Maria van Aelst's immediate successor was Levijntje Polet (written Livina Poleth in some sources), a native of Breda. It was in Batavia that she married Cornelis van der Lijn in 1630. In the course of many years in Asia both husband and wife had acquired a taste for luxury that the directors could never hope to legislate away. There exists an account of the state they maintained written by the Parisian-born merchant-adventurer Jean-Baptiste Tavernier. Shortly after his arrival in Batavia in 1648, Tavernier was invited by Governor-General van der Lijn to dine with him and his party and then to join them in an outing. "Two trumpets began blazing," he writes:

> "My Lord Governor and My Lady with the four wives of the Councillors stepped into a carriage drawn by six horses and the Councillors mounted horses. One was led to me, saddled and bridled in the Persian style, with an extremely attractive

harness. There are always forty or fifty horses in the General's stables, for there is not a ship that does not bring in several, whether from Arabia, Persia or other places. A company of cavalry rode before the General's carriage; each horseman having a collar of buffalo hide and scarlet breeches with silver braid, a plumed hat and a sash of silver lace, sword-sheath and spurs of solid silver, and all their horses in very handsome harness. Three guardsmen marched alongside each carriage with halberd and very well hatted. Each wore a doublet of yellow satin and scarlet breeches trimmed with silver stripes, yellow silk hose, and fine linen. A company of infantry marched behind the carriage; another had left an hour earlier in order to reconnoitre the route."[4]

Passages describing the governor-general's procession occur repeatedly in accounts of settlement life. On the surface the display seems to confirm the reasoning used to combat sponsored female migration from Holland: that Dutchwomen would make excessive demands on their husbands' purses. In fact, female immigration had little to do with it. Men who spent thirty and more years in Asia could not fail to be influenced by their immediate surroundings more than they were by the manners of a country they had left as children. Senior officials of the Company assumed great pomp in dress and in number and variety of attendants when waiting on Asian rulers, and on these occasions no woman was present.

The habits of European men were quite different from those of their parents in the Netherlands. In place of the Dutch maidservant were numbers of retainers of a different race, owned not hired, who shared no common culture with the household head. Within the Batavian household there could scarcely develop that family life so celebrated by Dutch artists of the seventeenth century, who depicted homogeneous groups of kin, soberly dressed, engaged in domestic activities in small, simply furnished chambers. When officials of the Company came to marry, as distinct from selecting a concubine, they chose their brides from among the daughters of their peers or superiors, girls therefore often many years their junior. It should be noted that Batavia's senior officials did not seek to demonstrate their status by bringing proxy brides from the Netherlands. The accession of Creoles to the dignity of first lady, as the century wore on, testifies to the development of a settled society with its own distinctive habits.

The colonial female elite was greater, of course, than the sum of its first ladies. It included, broadly, the wives, widows, and daughters of men ranking as senior merchants, warehouse administrators, presidents or chiefs of factories, fiscals, justices, and councillors. Some of these great ladies had their portraits painted. One was Maria Isaacs Scipio, second wife of Jan van Riebeeck, who was then secretary of Batavia's government (1665–1677), a former president of Malacca and founder of the Cape settlement.[5] The portrait shows a

1. Couple with Servant. By the Dutch painter Albert Cuijp (1620–91) and dating from the decade 1640–50. The woman is dressed in Dutch style, but with pearls at both wrists and in her hair. The slave or servant holding the Asian symbol of status, the parasol, above the couple is dressed in European costume. (From F. de Haan, *Oud Batavia Gedenkboek: Platenalbum*, plate L4.)

heavy-set woman in black, the usual costume worn by Dutch ladies in portraits painted in Holland at that time. Where Maria Scipio's portrait differs from the ladies of Frans Hals, for example, is in the quantity of jewelry which the Batavian lady selected for the sitting. The same costume with ornaments of pearl and amber is recorded in a portrait, painted by Albert Cuijp, of a Batavian woman and her husband sometime in the decade 1640–50.[6] Behind them a dark-skinned servant in European dress holds a *payung* or parasol, the Asian symbol of status, above them.

In addition to the evidence of the portraits and the complaints of the directors about this quickly established, wealthy colonial class, there are letters in family archives that suggest its style of living and values. One that survives was written by Cornelia Johanna van Beveren, a Dutchwoman who was married in Batavia to the Malaccan Juriaen Beek on 27 October 1689. The letter gives an account of the wedding celebrations, her costume, and the furnishings of the house which Beek gave her. He was twenty-nine and a free townsman at the time. "My bridal gown," Cornelia wrote to her aunt, "was of black velvet with a train one and a half yards long. The underskirt was of white satin embroidered from top to bottom with gold lace, and the undersleeves were of the same material and lace, with bows of pearls and diamond buttons. The crowns that I was married with were made entirely of mother-of-pearl and diamonds which my bridegroom had given me for the purpose. Seven ropes of pearls were twisted through my hair, and the jewels at my throat and bosom were also very costly."[7]

The tone of self-congratulation courses throughout the letter, which describes in detail the decorations of the church and the bridal apartment. What makes this fragment so remarkable is its very rarity, and the glimpse it gives into the life of the female elite by a member of it. For the most part one has to rely on the accounts of all sorts of men for information about upper-class women. On this subject the opinions of the men are curiously uniform in wholehearted condemnation and even revulsion.

One passage that occurs again and again in the narratives of travelers to Batavia is the description of a grand lady proceeding to church. The focus on this single event stems from the fact that church attendance was one of the few outings elite women took. The tendency to cloister women of the upper class became characteristic of Dutch society in Asia within a few decades of settlement. It grew, not from imitation of the bourgeoisie in the Netherlands, but from increased familiarity with Asian civilizations and with the habits of the Portuguese overseas. For such a description one can do little better than turn to Nicolaus de Graaff. The scene he paints is a composite of the Iberian and South Asian, and shows how quickly the two mingled to produce a Mestizo culture that was to be most fully developed in Holland's Asian cities of the following

2. Eurasian Lady Going to Church. In procession to the Dutch Reformed Church, this Eurasian woman is surrounded by symbols of status from the Asian world: a woman slave carrying the betel box and a male slave bearing the parasol. The male slave had probably been brought from the Dutch settlement at the Cape of Good Hope. F. de Haan believes the portrait to be set in Colombo, on the evidence of the style of buildings in the background. (From F. de Haan, *Platenalbum*, plate M3. De Haan attributes the painting to J. Haafner's *Reize in eenen palanquin*, vol. 2.)

century. "What most astounds one in Batavia," he says by way of introduction,

> "is the extreme splendor and hauteur which the women in Batavia—Dutch, Mestiza and Half-Caste too—display, especially upon going to and from church . . . for on such occasions each is decked out more expensively than at any other time. . . . Thus they sit by the hundred in church making a show like lacquered dolls. The least of them looks more like a Princess than a burgher's wife or daughter, so that Heaven itself is filled with loathing, especially as they go and come from church, when even the most inferior has her slave follow behind to carry a parasol or sunshade above her against the fierce heat. Many of these have great hanging silken flaps embroidered with golden dragons and ornamental foliage."[8]

It remains for Tavernier to complete the picture with a further description of the ladies' attendants. In addition to the parasol bearer would be several slave women carrying their mistress's hymn book, fan, betel box, and cuspidor. Of betel he adds:

> Men and women always chew it when they go out, even in church; and that's how these ladies piously say their prayers. It is an infamous sight, for their mouths are always full of red spittle, as if their teeth had been smashed.[9]

Every traveler comments with disgust on addiction to betel and on its characteristic of stimulating the flow of saliva and staining the saliva red. Taking betel was peculiar to Eastern cultures; its appearance among the Dutch signals a mingling of the races and adoption of both the indulgences and the symbols of status of the Asian. One of these symbols was the betel box, which was not merely a receptacle for the nut, lime, and leaves but often an elaborately embossed and jeweled container. The betel box is always prominently displayed in paintings of wives of Dutchmen of this time.[10]

Another perversity noted by European visitors—for they could discern no virtue worth recording—was the custom of women raised in Asia of bathing several times daily. It was long before Dutch migrants adopted habits of personal cleanliness in the tropics. They were scandalized by the sight of their mistresses washing themselves in public view in the Ciliwung. Old Batavia houses had bathing boxes built beside the canals for this purpose, with a closed room for changing and steps leading to the water.

The other characteristic of local women with European status, one that was to become legendary in histories and novels, was indolence and its opposite face, viciousness. De Graaff introduces the idea with these lines:

> These little ladies in general, Dutch, but also Half-Castes and Mestizas, and especially in Batavia . . . let themselves be waited on like princesses, and some have many slaves, men and women, in their service who must watch over them like guard dogs night and day . . . and they are so lazy that they will not lift a hand for anything, not even a straw on the floor close to them, but they call out at once for one of their slaves to do it, and if they do not come quickly they are abused, called

41

"common whore," "whore's child," "child of a dog," and sometimes even worse; and if their slaves displease them in any way, even a minor offense, they have them bound to a stake or pole and flogged and beaten with a sharp jagged rattan till their blood flows and the skin hangs lacerated.[11]

The expression "with European status" used above to single out certain Asia-born women draws attention to another point. All women followed the national status of their husbands, so that at any time the European group could include among its female members native Netherlanders, Creoles, Eurasians, and Asians. Not that residents were blind to a person's racial heritage; de Graaff's vulgar definitions and their complexity should settle that question.[12] But upper-class Eurasian women, in these early decades of VOC rule, took on the appearance of Europeans in the dress they donned for their outings and in social consequence, as well as in their names.

Such women are represented in a family portrait by J. J. Coeman which hangs in the Rijksmuseum. The group has been identified as Cornelia van Nieuwenroode with her husband Pieter Cnoll and two of their nine daughters.[13] Cornelia was one of two daughters born to a Japanese woman by Cornelis van Neyenrode,[14] head of the Hirado factory in southern Japan from 1623 to 1632. In 1632 he sent the girls to Batavia. There Cornelia was to marry Cnoll, who held the lucrative post of first senior merchant of the Castle and was to leave her an enormous fortune upon his death in 1672. The portrait shows a thickset Dutchman by the side of a slender, obviously part-Asian woman. Cornelia stands dressed in black, her face a delicately drawn oval, eyes slanted. The painter's attention to visual truth is continued in the depiction of one of the daughters, whose features closely resemble the mother's. The three women are richly gowned in the European style; one of them holds a jeweled box. It is one of the most tender portraits from Batavia.

At this point one can profitably diverge to consider how the young were being raised in this growing municipality of Batavia. Travelers were eloquent on the subject. They were as little able to divorce themselves from racial prejudice in their efforts to describe child-rearing as in their evocation of Mestizo manners. Nevertheless, some passages are worth consulting as testimony to a characteristic of settlement life already noted, the predominance of Portuguese or Asian tongues as the languages of daily life. De Graaff explains the situation in this passage:

> Those born in the Indies especially are incapable, or rather too lazy, to raise their own children. Instead, as soon as they come into the world [the mothers] hand them over to a Black wetnurse, a slave whore, or to one of their women Slaves to nurse and rear, so that they trouble themselves little with their own children; which is why children prefer being with their Black nurse and the men and women slaves to being with their parents. Since they are raised by [slaves] and imbibe all their manners,

their nature and all their qualities, they therefore speak Malabarese, Singhalese, Bengali, and pidgin Portuguese as well as the slaves themselves, and when they reach adulthood they can scarcely speak a word of Dutch decently, far less maintain a rational conversation without mixing many words of pidgin Portuguese in it.[15]

Governor-General Maetsuyker was in complete agreement with de Graaff on the ill consequences of raising children among slaves. Maetsuyker also attributed the fault to the supposed character of individual slaves rather than to the institution of slavery itself and the relationship of owner and owned. He saw well-run schools and careful supervision by parents as means to combat vice in the Indies-born, however.[16] In this he differed from de Graaff and others of his contemporaries who found in mixed racial heritage itself the major cause of the defects of character they listed.

The point to be settled here is not the relation of character to race, but the fact that in Batavia the offspring of European men were raised by people with non-European origins, manners, tongue, culture, and religious beliefs, people whose relation to their charges, that of chattel, did not exist in the Netherlands. Men who wished to pass on their own cultural heritage to their children sent them to Europe at the early age of two or three years.

The fortunes of the Caron children illustrate these points. They were born in Hirado, part-Japanese through their mother and part-European through their father. The latter was François Caron, who spent twenty-two years as a Company employee in Japan, rising from assistant and interpreter to president of Hirado in 1639. In 1641 Caron père was back in Batavia with his children and their mother. As a convert to Roman Catholicism, the Japanese mother had been forced to leave her country of birth under the terms of Iyemitsu's expulsion edicts. Five of their six children were still living. Caron had publicly acknowledged them, giving them Dutch names and raising them as Europeans and Christians. In 1643, however, upon returning from leave in Holland, Caron took a further step and applied to Batavia's government for a certificate of legitimacy for the five. His request described government action as the only way in which he could accomplish his aim: he had hastened his return to Batavia, he said, in order to marry the children's mother and thus make their social position secure, but she was, "to his excessive sorrow," already dead. The government complied, legitimizing Daniel, Tobias, François, Petronella, and Maria by a decree of 26 September 1643. A similar act of legitimation was later obtained from the directors in Holland also.[17]

With his children thus securely European and legitimate by proclamation, Caron set about promoting their futures. The two surviving boys he sent to Europe for schooling (Tobias had died some time after 1643). Daniel (b. 1622) was enrolled in Leiden in the very respectable school of theology in 1643; François (b. 1634) entered Leiden University some eleven years later. In 1649

Daniel enlisted in the VOC's service as a common soldier. The interlude was brief, however, for he applied to the church authorities in Batavia for permission to enter the ministry, and was examined and accepted as a candidate for ordination in August of 1650. In 1658 he was assigned to Taiwan, where his father's brother-in-law, Frederik Coyett, was governor (1656–62). It is probable that Daniel lost his life during Koxinga's attack in 1661.

Caron's other son, François, set out for the Indies in 1660, where he was to act as dominie in Ambon for fourteen years and become known as a Malay scholar, composing many religious works in the island's dialect. In 1673 he requested permission to "repatriate," by which he meant return to the Netherlands, not Japan. He departed for Europe with his Asia-born wife and family in 1675. It seems that his ethnic origins were no obstacle in Holland, for he was called to the pulpit of Leksmond near Tiel. A collection of his Malay religious tracts was published in Amsterdam in 1693, and he died in Holland twelve years later.

By contrast, neither Petronella nor Maria Caron was sent to the Netherlands for schooling. They were raised in Hirado and Batavia, and destined to be wives to native Hollanders. Very little is known about them, and the information we have is contradictory. According to Wijnaendts van Resandt, Maria was married in Batavia to the merchant Nicolaas de Voocht, and in 1657 accompanied him to Tonkin (northern Vietnam), where he was head of trade. Boxer has her sister Petronella marrying de Voocht, living in Batavia over the years 1657–65, and later marrying justice Jacob van Dam. He says that Maria Caron was married to Isaac Soolman around the year 1668.[18]

The actual details are of little importance here. What matters is the contrast between the careers charted for part-Asian children of distinguished VOC officials. In the case of the Caron girls we see that Eurasian daughters remained in Asia. Although they had European status and privileges, they were destined for a lifetime in one or the other of the VOC's Asian factories. Caron left these half-Japanese daughters behind when he was recalled to Holland by the directors in 1650 on charges of smuggling. He did, however, take back to the Netherlands all the children, daughters as well as sons, born to his Dutch bride, Constantia Boudaen, whom he had married by proxy and had brought out to Batavia in 1645.

Nothing is known of Daniel Caron after 1658. The younger François Caron married a woman who was either Ambonese or of mixed race. While a part-Asian woman could improve her status by marriage to a European of good ranking in the Company, a part-Asian male had to achieve his status through employment. In the case of the Caron boys, neither was taken into the Company on the one route to high position, the civilian hierarchy of merchants. It can be argued that in 1666, when François went out as a minister, he had no powerfully placed relatives to promote him, his father having been dismissed and his step-uncle exiled to Ay in the Banda Islands. But Daniel was only a soldier in 1649 when his father was at the height of his VOC career, but one step away from the governor-generalship itself.

Many examples could be brought forward in support of the conclusion that very early on, some rich and powerful officers of the Company acted upon paternal inclination in favor of their illegitimate Eurasian children. For the boys there was schooling in Europe, and many never returned, or if they did, spent only a part of their careers in Asia, looking to the Netherlands as their homeland and the country of their descendants. The girls were usually left in Asia, but married Netherlanders. Their final resting place was then determined by their husband's career and disposition. The Eurasian man reared in the Indies could hope for employment by the Company and marriage to a Eurasian woman. It was rare for Eurasian men to marry immigrants, both because of the small numbers of such women available as brides and because such a match was regarded as demeaning the woman. Evidently these matches did take place, however, when the man's origins were compensated for by wealth, as in the case of the Beek-van Beveren alliance. Upon occasion, Creole daughters might also be sent to the Netherlands. In 1659, for example, Cornelis Speelman won permission from the Indies Council to "send his little daughter, aged about two, to the fatherland, together with her *amme* or wetnurse."[19]

These examples are, however, exceptions to Company policy, which was to keep Creoles and Eurasians in the settlements as an intermediate group between the mass of Asians and the thin layer of immigrants in the top positions. Those senior servants of the Company who bent rules to their needs still thought of an Asian settlement as the proper place for their daughters, and attempted to secure their girls' future by marriage to men who were white and privileged office-holders. Their sons they groomed either to become members of Dutch society in Europe, by removing them as lads from their homeland, or to hold positions of modest respectability in the colony. In either case, it was the boys who were trained to look upon Holland as their home country.

The Christian Asian community also represents a new social and cultural group springing from the contact between East and West. It came into existence in the most natural way. Portuguese religious had taken the Gospel to Indonesia's islands from their bases in India all during the sixteenth century. They established Christian settlements in the islands east of Java, especially in Flores and Timor, and in the Moluccas. Francis Xavier, for instance, arrived in the Moluccan islands in 1545. Indonesians who adopted the new religion symbolized their spiritual rebirth by exchanging their personal names for those of the saints or biblical characters, in their Portuguese form.

This nucleus of a Christian community was the object of especial attention from the Dutch. In their homeland they were fighting a national and civil war against Roman Catholic Spain and Portugal, so it is understandable that they should concern themselves with local peoples who had taken the faith of their enemies. Portuguese religious were expelled and conversion to the beliefs and practices of the Dutch Reformed Church demanded. Some converts still took Portuguese names, but many more adopted Christian names in their Dutch form.

Still, Portuguese remained the tongue of Asian Christian communities in areas like Timor where priests and friars continued to guide congregations, and in Batavia where a separate parish was created for people from Indian ports and their descendants. Malay quickly displaced Portuguese as the language of religion among Indonesian Christians, however. A knowledge of Malay or Portuguese was required of clerics appointed to work with Asian converts.

Since Malay was not usually the first tongue of Indonesian converts, European dominies expressed doubts about the efficacy of their preaching and of catechism classes. Indonesians came to be appointed as lay officers with the duty of giving religious instruction in the vernaculars. Some were men of considerable learning, such as the Ambonese Amos Pieterszoon Thenoe, who had been a pupil of Valentijn, spoke Dutch fluently, and wrote Malay in both the Roman and Arabic scripts. Most, however, had little education, were poorly paid by the Company, and were treated with scorn by the European clergy, who at first doubted the very fitness of any Asian to partake of the sacraments. That debate was resolved in favor of confirming Asians as members of the church. Their lay officers, however, were never admitted to church synods and rarely ordained into the ministry.

European views were never solidly united, so that there were some among the Dutch who sought to foster learning and truth as they saw it among the Asians with whom they lived. It had begun with Xavier, who took several Indonesian boys to Goa in India in 1547 with the intention of training them as evangelists to their home communities. From time to time small groups of Indonesians were sent to the Netherlands at the Company's expense for the same purpose.

The names of certain Hollanders in particular have been associated with the European education of Indonesians early in the seventeenth century. Matelief took three Ambonese to the Netherlands in 1608, in the hope that they would return as schoolteachers to spread Dutch culture as well as religion. Another five were taken to the Netherlands in 1630 in the care of the lay officer Johannes Gerritszoon Bloem. The first Javanese to be sent to study theology in the Netherlands went under the baptismal name of Pieter Ducot. He was a nephew of the harbor master of Japara, and had converted while a prisoner of the Dutch on Banda.

From the first, religion and culture were understood as inseparable; hence the efforts made to associate Christian Asians with the Dutch. The first schools and church services for Asians were conducted in Dutch, a fact reflecting not cultural chauvinism and ignorance of local tongues so much as a desire to foster the Dutch tongue among all political allies of the Netherlands. It is amply documented that in the late-nineteenth century colony many Dutch people resented Indonesians speaking their tongue; but Company officials thought quite differently on the matter and sought to expand its use during the VOC centuries. They gave lucrative and prestigious civic posts only to those Asians who could speak Dutch, and only Dutch speakers were entitled to wear certain exceptional articles of dress such as the Western hat. Furthermore, Christians might manumit only such slaves as could speak Dutch.[20] As late as the 1770s VOC officials made attendance at language classes mandatory for all Indonesian lay officers of the church, punishing the laggards with deduction of half their monthly pay.[21]

Some Asian Christians prospered under the Dutch, and their relatives and friends were able to raise monuments to their memory that are impressive in their size and claims. These monuments were erected in the churchyards of the Malay and Portuguese communities that grew up within and around the original walls of Batavia. They proclaim the offices once held, and sometimes combine initials of spouses with designs to form a family crest in the Dutch manner. Other relatives gave the church vessels and plate stamped with the names and worldly degree of the person they so honored. De Haan has included in his album a photograph of a large silver baptismal font bearing the inscription (in Dutch), "In memory of the Native Burgher Thomas Anthonits bequeathed to the Portuguese Church in Batavia on 15 February 1733, valued at 755 reales 9 stuivers."[22]

The deceased and the mourners cherishing his memory belonged to the group of non-Indonesian Asians whose members were the principal patrons of the Portuguese church. They were known as Mardijkers, which is an old Dutch rendering of the Portuguese version of *Maharddhika* (Sanskrit for "great man," "high and mighty") and which acquired in Indonesia the meaning of free(d) person. For a long time this group was distinct from the Indonesians, as freed slaves of non-Indonesian descent and as baptismal members of the Reformed Church. Most traced their history back to the coasts of India and settlements dominated by the Portuguese in the sixteenth century. In Batavia they clung to their separate status, encouraged by the Company, which legislated for them as a distinct group.

As heirs to a Mestizo culture formed in Portugal's Indian settlements, Mardijker men typically combined elements of the European and Asian in their costume; that is to say, they wore Portuguese silk shirts and plumed hats but went without shoes. In the eyes of some of their Dutch contemporaries it was an absurd and pretentious apparel. Every visitor to Batavia commented on the appearance of Mardijker men, at times in a language as spiteful as that used to depict Eurasian women. The traveler Jacob Haafner was most struck by the

47

bare feet, and has left us this description: "The black Portuguese who are rich parade it excessively, especially in their dress; still, for those not used to such a sight there is no stranger or more contradictory display to be seen than these people in the richest clothing, with ruffles at their wrists, but bare feet, wandering along the streets with neither shoes nor stockings." [23]

In Batavia the men were self-employed as traders and shopkeepers or they raised sugar on estates ringing the city, estates which they purchased or leased. Since all groups of any size were required to live in their own quarters of the city, Mardijkers were able to maintain their own language, a form of Portuguese. They helped perpetuate Creole Portuguese as a lingua franca of Dutch settlements far into the late eighteenth century, as did the Company itself by appointing Portuguese speakers to their pulpits and to the catechism classes organized for their children.

Batavia's first Portuguese church had been built next to the vegetable and poultry market in 1634. In 1693 a new church was begun outside the city walls on the southeast side, its first stone laid by the retired councillor Pieter van Hoorn. The Portuguese churches were to have patrons from the highest ranks of VOC society. Many of Batavia's distinguished citizens were honored after their death by memorial plaques hung on the walls of the inner church, [24] and Governor-General Hendrik Zwaardecroon chose to be buried there rather than in the Dutch church. Another patron was Camphuys, who left a set of silver plate to the parish in 1695 inscribed, "In honor of the new Church for the Portuguese or Native community endowed and bequeathed by Joannes Camphuys, born in Haarlem 18 July 1634, being from 11 January 1684 to 24 September 1691 Governor-General of Netherlands India, died at Batavia 18 July 1695." [25]

It is interesting to note the description of the Mardijkers as the "Portuguese or Native community" in this inscription. This was at the close of the seventeenth century. The Mardijkers were to remain a separate group for nearly another century, but the association with Indonesians accurately foreshadowed the trend to come. To retain a separate identity, there had to be a constant influx of Asians from India having some acquaintance with Portuguese language and culture. Even had this been so, there was still the developing metropolitan culture of Batavia that came to envelop all its inhabitants as the years wore on. Within the Asian quarters differences between the many ethnic groups became less marked. Daily mixing, use of Malay, common experience of Company law—all contributed to the making of the Batavian.

The disappearance of a distinct Mardijker community through fusion of Mardijker and Indonesian Christian groups was a natural development. The Company recognized it in 1797 when it dissolved two of the four militia companies of Mardijkers on account of the declining numbers of those so identifying themselves. [26] In organization, Mardijkers yet survived the Netherlands East Indies Company by a decade or two. In 1808, when Abraham

Anthonij Engelbrecht, minister to Batavia's Portuguese church, died, there was none to succeed him. Services and catechism classes in Portuguese ceased from that time. The post of Mardijker captain, or head and spokesman for the community, continued a little longer. Its last bearer was the wealthy landowner Augustijn Michiels. With his death in 1833 the post was allowed to lapse. But from the beginning some Mardijkers had taken the ultimate step towards complete assimilation with the Asian majority of Batavia by becoming Muslim. And some had never been Christian at all. Among the Indian slaves captured from the Portuguese (listed in chapter 1) there was an Ysmael, along with the Rodrigos.

In sum, then, there was no ethnic or racial unity among Asian Christians in the seventeenth century. Individuals came from the smaller islands of Indonesia or from India's coastal cities. Their establishment in Batavia was the result of various circumstances. Some had come as free settlers, expecting economic advantage from their common religious profession with Batavia's rulers. Others were former slaves, freed upon conversion. Some had reached Batavia through capture and had there been transformed, at least externally, from Roman Catholics to Protestants. Still others had taken up the new religion as a result of evangelization or upon legal marriage to a European man. Some Asian Christians had a command of the Dutch language and an insight into Dutch culture, while a very few had seen it at first hand in Europe. But all Asian Christians had a special relation to the Company as co-religionists of the Dutch. This attachment gave them certain privileges such as a claim on poor relief, an opportunity for formal schooling, and the chance for employment as religious teachers.

In daily living, converts differed less clearly from the other Indonesian inhabitants of Batavia. Women, particularly, differed little in dress, and in habit and manners not at all. Many classified as Mardijkers may have been Indonesian, since under Dutch law women followed the nationality of their husbands. In the Mardijker wards, they raised their children not according to the Indian customs of their husbands' home cities, nor yet exactly as in their own ethnic communities in Indonesia, but in the ways of the population indigenous to Batavia that was coming to develop a culture of its own. Only the wealthy few stood out in any marked way, the ones who fashioned coats-of-arms for themselves and modeled their manners on those of the Dutch colonial elite. The great majority of Mardijkers and Christian Indonesians passed their lives in Batavia in the same manner as their fellow Asians.

The average VOC clerk and soldier knew little about the religions and histories of the Asians amongst whom they lived. All the same, they were not entirely ignorant of the world around them. The daily stroll made them aware of the great variety of peoples and customs, and many gained more than a passing familiarity with Asian languages and traditions from their slaves, mistresses,

49

and part-Asian kin. Valentijn's description of the languages heard in Batavia may be taken as a summary of the average Hollanders' reckoning with their environs at the close of the century: "The languages one ordinarily uses in Batavia are Portuguese, low Malay, and Dutch. There are also Javanese, Chinese, and all the other languages of the peoples who reside here; but these are used only when speaking among themselves, never being used by other nationals; but Portuguese and Malay are the two languages one can communicate in easily with all manner of peoples, not only in Batavia, but throughout all India as far as Persia."[27]

The seventeenth century closes on societies very different from those planted in its opening years. The larger of them had the appearance of cities, with streets laid, churches and hospitals built, and a visible government. Batavia was now secure and expanding beyond its outer walls, as new fields were brought under cultivation and sugar mills erected along the Ciliwung. Its inhabitants were similarly transformed. The rough and ready soldiers and merchants had become a more orderly citizenry. Domestic habits had triumphed in some circles, so that adventurers were now family men bent on promoting the future of their children and relatives by marriage. From a Dutch Calvinist point of view, of course, senior officers of the Company set a lamentable example still, taking concubines, then late in life marrying young girls for political or financial reasons.

Daily life in all the VOC settlements involved a recognition of the diversity of human behavior and traditions. Some consciously exchanged one code for another: Europeans adopted language and slavery from Asians; some Asians acquired names, dress, manners, occupations, religion from the Europeans. New alliances had been formed between groups, based, not on mutual esteem, but on shared attachment to belief and power. One cannot therefore readily distinguish in the mature seventeenth-century settlement such clearcut groups as Dutch, Indonesian (in the geographical sense), and Foreign Oriental. More complex and numerous groups than these had developed, sharing some characteristics but differing in others.

In the middle years of the century there was still considerable movement by Europeans between Holland and the Asian settlements. Between the years 1645 and 1651 Constantia Caron-Boudaen, for instance, traveled from The Hague to Batavia, to Taiwan, to Batavia, and back to the Netherlands before finally settling in Paris. Holland was still the homeland of the migrants and the adopted land of their children. Even a man like Cornelis Speelman, who spent forty of his fifty-seven years in Asia, made several plans for a return to Europe and remained in the East only by reason of successive appointments to lucrative and prestigious posts.

With Camphuys is revealed a new development within colonial society, that of an elite choosing permanent settlement on Java, a choice less-fortunate Europeans had been unable to reject. Camphuys, too, spent the greatest part of his life in Asia. Having survived the first years of governor-generalship and looking forward to a life in retirement, he recognized, perhaps, that Europe had little attraction for him anymore, or perhaps that he was unfitted by his long sojourn in Asia to take up life there again. His wish to retire in Indonesia was granted by the directors. Camphuys set a pattern in a preference for Indonesia over Holland, a taste for seigneurial life on a country estate, an appreciation of oriental civilization. This style, most fully developed in the eighteenth century, represents the culmination of trends already apparent in some Company settlements by the fifth and sixth decades of the seventeenth. In some respects it was to be a closed society, isolated from Europe and elaborating those aspects borrowed early from an Iberian and Asian cultural medley. This development is the subject of the next chapter.

3

The Web of Colonial Society: Batavia and Environs in the Eighteenth Century

THE COMPANY SEAMAN AND POET Jan de Marre first sailed to Batavia early in the eighteenth century. Something of the impression the city made on the visitor after months at sea can be felt in this excerpt from his long poem "Batavia":

> O lovely Batavia, that holds me spellbound,
> There your Town Hall with its proudly arching vaults
> Rears its profile! How splendid is your situation!
> Your broad Canals, replenished with fresh water,
>   beautifully planted,
> Need bend before no city in the Netherlands . . .
> The Tiger's Canal, of which Batavia well may boast,
> Throws up proudly to the skies a row of Palaces
> And glitters from end to end with jewels of architecture . . .
> O'ershadowed by an avenue of eternal spring green . . .
> How does Batavia charm the stroller then![1]

These were to be the last years of the city's prosperity, although individuals made fortunes at the Company's expense throughout the eighteenth century. Conditions in Batavia itself—its location on malarial swamps, its crowded quarters, the unsanitary life style of the immigrant Dutch—combined with cholera and typhoid epidemics to decimate the city's population. Such mortal dangers emptied Batavia of its wealthy, encouraging them to build spacious, airy villas beyond the limits of the old settlement. By mid-century the country houses of Batavia's elite extended as far south as Bogor. It was not merely health they sought. Landed estates gave rich Batavians novel ways to display their fortunes and provided a fresh context for the elaboration of a peculiarly Eurasian culture.

The move away from the old city had, in fact, begun long since. Petronella Speelman-Wonderaer described herself in 1680 as living on her "estate, named Wonderwel, outside this city of Batavia."[2] Thirty years earlier Tavernier had spoken of councillors as "each one having his garden" along the river to which they journeyed by boat. De Graaff had also noted the preference for a residence in the country lying south of Batavia. "Outside the Town," he had written, "one finds many beautiful Pastures, Rivers, Rice and Sugar fields and Estates, all of them planted to fruit trees, and some with splendid houses and delightful pleasure gardens."[3]

At first, country estates were principally used for a few hours' relaxation, the owner returning to the safety of Batavia's walls by nightfall. Outings by the city's prominent citizens are often noted in the *Daily Register*, as in this entry for 27 September 1648: "This afternoon the noble Governor-General [van der Lijn] and his wife and children, together with the Councillors of the Indies and their wives, journeyed in two large praus upriver to Mr. Caron's newly laid out estate, being invited there by that gentleman, and were splendidly entertained and regaled, floating back down the river in the cool of the evening, and the whole company arrived back here inside the castle at 8 o'clock."[4]

Only in the eighteenth century did fashionable society spend weeks at a time in the country and retired officials take up permanent residence in country villas. This change in living habits depended in part on two conditions. One was the accord signed with Bantam in 1684 which guaranteed Batavia from attack. The other was the transformation of Batavia's environs into cultivated fields.[5] The advance on the heavy vegetation surrounding the city lessened the dangers to life and property from wild animals and from runaway slaves. Accordingly, colonial society, which in the seventeenth century had been merely perched on the edge of Java and "outward-looking," connected by sea lanes to the European homeland, now turned to look inland, extending beyond the city's walls in ever-widening arcs.

Around 1700 the Dutch painter Cornelis de Bruijn began his travels round the world, reaching Batavia early in 1706. He carried letters of introduction and so was at once presented to the current governor-general, Joan van Hoorn, to other high officials, and to former governor-general Willem van Outhoorn, who was living in retirement in a "villa situated a little distance from the town." One of de Bruijn's social engagements was a dinner given by Councillor Abraham van Riebeeck in celebration of his wife's birthday at his estate situated, in the traveling time of the day, "about one and a half hours to the South." "The whole countryside is planted to rice," de Bruijn wrote. "One also saw all sorts of fruit and other trees on this estate, although they had not yet reached maturity, and the land was being worked daily. Although the house is already completed, the stables and kitchen have still to be built."[6]

De Bruijn was also a guest of Cornelis Chastelein on his Depok property. Chastelein (1657–1714) had emigrated with the rank of accountant, accompanied by his sisters. He continued in the Company's employ until his death, by which time he was a full councillor. He had started his Indies career in the privileged capacity of son of an important shareholder in the Company, and smoothed his climb up the hierarchy by marrying the Indies-born daughter of

Councillor Cornelis van Qualberg. His legitimate son Anthonij married a daughter of Mattheus de Haan (governor-general 1725–29). Chastelein also recognized Maria and Catharina as his daughters by the slave Leonora van Bali. De Bruijn described Chastelein's villa as two-storeyed and constructed of wood, set amidst fields under sugar and pepper cultivation. He noted that the slave retainers were numerous and included many Balinese. Chastelein emancipated them in his will, and Depok was to remain a distinct Indonesian Christian community for two centuries.[7]

Besides the traveler's narrative, there is information on the country estate from ground plans of villas and their gardens, contemporary paintings, and photographs, taken this century of such houses as still existed. The work of Johannes Rach and beautiful photographic records assembled by V. I. van de Wall and F. de Haan are particularly instructive. Three distinctive country houses will be briefly described here in connection with their principal owners.

Gunung Sari was built by Frederik Julius Coyett in the third decade of the eighteenth century.[8] Coyett was a grandson of Governor Frederik Coyett of Taiwan and of Susanna Boudaen, sister of Caron's proxy bride. The grandson Coyett had been born in Asia, but went to Holland in 1707 after commencing employment with the Company as an assistant. Upon his return he swiftly reached high offices—senior merchant, governor of Java's North Coast Province, councillor extraordinary (1737)—amassing a fortune along the way. He journeyed further into Java than most of his contemporaries, visiting Solo in 1733 and touring the Mataram territories. Given his family history (he was second generation Indies-born) and long years in Java, it is understandable that the house he built should incorporate Indonesian features. Gunung Sari was made up of a closed inner core, to which were added large front and back pillared verandas with marble floors and peaked roofs,—a modification of the Javanese *pendopo* or reception hall. Into the walls and about the grounds were placed Hindu statues from the Prambanan temples which Coyett had fancied during his travels and transported to Batavia.

On Coyett's death Gunung Sari passed to Geertruida Margaretha Goossens, to whom he was betrothed. The house was to change owners another four times before being sold to Batavia's Captain China of 1761, Lim Tjipko. From that time on it served as a temple and burial ground for the capital's Chinese and was called Klenteng Sentiong.

Gunung Sari was fairly modest in size and ornamentation, and so the contrast with the house that Governor-General P. A. van der Parra built himself is startling. As Rach painted it,[9] the building was imposing in its size and fantastic appearance, with a central part of two storeys topped by eagles, and with ornamental pots and arches. Heavy monumental gates fronted it, again with a variety of statuary. To both sides and set back were separate buildings—guest accommodations, slaves' quarters, stables, and so forth—a typical feature of

3. Country House of Governor-General P. A. van der Parra. Painted by Johannes Rach (1720–83). Rach went out to Indonesia as an artillery gunner for the VOC in 1762, but was employed upon arrival as an official painter for the Company. (From F. de Haan, *Platenalbum*, plate K22.)

the Indies house and again a development on Javanese styles. The house gave on to the Ciliwung River, and bathing stalls were erected at its edge, with the whole approached by an avenue of tamarind trees.

Now van der Parra, like Coyett, came from a well-established Asian family. His term as governor-general (1761–75) coincides with the period of the colony's greatest insulation (or independence) from Europe, when Eurasian culture was its most elaborate. It is not surprising, then, that the ostentation and pomp van der Parra and his contemporaries brought to their houses should be quite distinct from another architectural type, exemplified by men who associated themselves publicly with ideas stemming from the Enlightenment movement in Europe.

The mansion which Reynier de Klerk erected around 1760, and which has survived through many hands to house the archives of the Republic of Indonesia, is such an example. It is a solid, well-proportioned building, two-storeyed, with great ornamental doors and deep mullioned windows.[10] Gone are the embellishments, as are also the verandas, in favor of the close privacy of the Dutch house. By a peculiarly Indies coincidence, de Klerk's wife was daughter to the Geertruida Goossens of Gunung Sari, and the house passed to his protégé J. C. M. Radermacher, who was husband of de Klerk's wife's daughter, Margaretha Sophia Verijssel, by an earlier marriage.

While they differed markedly in design, eighteenth-century villas all shared certain characteristics. First, they were set in huge grounds. Second, they were built beyond the Castle's walls, in the heart of today's Jakarta but at that time often one or two hours' distant by boat or carriage. Third, they were maintained by large retinues of slaves and their owners continued traditional Indonesian practice in drawing upon the labor of inhabitants of the lands they leased or purchased. Their owners lived in a grand seigneurial manner that struck the eighteenth-century observer forcibly. That living style will be examined in the following sections dealing with the great property owners of the period, members of all the major divisions within the colonial elite: native European, Eurasian, Creole, and Asian Christian.

Let us first take a look at the position of a VOC official after his appointment as governor-general. We have already seen the governor-general in Tavernier's *Travels* (pp. 36–37), riding out with his trumpeters, guard, liveried attendants, and suite of ladies and gentlemen. This entourage, larger and more elaborate, accompanied the eighteenth-century chief official. After 1719 it became obligatory for all to alight from their carriages or to dismount upon announcement of the progress of the governor-general or a councillor.[11] Every group was required to make obeisance in the manner of its culture: men with European status would make their bow, baring their heads; Indonesians squatted, hands clasped, as they did before their own nobility. The same attentions were paid wives of members of the government. In this manner the congested, narrow streets of the inner city were used for enhancement of the governor-general's position. Another regulation issued in the early days of Batavia and originally introduced for reasons of state security was similarly adapted for display. After 1729 only the highest officials and their wives might enter the Castle on horseback or by carriage.[12] All lesser mortals had to cross the bridge into the Castle on foot.

Governors-general carried their need for public respect into the realm of religion, too. When a governor-general entered church, at whatever point during the service, the entire congregation was expected to rise and bow until he had taken his seat.[13] The same consequence attended his wife. The ceremony, slightly modified, extended to councillors, for whom men alone had to rise from their devotions.

Some who reached the lofty position of governor-general had odes composed in their honor. Verse in praise of Governor-General Willem van Outhoorn (1691–1704) will be quoted here. Van Outhoorn was one of only seven men born outside Europe who reached the governor-generalship in all Indonesia's colonial period. He had been born at Larike on Ambon in 1635 to Cornelis van Outhoorn and the Dutch immigrant Agnetha Tielmans. His schooling was in the Netherlands and he returned East in 1659 as junior merchant at Malacca. A year later he was transferred to Batavia, where he was posted until his retirement from the governor-generalship in 1704. He had climbed the ranks and held such honorary posts as colonel of the town's militia before passing his last fifteen years on his country estate south of Batavia. His poet was the Company surgeon Abraham Bogaert. After van Outhoorn had elevated Bogaert to the supervisory post of grand inspector, his protégé penned these lines in his patron's praise:

> Thus noble Outhoorn, thus rose, thus mounted
> Your glorious sun above the horizon yonder in the East . . .
> The entire kingdom fell to its knees before this luster,
> And knew no limit or measure in admiration.
> What speak I of Siamese, Timorese,
> Amboners, Malays, Makassars?
> What speak I of Bengalis, Singhalese,
> And Malabars, and other Barbarians?
> The entire East, gladdened by your glory-sun
> Bathed in the light of your mighty power,
> Burned incense on the altar of your virtue
> With deep reverence and downcast eyes.[14]

The apotheosis of the governor-general was well underway. Valentijn says of the Africa-born Abraham van Riebeeck that he was a "hater of all pomp"; but he, too, took advantage of his wealth and position to indulge a passion for acquiring race horses, and he liked to be followed, when he rode out, by a great train of slave women on donkeys.[15]

The massive, intricately carved furniture found in colonial collections of museums and photographed in de Haan's *Platenalbum* and other books on this period[16] also attests to the wealth and tastes of Batavia's elite. So do the fine porcelain sets members ordered from China. Often the plates were painted with Asian designs, but frequently they bore the insignia of the VOC or the purchaser's family. Governors-general, and all who aspired to follow their style, had memorial trays or plates inscribed with their names to mark special occasions in their families, and issued medals to their colleagues commemorating accession to office.[17]

More than any other, Petrus Albertus van der Parra epitomizes the magnificence of the eighteenth-century Company official and the remoteness of Batavians' lives from native Dutch practice. He had been born in Colombo in 1714, son of Cornelis Romboutsz. van der Parra and of the Dutch-born Geertruida Susanna Spanuyt (or Spanijt).* His father Cornelis had also been born in Ceylon, where he was secretary to that island's colonial government, and his father before him had been a VOC employee in Ceylon also. This founder of the clan, Rombout van der Parra, had married there a Henrietta Wichelman, who had been born to Dutch parents in Ceylon in 1676. In the paternal line, then, P. A. van der Parra had strong roots in Asia. His father died when he was young, and his mother followed the VOC habit in quickly remarrying. Van der Parra's stepfather was the Netherlander Adriaan Maten, who rose to be commander of Malabar in 1731 and was later called to Batavia as councillor.

The future governor-general entered the VOC's service at fourteen. He had had no schooling in Europe, and doubtless owed his employment as clerk and his swift rise to junior merchant at Colombo to family connections. For, it should be noted, he was taken on in 1728, the same year that Batavia's government reissued a decree banning the hiring of Creoles and Eurasians. In 1739 van der Parra was transferred to Batavia with the rank of merchant and was never to leave that city during his remaining thirty-six years. He climbed the hierarchy in the usual way: second secretary of government in 1741, councillor ten years later, and director-general of trade from 1755 until his assumption of the chief post in 1761.

The formal inauguration did not take place until 29 September 1763. Van der Parra's predecessor, Jacob Mossel, had died in office, so that some time elapsed while the directors were notified and could send letters of confirmation, and then there was a further postponement of three months because of van der Parra's desire that the ceremony should fall on his natal day. When the installation finally occurred it took the form of a great festival, and it was attended not only by all the notables of Batavia but also by Indonesian officials, the *bupatis*,

---

* All names marked with an asterisk in the text will be found in a family tree of appendix 1.

who administered the VOC territories in Priangan, Cirebon, along Java's north coast, and Madura. Representatives of the Solo and Yogyakarta sultanates were also present.[18] The occasion was celebrated, too, in all the Dutch settlements from Africa through Persia, India, and the archipelago to Japan. Van der Parra had a medal struck on the occasion. The text, which was in Latin, read, "To mark the inauguration of the noble and mighty man Petrus Albertus van der Parra, Governor-General of the Netherlands Indies; it was his forty-ninth birthday."[19]

The Batavian chronicler P. de Roo de la Faille gives a very full account of the evening audiences van der Parra presided over in the Castle. Men were received by the governor-general in the veranda and sat

> in a long row . . . each one according to his rank; and should it happen that one among them does not observe this, he will be addressed by the Commander [van der Parra] thus: "Sir, that is not your place, you must sit there." . . . Then the conversation begins, but in such a manner that one talks only with one's neighbor . . .
>
> The ladies are received by the Governor-General's lady and remain apart from the gentlemen. They, too, sit according to their husband's rank with the Governor's wife at the top. According to Indies ways, they are served tea in fine little Japanese cups with lids by smartly dressed slave women.[20]

Such experience of Batavian life amused and shocked eighteenth-century travelers and fed their convictions of the superiority of European birth and breeding. The contempt need not delay us here, except to note that it probably encouraged the colonial elite to ignore the behavior of upper-class circles in Dutch cities. A distinctively Indies pattern can be seen in this account: the reception of men took place in the front, public part of the residence, as in any Javanese kabupaten; women sat in the inner apartments.

It is not difficult to understand this segregation. Most of the ladies were part-Asian or Creole and all had been reared by Asians. Their model of behavior could not be that of the Calvinist housewife and mother. Both of van der Parra's wives, for instance, were Batavians by birth and spent their whole lives in VOC settlements in Asia. The first, Elisabeth Petronella van Aerden, had wed van der Parra in Colombo in 1733 while he was still a bookkeeper. She did not survive by long their transfer to Batavia, dying in her home city in 1741.

Van der Parra's second wife, and first lady of Holland's Eastern possessions, was Adriana Johanna Bake, daughter of the Dutch governor of Ambon and of the Indies-born Ida Dudde. She married van der Parra in 1743. Seventeen years later the only child of the marriage was born, the younger Petrus Albertus, who was to be the governor-general's sole heir, for his children by Elisabeth van Aerden had died in infancy. On one side of a medal issued by Governor-General van der Parra in 1768 on the occasion of his twenty-fifth wedding anniversary this surviving child was shown in the manner of a prince, placing a floral wreath on the family coat-of-arms. The boy was then eight. By thirteen he was on the VOC payroll as clerk to the government secretariat, and by the time of van der Parra's death, the twenty-three year old was VOC inspector.[21]

Van der Parra's term as governor-general—fourteen years—was long by eighteenth-century standards. He had come to that office at forty-nine. His whole world was bounded by Ceylon and Java, and it was in the Indies that he sought to promote his son, rather than using his influence to make a place for his heir in Netherlands society. The governor-general was not admired by contemporaries in Europe whose judgments have passed into acceptance. "Vain, self-important, and autocratic" are the terms describing him in the *New Netherlands Biographical Dictionary*.[22] In his own society, however, one quality of the grand courtier was particularly esteemed, his generosity as patron of the church.

Most governors-general patronized the church in one way or another. Joan van Hoorn, for instance, rewarded the Reverend Godefridus van Holten with the sum of 1,000 rix dollars for a gratifying sermon preached on the occasion of his third marriage. Wives and widows of governors-general also endowed the church. But van der Parra consistently favored the clergy, making them gifts of clothing and money, taking on the cost of educating their sons, and generally easing the way of ministers into the tight little societies of other settlements. He was also capable of signaling special favor with éclat. The Reverend Theodorus Vermeer's first sermon, preached in Batavia in 1771, was followed by the gift of a gilded carriage, two Spanish horses, and a coachman.

The major direction of van der Parra's charities reveals him to be a man of Dutch Asia. He never forgot to look upon Ceylon, rather that the country of his great-grandparents, as his homeland. His chief legacy went to the widows of Colombo and a smaller one to the poor of Batavia. Moreover, when he commissioned a new translation of the Psalms and Gospels and had it published at his own expense, the text was in Portuguese, the language van der Parra himself may habitually have spoken in his early years.

While many of the colony's elite modeled themselves on memories of European *grands seigneurs*, P. A. van der Parra and others like him who had never lived in Europe were more immediately influenced by the living styles of some members of the Mardijker group. Descendants of settlers from Portugal's territories in India who grew wealthy in trade rose to social prominence in Batavia in the eighteenth century, and they, too, bought estates in the city's environs, where they lived according to their memories of Asian-Iberian grandees. F. de Haan has traced the fortunes of the most distinguished of these Mardijker clans, the Michiels family.[23]

It began when the free man Titus van Bengala (from Bengal) took the baptismal name of Titus Michielsz. upon conversion in 1694 in Batavia.

Through marriage to the Indian Christian Martha Pieters he had numerous descendants. His sons, grandsons, and great-grandsons held high posts under the Company as spokesmen for the Mardijker community and as heads of their militia companies. The clan reached the peak of fashion with Jonathon Michielsz. (1737–88), a contemporary of van der Parra. He took a family coat-of-arms and consolidated the clan's fortunes through acquisition of large landholdings. The fortune passed to the most famous of all the clan, Augustijn Michiels (he dropped the "z" from the surname), who was a great-grandson of the Bengali Titus and who as head of the Mardijkers was popularly known as "Majoor Jantje."

The family was still almost wholly Asian, being composed of descendants of the original immigrants from India and their Indonesian wives and concubines. Its first member with European status was admitted in 1809, when the Creole Jacobus Anthonij Beijvanck married Augustijn Michiels's legitimate daughter Agraphina Augustijna.[24] At the same time, the alliance gave a descendant of Mardijker immigrants full European status in her own right. But there was already considerable social mixing between members of the two elites. While Augustijn Michiels maintained a house in Batavia's Mardijker neighborhood, which was located around the Portuguese outer church, he spent much of his later years at his favorite country estates, Citrap and Semper Idem. There he entertained leading members of the Dutch community including, in 1828, Governor-General L. P. J. du Bus de Gisignies.

Michiels's arrival on one of his estates was like the triumphant progress of royalty, with inhabitants of his lands playing the *gamelan* (an ensemble of Javanese musical instruments) in welcome and all the hamlet heads in procession. Michiels dressed in Indonesian costume and preferred to sit on a mat rather than a chair. His food was Indonesian and his day punctuated with the afternoon siesta. Female slaves waited at table, and his guests were entertained with music from his slave orchestras and by troupes of *ronggeng* (women dancers). At Citrap he also kept *topeng* (masked) dancers in his employ, and his retainers there numbered 117 house slaves and 48 free servants, in addition to the stable hands and outdoors staff.[25]

Colonial society of VOC times and a little later, then, was made up of groups whose externals alone were European. Since Asian, Eurasian, and Creole constituted the majority, they strongly influenced the immigrant minority of Dutchmen in manners, style of living, and recreation. When an immigrant married into one of these local groups, that influence extended into domestic arrangements, styles of furniture, and the like. And of course, whatever the bride's nationality, the Asian influence was never absent on account of the household slaves. The eighteenth-century contribution to colonial culture was the very public elevation of such styles to the governor-general's court. Of all the first ladies in that century, one alone was Dutch by birth.

61

The eighteenth century yields a little information on the grand ladies of VOC settlements from sources as various as marriage odes and funeral orations, wills and portraits. Then there are the accounts of travelers, records of family alliances, and decrees issued from the Castle dealing particularly with women. From such sources one can piece together an idea of the manner of their lives, without, however, the benefit of a direct observation from one of their number. This is hardly surprising. The Company's major endeavors to promote schooling for girls came late in the century. For the most part, girls raised in the colonies had no formal education outside the household, and their training in the home was supervised by slave women or by mothers who were themselves unschooled.

As first lady, Adriana Bake* emerges partway from the obscurity that hides most eighteenth-century women. We have already seen that she was a daughter of Ida Dudde (who was probably part-Asian) from the mother's second marriage to the Hollander David Bake.[26] Adriana was the widow of VOC commander Anthonij Guldenarm when she married van der Parra in 1743. We see her in paintings by Rach, standing before the governor-general's great house, surrounded by ladies, a parasol held above her by an Indonesian slave. It is her costume that attracts attention, for she is garbed each time in a crinoline, as are her companions.[27]

This selection in dress is not the contradiction it may seem. European costume is but one more example of the medley of elements making up Mestizo culture in Batavia and all the Dutch settlements in Asia. The point is more clearly grasped from another Rach painting, this one of Willem Arnold Alting and his wife standing before their Batavia residence.[28] Once again the woman is shown in European dress, a walking-out costume with narrow skirt, a hat, and a patch on her cheek. Quite naturally complementing this picture of European privilege are the Asian symbols of status: the slave attendant and the betel box.

It is possible that the woman on Alting's arm is Maria Susanna Grebel.* Alting's first wife, the abandoned daughter of a Company soldier who was baptized and reared as Hendrina Maria Knabe, died in 1774. She had married the Dutch lawyer and merchant Alting at thirteen (when he was thirty), and had borne him ten children. Five girls survived to adulthood, and they married Netherlanders who subsequently received appointments to lucrative posts. In 1776 Alting remarried. Maria Grebel was the daughter of the freed slave Susanna van Makassar and the widow of Alting's fellow councillor, Huybert Senn van Basel, who was the founder of a family that was to be prominent in Batavia at the turn of the century. She died in 1780, the year of Alting's elevation to the governor-generalship. Maria's daughter from her first marriage, Maria Wilhelmina Senn van Basel, was later married to Alting's nephew, Nicolaas Engelhard. Whatever the identity of the woman in Rach's

4. Governor-General W. A. Alting and Wife. Painted by Johannes Rach. The lady in the portrait is probably Alting's second wife, the Eurasian Maria Susanna Grebel (d. 1780). She wears European costume, but is followed by a slave carrying her betel box. (From F. de Haan, *Platenalbum*, plate K32.)

painting, the point remains that in the eighteenth century, grand Eurasian and Creole ladies did not discard the symbols giving them status in the eyes of the Asian population when they moved in public as Europeans.

The supreme government took care to uphold the dignity of members' wives, resolving on procedures for their suites and on the deference to be paid them. All councillors, for instance, wore black for Catharina Huysman, wife of Governor-General van Imhoff, when she died in 1744, and by decree they observed mourning for six weeks. In other ways, too, government members elevated their female kin. Mossel named forts Philippineburg and Grietenburg for two of his daughters, and Governor-General van Hoorn's daughter Petronella laid the foundation stone of Batavia's new town hall in 1707. Few eighteenth-century governors-general had sons surviving to adulthood. It was for their daughters that the great expenditures and public celebration of family events were made.

Nor were the illegitimate daughters of ruling families necessarily forgotten. Mossel recognized a girl born to one of his household slaves named Jasmina van Soembawa. This daughter, Arnolda, was born in 1751 and given the surname Schulp, a name that indirectly states the family connection, for *schulp* translates as "shell" and *mossel* is Dutch for "mussel"! Mossel left her a country property and house named Batenburg at his death in 1761. Eighteen years later, some 10,000 rix dollars were restored to her by the trustee of wills, confirming Arnolda's status of acknowledged child.[29] She was accorded the dignities of her half-sisters, including the title *juffrouw*.[30] She survived them all, dying in Batavia at the age of seventy-three.

All these women represent the Creole and Eurasian branches of colonial society. Asian women were sometimes counted among the elite too. Take Anjelina Catharina Valentijn, one of the owners of the Citrap estate before it passed to Augustijn Michiels. She had been born into slavery as Anjelina van Batavia, but had been baptized at three under the sponsorship of one Margaretha Catharina Wargaren[31] and raised as a European. She married the German burgher and militia ensign Johan Samuel Heinrich Wüstenberg, owner of Citrap since 1790. After Wüstenberg's death Anjelina married two more times, and again, European men. Baptism, emancipation, and marriage to wealthy European men combined to make of Anjelina a woman of some consequence in colonial Batavia.

On the whole, race was irrelevant in determining the style of the female elite, since all of its members were raised by the same Asian retainers. European visitors confirm this point by describing them, Eurasians and Creoles, in much the same way. To summarize this section on elite women we can therefore conveniently turn to Stavorinus. Most ladies, he says,[32] were married at twelve and thirteen, had no notion of running a household, could neither read nor write, and had no idea of religion or of the social proprieties. Early marriage

5. Joanna van Riebeeck. Portrait attributed by J. de Loos-Haaxman to Jacob Janssen Coeman, a seventeenth-century lay minister of the Batavian church. Joanna, who was born at the Cape of Good Hope in 1662, is shown in European costume. She was a sister of the future governor-general, Abraham van Riebeeck. (From J. de Loos-Haaxman, *Verlaat Rapport Indie*, plate 10. Print courtesy J.J.C. van der Wilk.)

and premature childbearing robbed them of their looks. He noted that all women raised in the East sat at ease on their feet. Their dress he described as composed of the Indonesian sarong and a kebaya which reached the knees. When they visited a lady with the rank of councillor's wife, they exchanged the shorter kebaya for one falling to their ankles. On Sundays they would wear European costume, but looked, to Stavorinus, gauche and uncomfortable. For the rest, all Indies ladies passed lives bent on the pursuit of pleasure and lavish consumption, never admitting men into their society except at weddings.

Wealth and its public demonstration preoccupied Batavia's government too. Concern did not arise from distaste, as with the travelers, but rather from an aversion to the notion that members of a hierarchically ranked society should appear equal in affluence. With the prescriptions of Javanese and Japanese court societies as their models, Batavia's rulers set about spelling out degrees and forms of magnificence appropriate to each rung in society for Company employee and free burgher alike.

Governor-General Rijcklof van Goens (1678–81) is one of the earliest to legislate on personal habiliments, reserving for members of the supreme government and their wives and children the right to wear pearls, other jewelry, and gold and silver trimmings on their apparel.[33] He also banned lower grades of officials and all free burghers from keeping a carriage.

Such inhibitions on personal pride were evidently not suffered gladly and were disregarded, leading Governor-General Diederik Durven to lament that it was impossible to distinguish councillor from tavern-keeper. To set matters to rights he legislated privileges to two of the most visible symbols of wealth, carriages and parasols.[34] But the great codifier of the eighteenth century was Jacob Mossel. One hundred and twelve years after his predecessor Antonio van Diemen set about introducing order to Batavia's existing statutes and decrees, Mossel devoted himself to a similar undertaking, but this time with the purpose of standardizing personal vanity. The two codifications of statutes mark, then, distinct grades in VOC history and in the course of settlement. The one, established to deal with questions of municipal organization, was intended to bring practice into line with Dutch habits, while the other marks a colony that had renounced the pretense of being Dutch in spirit.

Mossel's code, entitled "Measures for Curbing Pomp and Circumstance," was issued on 30 December 1754.[35] It is an immense piece of legislation, containing twelve major clauses, each subdivided into articles, and is a remarkable document on colonial society. Not surprisingly, the code opened with articles dealing with "carriages and related matters, horses, etc.," some twenty-nine in all. Reserved to the governor-general and councillors alone were glass coaches and coupés with family crests emblazoned on them. Six horses might draw the governor-general's coach, four, the councillors. Within three months of the date of promulgation, persons lower than retired directors of secondary settlements must strip their carriages of gilt and silver. All must dismiss coachmen who were native Europeans; the privilege of employing Europeans was reserved for the governor-general and councillors and their wives and widows and for the president of the supreme court, former governors, secretaries to the government, and the brigadier of the VOC militia. A curious sidelight, this, on the eighteenth-century view of race and status, for it set service by a European above that of a slave, and that service was often to non-Europeans. Mossel's wife was already dead, but wives of his colleagues in Council—Sophia de Klerk-Westpalm, Hendrina Alting-Knabe, Adriana van der Parra-Bake, and Adriana van Riemsdijk-Helvetius—were none of them European by birth. Nor was the Governor-General van der Parra.

Other regulations on transport dealt with the carriage tax and reserved the use of litters to members of the supreme government and their wives and children; only the relatives of such celebrated persons might dress their carriages and attendants in mourning at their decease. By contrast, the section on parasols relaxed restrictions, permitting junior merchants the privilege of a parasol carried by a slave, and allowing wives down to those of ensigns, as well as of "native, Chinese, and Mohammedan officers," the same. All others must carry their own small umbrellas.

Van Goens's code had introduced hierarchy into matters of carriages, parasols, and jewelry. Mossel's paid particular attention to dress. The clause on men's apparel is composed of nine articles. The first of these reserves embroidery in gold and silver to the high government and president of the bench. One gold or silver button might adorn the clothing of former governors, secretaries to Batavia's government, all justices, and directors of subsidiary posts, and these dignitaries could also wear shirts and camisoles made of silk. None below the rank of junior merchant could wear golden shoe buckles.

The item on women's apparel dealt chiefly with jewelry, not spelling out European or Indonesian costume according to rank and race. To those on the top rung—the wives and widows of the governor-general, councillors, and court president—were reserved diamond necklaces, diamond-studded watches, massive gold betel boxes and boxes set with precious stones, necklaces of top quality pearls in two strands, and costly jewels. Those a step lower, the wives of directors of the outlying posts, could wear pearls not exceeding 6,000 rix dollars in value, while pearls owned by wives and widows of senior merchants could be worth no more than 4,000. Frocks of velvet, silk, and linen, and lace trimmings, were reserved to these ladies. In recognition of the social mobility of women, a bride was permitted to dress in the manner allowed a lady of her husband's rank rather than of her father's.

Another item dealt with the numbers of female slaves permissible in public gatherings and the quality of their apparel and ornaments. Three were assigned wives and widows of the supreme government and chief justice, and they could be adorned with diamond earrings of average quality, a gold hairpin, chains of gold and corral, and gold and silver gauze cloth. For the women in senior merchants' families were reserved two female attendants, and for all lower, one dressed in cotton and linen, false pearls, gold hairpins, and small diamonds. The liveries of coachmen and male attendants were also prescribed by rank of the employer.

A new feature was the tax imposed on family celebrations, bearing heaviest on the socially inferior. The tax was assessed on the number of coaches proceeding to a christening and on the number of guests at a wedding feast. Anyone wishing to erect festive arches for a daughter's wedding had to pay fifty rix dollars to the mid-century theological seminary. No such charge was made on members of the supreme government, however. Furthermore, they alone could have trumpets, tympans, and drums in the orchestras playing at their dinner tables.

It would be tedious to relate all the other provisions, which have to do with ceremonial at the graveside, announcement of wedding banns, number of bridesmaids, and so on. Needless to say, the higher the rank, the greater the pomp and quantity of costly items or attendants allowed. Attention should, however, be directed to the last section entitled "On the Outer Offices of the Indies," for it is here that the legislators explicitly recognized the dominant Asian influence in daily life in the VOC settlements. There, from the director down, VOC employees might dress "according to native custom." So, too, might their wives. But when any of these officials came to Batavia, they and their spouses had to observe the proper distinctions in terms of silks and velvets, gold buttons, attendants, and the like, and the men were expected to don European costume.

It is easier to understand the intention of this type of legislation than estimate its effect. Certainly it could be promulgated only in a society that was autocratic and hierarchic. It portrayed and catered to a society whose members knew their place. To a far greater degree than Netherlands society at the same period, colonial society was one in which habitual relations were understood as between superior and inferior. It was, in fact, a society superficially like the Javanese but without its "mystical" underpinnings. Colonial society was a medley of borrowed forms; it created its own meanings that can be understood as neither Dutch nor Asian but as Mestizo.

Sumptuary laws did not survive the Company. They were revoked by Governor-General Alting in December 1795 in response to new demands for abolition of outer distinctions between citizens.[36] Their revocation reflects the contradictory nature of Indies society; privileges regarding horse and carriage were maintained, and new sumptuary laws were devised in the nineteenth century assigning Javanese titles to Dutch civil servants and setting the number and color of parasols allowed each in ceremonies. No succeeding government ever brought in such all-encompassing regulations as the Mossel code, however. The 1754 sumptuary laws mark the triumph of a style of society as surely as they signal its inner nature.

The sumptuary laws caught up all residents, since none could escape Company edicts. Not even the clergy was exempt, but ranked with surgeons in matters of gold buckles and braid. There were few ministers who railed against the vanity and pomp of eighteenth-century colonial society. Even the Reverend Johannes Lipsius, who criticized the extravagance and self-indulgence of his Semarang parishioners, spoke with evident satisfaction of his manse as being ''save the Governor's residence, the most distinguished building of the whole town.''[37] Nor did he scruple to accept van der Parra's gifts.

From decrees passed at Batavia in the second half of the century come traces of official concern or small proofs of a movement away from the dominant morality of earlier decades. Religious enthusiasm was wanting even in the Batavia synod itself, so that the government in 1755 determined on fining church elders half a rix dollar for failure to attend meetings, and two shillings for late arrival. In 1768 the government complained to the directors that there were too few ministers, and that they were too sickly and unable to keep the populace from turning to Islam or ''popery'' or from lapsing into heathendom. Poor attendance forced ending of the Wednesday evening service after 1776.[38]

The protests of certain clerics and travelers against impiety and superstition should be taken cautiously, however, since their standard of judgment was the ''true religion.'' When Stavorinus, for instance, said that Batavian ladies with European status had no idea of religion or of the social proprieties, he was thinking of Dutch Christianity and the European drawing room. It is evident that these ladies were well rehearsed in civilities of a different kind—the tea ceremony, for instance, offering of betel, observance of rank, discreet withdrawal from the company of men. It is difficult to demonstrate, but still arguable, that those who did not know the Heidelberg Confession did know the divining of good and evil days and proper observance of ritual to propitiate the spirits, and that through their maids they had been steeped in a folklore that carried its own morality. Such were not the conclusions of the eighteenth-century observers whom we read today. They were alike in pointing to the decline in public observance of Christianity and in describing Batavians as obsessed with accumulating wealth and with its display.

Wealth, and the leisure following from it, were demonstrated by the ownership of slaves. This is the other face of the society of sumptuary codes and of country estates. In the discussion so far, we have considered slavery chiefly as a symbol of status for Europeans, and little has been said of the treatment of

69

slaves or of the laws governing them. The Batavian government, which employed vast numbers, was not moved to deal with such matters as fair rations and decent accommodations until 1803. Before that time there is scant reference to conditions of those enslaved, and the compassionate or outraged observer is usually wanting. Occasional references in the *Daily Register*, however, suggest that slaves were often grossly mistreated and that there was shocking loss of human life.

Slaves always made up a large part of Batavia's population. In 1757 a limit of 1200 was set to the number of slaves within the Castle and of 300 on Onrust Island (one of the islands in Jakarta Bay now called Pulau Kapal). After January 1, 1758, no slaves from the archipelago younger than fourteen years might be brought into Batavia because of the "enormous number" then in the city.[39] The slave market was a Batavian institution until import and trade in slaves was stopped in 1818. It was not until 1860, however, that slavery was finally abolished on Java. Like all major articles of commerce, slaves were a monopoly of the VOC, although illegal slave trading was both profitable and apparently common.

Batavia's slaves were purchased by residents for household use and were totally under their control. There being no provisions on slavery in Dutch charters, Roman law was followed in the Asian settlements. It underwent modifications having to do with resale of slaves and with rights of slaves in Christian households. In principle, slave owners of European status were to seek to convert all slaves in their possession and to manumit the new Christians, or at least provide for eventual emancipation in their wills. This was in fact done. Sophia Westpalm, for instance, was found to have granted release to many of her slaves when her last testament was opened in 1784; but she directed that many more—over one hundred—be put up for sale.[40]

Emancipation gratified only the conscience; economically it was a complete loss. Laws were still necessary forbidding the sale of slaves from Christian households to Jews, Muslims, and "Heathens."[41] Nor did a filial relationship give slave children any privileges. Under Roman law they followed the nationality and status of their mothers. Not until 1766 was a law passed forbidding the sale of children begotten by Christians on slave women, and then because of "concern for Christian blood." And only in 1772 was a decree enacted automatically freeing a woman upon the death of a Christian master if she had borne him children.[42] Unrecognized children and children of male slaves would be put up for sale, with their mothers, in batches.

A few among the slave-concubines prospered by the connection. Augustijn Michiels's second wife, Davida Elisabeth Augustijns,[43] is an example. For many years she was a concubine, described in an early will Michiels made with his first wife as the "freed Christian woman living in his house." Michiels

70

married her in 1819 when their daughter Augustijna, whom he had already formally adopted, was eighteen years of age.

Davida Michiels-Augustijns represents the favored minority. Reality was much grimmer for most, with harsh punishments and lurid tortures within the privacy of the house the order of the day, if Stavorinus is to be believed. At any rate, the government in the second half of the eighteenth century concerned itself this much: it required removal and sale of all slaves related to one killed by their owner.[44] Perhaps this decree was designed to protect the owner from revenge; but in certain cases the government came down clearly on the side of the enslaved. In 1742, for example, a burgher was exiled from all VOC territories for having shot one slave dead and tortured three others. Occasionally a person with European status would be banned from slave ownership altogether because of grotesque abuses.[45]

Nineteenth-century apologists argued that household slavery was milder than the plantation system and even a benevolent institution in Indonesia.[46] Nevertheless, the Dutch in Batavia feared their slaves. This is the reason, quite as much as overcrowding, for limits set to the slave population within the Castle. It is also the motive behind such legislation as that banning slaves from gathering in public places, carrying concealed weapons, and purchasing alcohol and opium.[47]

The foregoing is not in denial of another aspect of Indies slavery: lives of free and enslaved were closely entwined. It exists side-by-side with the fact that slave men and women reared the children of their owners, thereby creating ambiguous ties. From their slaves the "Europeans" absorbed much that was reflected in how they lived and what they thought important or prestigious. Slaves might be bequeathed to children rather than emancipated, which could mean loss of shelter and sustenance and forced reliance on municipal charities. Whatever the nature of individual relationships, VOC society was based on slave ownership. The concept was a borrowed one for the Dutch. Its incorporation into colonial settlements altered the Europeans and profoundly shaped the culture of succeeding generations.

The glue that held this society together was the family system. Under the VOC political and economic structure, promotions were largely controlled by patronage in which family relationship played a key part. Because of the Company's peculiar policies on immigration and intermarriage, the crucial family links were not those between father and son but between a man and his in-laws. At the heart of the Indies clan were women, locally born and raised, who brought men into relationships of patron and protégé as father-in-law, son-in-law, and brothers-in-law. Such alliances could be far-reaching when high death rates and remarriage meant that spouses circulated. And since, under

Dutch law, women could be named sole inheritor of a man's property, widows were sought after for the fortune they brought to a marriage.

The mode of family and political alliance was ordained as the seventeenth century turned into the eighteenth, years when Governors-General Willem van Outhoorn, Joan van Hoorn, and Abraham van Riebeeck governed. The pivotal figure in this trio is van Hoorn. He had migrated with his family at nine and owed his early rise in the VOC's service to his father, who was a councillor.[48] He served as secretary to the Indies Council under van Goens, Speelman, and Camphuys and was a full member of the Council and supporter of the latter in the feuding that was to mark Councils over the next four decades. From his marriage to Anna Struijs, daughter of a Batavia burgher, van Hoorn had acquired a fortune. By 1691, however, she was dead, and van Hoorn, who was then first councillor and director-general of trade, lost no time in marrying Susanna van Outhoorn, daughter of the ruling governor-general. Within ten years his father-in-law had nominated him as successor. Van Hoorn insisted on permission to add three supporters to the Council before accepting the position from van Outhoorn in 1704.

On the Council, Governor-General van Hoorn met with continuing opposition from several members, led by Councillor Abraham van Riebeeck. The governor-general was able to control his opposition through a marriage alliance. Widowed providentially a second time, he chose as his new bride Johanna Maria van Riebeeck, daughter of his chief opponent and widow of Gerrit de Heere, governor of Ceylon. That this was a political match is clear from Valentijn, who was in the Indies at the time and says that it was contracted "to everyone's astonishment."[49] Evidently it was a successful strategem, and the governor-general's father-in-law followed him in office in 1709.

All this was too much for the directors. They responded by insisting that van Hoorn repatriate immediately upon retirement rather than emulate father-in-law van Outhoorn by spending the rest of his life in the country where he had already passed forty-six years. And they decreed that no men related by blood or marriage might sit together on governing boards. In the small, closed society of Batavia, this provision would have been impossible to enforce, even had there been the will in the elite to do so. The VOC's Asian empire continued to be governed by cliques that feuded among themselves and used marriage to cement alliances.

The control of Holland's towns was also in the hands of oligarchies at this period. What was distinctive about the Indies pattern was the small number of actors involved and the type of woman who linked the men together. A list of some of the beneficiaries named in the will of Governor-General Abraham Patras (1735–37) provides a brief illustration of the first point: Anthonia Lengele, widow of his predecessor, Dirk van Cloon; Johannes Thedens, then councillor and later acting governor-general (1741–43); councillor and future governor-general G. W. van Imhoff; and Geertruida Goossens, who was wife successively to two councillors and an acting governor-general, mother-in-law of Councillor Hugo Verijssel and of future governor-general R. de Klerk, and godmother of the children of Governor-General Jacob Mossel.

The van Riemsdijk clan* most clearly demonstrates the political importance of family alliances and the contribution of part-Asians to colonial culture. It begins with Jeremias van Riemsdijk, a native of Utrecht born in 1712, who enlisted as a sergeant in the VOC's army. He was twenty-three years old when he reached Batavia. Immediately upon his arrival he was transferred to the civilian service, and within seven years he had been raised to first senior merchant of the Castle. Promotion as councillor extraordinary and full councillor followed, and in 1775 the former soldier succeeded P. A. van der Parra as governor-general. He died in office in 1777 after forty-two years of unbroken service to the Company, all of them passed in Batavia.

In the course of his life van Riemsdijk married five times. His first three wives all died in childbirth within a year or two of marriage. The fourth wife, Adriana Louisa Helvetius, was to survive eleven births and twenty-one years of married life. In 1774 van Riemsdijk married a fifth and final time, his choice being Theodora Rotgers.

Reviewing van Riemsdijk's career in the light of his family connections, it is clear that in his early career he was promoted by his uncle, councillor and then governor-general Adriaen Valckenier. Van Riemsdijk's continued rise was slowed by his patron's fall, but obstacles were removed when he made his fourth marriage. Up to that time his wives had been daughters of middle-level VOC employees, but Adriana Helvetius was granddaughter of a councillor and daughter of Batavia's chief justice. One of her sisters had been wife to a governor of Ceylon. Within four years of marriage to Adriana, van Riemsdijk was made councillor extraordinary. Theodora Rotgers also brought van Riemsdijk the advantage of connections to important men in Batavia. Her second husband had been the lawyer Maurits Theodorus Hilgers, councillor extraordinary, president of the orphanage trustees and a relative by marriage of the Hartingh-Mossel families.

It should be noted that all of van Riemsdijk's marriages were contracted with women born in Batavia. Politically speaking, their connections were all in the capital city and in secondary settlements of the VOC empire. Culturally, it is important to note that none was a Hollander. Van Riemsdijk chose women who had no firsthand knowledge of his home country, culture, and tongue. All had been raised by Asians, led the semisegregated life of the Indies lady, and were probably more familiar with legends, stories, and religious beliefs of the East than with those of northern Europe. These facts are important, for the fourth and fifth wives were leading ladies in Holland's Asian empire, setting standards of manners and taste. And since van Riemsdijk shared nothing with his brides except his privileged status as a European, he was unable to reproduce in Batavia the household atmosphere and spirit of his native Holland. Little is known of his first wives beyond their names and the fact that their fathers were Netherlanders, but the background of his fourth wife is open to inspection, and it tends to confirm the assumptions just made.

It stretches back five generations to an unknown Asian woman who in 1664 gave birth to a daughter by a Company soldier surnamed de Bollan. De Bollan recognized the girl, christened her Johanna Magdalena, and raised her as a member of the European group. In 1685 she married the Netherlander Johannes Maurits van Happel, a former commanding officer of Sumatra's west coast and head of the Japan factory in 1688 and 1689. One of their daughters, Anna Catharina, married the Dutch lawyer and councillor Laurens Tolling. Their daughter, Egidia Cornelia Tolling, in her turn married a Dutch lawyer and president of Batavia's supreme court, Willem Vincent Helvetius. Adriana was one of the children of this marriage.

Underlining the political significance of her marriage to van Riemsdijk is Adriana Helvetius's age. She was just fifteen, her husband thirty-nine. Her youth at marriage is to be attributed to Indies custom. Borrowing from Oriental societies' prescriptions concerning seclusion of upper-class unmarried girls and their early marriage, Batavia's leading families married their daughters off when they were barely teenagers. They made matches for their girls with much older men, men who were colleagues in government and who offered advantages of secure partnership if it were sealed through family ties.

The development of Indies clan patterns can be traced in the next generation. Six of van Riemsdijk's children survived infancy. The oldest surviving son was Isebrandus Johannes Faber van Riemsdijk, one of three children born to Cornelia van Vianen, the second wife. His career followed a course now familiar in that he was sent in early childhood to the Netherlands. He was never to return to Indonesia, instead settling permanently in the Netherlands and marrying there. Johanna Maria, daughter of the third wife, was raised in Batavia. At fifteen, also according to form, she was married to a native Netherlander, Paulus Godefridus van der Voort. At the time of their marriage he was first secretary to Batavia's government and was later raised to the governorship of Makassar (1770–80).

By this time Jeremias van Riemsdijk lived in grand style. He celebrated his designation as director-general by ordering a new glass carriage from Europe to add to his two other glass coaches, his "English carriage with gauze netting instead of glass, three Berlins able to hold four, a Phaeton, four small carriages and two chaises." His Batavian household on the Tijgersgracht depended on the services of a "European coachman, two European caretakers and a European cook, besides 200 men and women slaves and their children."[50]

Four of van Riemsdijk's children by Adriana Helvetius lived to adulthood. The one daughter, Catharina Louysa (1758–1823), married an immigrant Netherlander. This was Mr. Arnoldus Constantijn Mom, a member of the Dutch nobility who migrated young and spent his whole life in the Indies. Two of the sons married Batavians. They died in their twenties in the VOC's service in the insignificant ranks of clerk and ensign, the approved levels, under VOC law, for part-Asian men with European status.

The career of the remaining son, Willem Vincent Helvetius van Riemsdijk (1752–1818), suggests a trend in Indies family and political life, a trend away from a matriarchal system and towards a system in which sons followed their fathers. W. V. H. van Riemsdijk, despite his Batavia schooling and reputation as "stupid and ignorant man,"[51] rose to become a councillor in 1799, amassing a fortune from his Company posts along the way. He was the progenitor of a large clan whose members in the nineteenth century stand for the ultimate development of Mestizo culture, when, as will be shown in chapter 6, Eurasians were cut out of political life by the new Dutch policies. Some of his descendants continued to marry Dutchmen, but most married among their own ethnic and social class or merged wholly with the Indonesian community.

The preceding notes illustrate the large and steady contribution of Asians and part-Asians to the culture of VOC settlements. The only way to break the hold of Mestizo society was to dispatch children to Europe. That recourse ceased to be desirable to some important Batavians in the second half of the eighteenth century. A pattern of promoting sons' careers in the VOC hierarchy has already been noted of officials in settlements subsidiary to Batavia. Too few leading officials had sons surviving infancy for a similar claim to be made convincingly for the Batavian elite, and its ascendancy was cut off early in the nineteenth century. All the same, a trend towards furthering a son's career in the East appears in some families in the late eighteenth century. Jeremias van Riemsdijk, for instance, was prompted to send only one of his boys to Holland and to fix him permanently there. The son, I. J. F. van Riemsdijk, was, moreover, a child born early in van Riemsdijk's Indies career, possibly before he had come to look on Java as his adoptive homeland. The other five children were to remain in Java and their descendants after them. It is possible that J. van Riemsdijk was planning an eventual succession by W. V. H. van Riemsdijk, as Governor-General van der Parra appears to have been planning one for his son, whose likeness he struck on medals and whose early climb in the VOC hierarchy he fostered.

This chapter opened with a look at the "breaching" of the city's walls, the movement of the elite to villas on country estates in the environs of Batavia. The significance of the movement is this: owners of estates brought into the countryside new populations in their slaves from Bali, Makassar, and India. The importance of these new inhabitants surpasses their actual numbers (perhaps fifty to one hundred to each great house), for the slaves introduced new ways and set new examples for the local population. At the same time, local peoples were caught up in the life of the estates too, principally as laborers and concubines, and they came into contact with a Mestizo culture that had first developed within the walls of Batavia. Country estates provided a new arena for that culture to develop, for local inhabitants deferred to the newcomers in their traditional Sundanese ways.

The new country elite were not so much landed gentry as they were landowners, since they displayed no real attachment to particular areas. Estates changed hands frequently, rarely remaining in a family's possession for more than a score of years. I have therefore described these owners in terms of office and family history and as patrons, and stressed the lack of lineage in the sense of office and property handed down from father to son.

The ruling elite was preoccupied by the definition of "European." Technically, included under the term were all persons born in Europe, all born in Asia to European parents (Creoles), women married to European men, legitimate children of European fathers, and all illegitimate children acknowledged by a European man. Fathers officially acknowledged illegitimate offspring by purchasing a certificate of legitimation or by formally adopting them before a notary.

The matter was never clearcut, however. While the government might occasionally "retrieve" children from their Asian mothers and place them in the orphanage when their European fathers were dead or had repatriated, it also discriminated against the part-Asian members of the European group. An example of distinction made between "Europeans" is the decision passed in a case heard to determine a point of etiquette. It involved two men of equivalent rank in the VOC hierarchy, Stephanus Versluys and de Witte van Schooten, and the problem was to determine which of them should walk ahead in public procession and should take the higher seat at table. The case was settled in favor of Versluys on the grounds that he alone had legitimate issue.[52]

To European visitors the Mestizo culture of the colonial settlement was foreign and disturbing. Their disapproval was communicated principally through books published in Europe, however, so that it had but fleeting effect on the local elite or went unnoticed altogether. Yet colonial society was never totally insulated from the Netherlands. Always there were zealots working to bend it to particular molds. In the first century of contact their efforts had been chiefly in the direction of establishing Dutch Calvinist culture. In the following century the assaults on colonial manners by a Coen or Candidius in the name of the "true religion" were succeeded by assaults from men who saw themselves as part of the Enlightenment movement of Europe. In the name of reason and science they sought to transform Mestizo society culturally through innovations in Batavia's school system, introduction of a newspaper, and establishment of learned societies. Their efforts and the results and the style of the reformers are subjects of the next chapter.

4

The Assault on Indies Culture

THE ENLIGHTENMENT IN BATAVIA

BY THE MID-EIGHTEENTH CENTURY, when Baron van Imhoff took office, Indies society was formed. Its culture was clearly not Dutch any longer. Netherlands society at the time may be defined broadly as racially homogeneous, Calvinist, and patriarchal, its cities run by oligarchies of prosperous businessmen and its industries controlled by guilds. Thrift and sobriety were highly prized qualities. Average Hollanders lived in narrow, closed houses and their diet was based on red meats, cheeses, and bread. The upper classes were literate in French and German as well as in Dutch.

By contrast, Indies society was exceedingly polyglot in composition, and its "European" elite secular before agnosticism was a common condition in Europe. This spirit did not derive from any intellectual revolt against established doctrine but was the result of life in a transplanted settlement. It was also a consequence of the immediate influence of Asian nursemaids, guardians, servants, and wives.

Nor was the colonial elite patriarchal. Landed property did not remain with a family for more than one or two generations; similarly, fathers did not usually pass positions to their sons but sent their heirs to Holland in earliest youth to make them members of Dutch society in the homeland. Economic life was not controlled by guilds of master craftsmen and merchants, but dominated by a monopolistic corporation. The route to wealth lay through promotion to senior posts in the East Indies Company bureaucracy, the office-holder winning at once power, prestige, and opportunity for illegal gain on a vast scale.

By the eighteenth century, access to these privileged positions was governed by connections, and the basis of connections was marriage into Indies families. The colonial ruling class was matrilineal in the sense that men passed on posts and privilege to their sons-in-law, the husbands of their daughters whom they kept in Asia. Women-based clans absorbed the immigrant males who came without wives; the clan enfolded the newcomer in a network of immigrants with locally born wives, Mestizo and Asian kin. At the same time, the clan eased adoption of Indies manners for the newcomers.

In contrast to the Calvinist, bourgeois thrift of Holland, there was the Mestizo luxury, the spending on a grand scale, the importance of display. The Indies elite lived in spacious, open villas and alongside Dutch food often ate spiced Indonesian dishes and rice. Many members, especially the women, were not literate; the languages they spoke were Malay and Portuguese, and they sponsored no written literature. In the arts they patronized woodcarvers, assembled slave orchestras, summoned ronggengs, and held performances of Indonesian and Chinese puppet plays. That is to say, the entertainments and arts enjoyed by the colonial elite were not yet divorced from the tastes of their Asian retainers.

The man set on changing this was Gustaaf Willem baron van Imhoff, member of an East Frisian patrician family who entered the VOC's employ in 1725. Well connected with the Company's directors and soon to be with the VOC Huysman family, van Imhoff rose swiftly in the hierarchy. Within a few months he was promoted from junior to merchant and chief of the accounts office. By 1730 he was senior merchant and second secretary to the government, and in 1736 he was sent to Ceylon as governor with the rank of councillor.[1] The background to his elevation as governor-general (1743–50) is the massacre of Batavia's Chinese, which occurred in 1740 when van Imhoff was back in the capital. From 1741 to 1743 the baron was in the Netherlands, explaining away his part in government actions that led to the murders and drawing up for the directors his *Considerations on the Present State of the Netherlands East Indies Company.*[2]

Van Imhoff's colonial program recalls J. P. Coen's proposals in many points, for he too wanted to develop a distinctively Dutch character in the colonial capital by bringing in burgher families as settlers and allowing them to trade in categories of goods and in ports hitherto under Company monopoly. Van Imhoff's program was also addressed to establishing conditions that would make permanent settlement attractive to the immigrant Dutch. Thus the early business of his government was to restore the Company's trade and revenues, encourage a return of Chinese retailers and market gardeners, build a second hospital, and provide for more medical assistants. The second part of his plan was devoted to keeping alive the culture of the homeland among immigrants and to supplanting the Mestizo culture among leaders of the locally born men with European status. This latter task was to be accomplished principally through establishing special schools for sons of selected Creole, Eurasian, and Asian Christian families.

The first of these schools was a theological seminary which was opened in 1745. As stated in the governing regulations,[3] the seminary's "foremost aim (with God's blessing)" was "to help foster the establishment of the Christian reformed religion in these parts" through training a "sufficient number" of young men for the ministry. Admission rules required that students be aged between eight and twelve, with no further discrimination as to "nation or race"

79

save that they be sons of "honest folk." Students were to follow a five-year course of study that would include Latin and would be equivalent to instruction offered by Dutch academies. Three or four outstanding graduates would be sent annually to the Netherlands at the Company's expense to complete their education and return to serve the Indies church.

The seminary was a boarding school, its rector, assistant, and junior master residing at the college too. Twelve male slaves were allocated from Company personnel to run the seminary, although teachers might also bring slaves for personal service. A lay religious officer was to supervise the pupils' spiritual growth. At the same time, the school was to admit paying day and boarding pupils enrolling for a general education.

The governor-general signalled the importance of the seminary by attending the opening ceremonies, which were held at the inner Portuguese church, a fact drawing attention to the school's cultural setting and illuminating van Imhoff's aims. The seminary is in no way to be thought of as a gentlemen's academy, training the sons of Batavia's elite for high office in the VOC hierarchy or fitting them as cultivated members of an overseas colony. Indeed, the school's founder sent his son Jan Willem van Imhoff, who was illegitimate and part-Indonesian, to the Netherlands before he was a year old, rather than have him reared in Batavia and educated there.

The school was, in fact, designed for a lower social class. This is patent from the article opening it to all classes and races of boys, as well as from its religious aims. The school's first rector, the Reverend Johan Maurits Mohr, was certainly a distinguished scholar and amateur astronomer, and he held a prominent position in Indies society. But most VOC clergy could never reach beyond their hierarchical slot, which was approximate to that of a merchant. Furthermore, seminarians could not aspire to a pulpit in the Netherlands nor think of their education as equipping them for a career in Europe. They were to be a locally bred and trained intelligentsia, Dutch in tongue, culture, and loyalties, and were to foster the VOC's interests, without hope of attaining a controlling voice in its Asian government.

As it turned out, the school did not survive to realize these aims. It was closed by executive order in 1755, after a peak enrollment of fifty-three day students and eighteen boarders in 1752.[4] One alone fulfilled van Imhoff's plan of study in the Netherlands and service in the Indies. This was Nicolaas (de) Graaij, who was enrolled at Leiden University and later returned as minister to Batavia's Asian Christian parish.

More remarkable than the theological seminary was van Imhoff's marine academy, for it had no precedent in either native Dutch or colonial practice. Its first object was to train Indies-born cadets in navigation and to improve technical knowledge of European youths already signed up with the Company. To this end a course of instruction was designed which included formal classroom work in mathematics, charting, navigation, and languages, and practical training at sea. Beyond raising the standards of seamanship, the academy was founded to create a naval officer caste that would not disgrace polite society. In giving their approval to the academy's regulations, the directors expressed the conviction that the new school would produce "experience, good manners, and polish among the Company's sea officers."[5]

The first class was to open with twenty-four boys from "respectable families" and of "regular birth"; that is to say, members of the future officer caste were not to be sons of concubines. They were to be boarders, subjected to the discipline of a resident governor and deputy drawn from the Company's navy. Ten to twelve paying boarders were to be admitted also to help the school's finances, and a few amateurs might follow instruction for a fee upon consent of the school board. Otherwise, classes were closed to the public. In this matter the marine academy differed from the theological seminary: it was strictly vocational and exclusive.

The academy's special orientation may be seen in the regulations concerning domestic arrangements. Household tasks were to be performed not by Asian slaves but by Europeans. Article 17 of the constitution puts it this way: "No natives or slaves shall be admitted into the Academy's house; its servants will comprise one European cook, taken from the fleet, one assistant cook, one house steward, also from the fleet, and six to eight European youths."[6] In other words, non-European cultural influences were to be held at bay. No Asian, Christian or otherwise, was to be enrolled. Admission was to be the privilege of the Creole and Eurasian of legitimate birth. In proscribing the Asian slaves and childhood companions of pupils from the academy, van Imhoff showed how well he understood the strength of Asian-derived beliefs, attachments, and manners.

It is not surprising, then, that article 18 should decree, "there shall be no native tongues spoken in the house." This meant that the new officer corps should use Dutch with ease in daily conversation, although it was assumed that recruits probably could not. It was not intended that they be ignorant of Asian tongues altogether; cadets had to study Malay, Malabar, and Persian in order to be able to command sailors used on Company ships. "Nevertheless," it made clear, "no use is to be made of the aforesaid languages in daily exchange among the others in the Academy without express leave from the Governors."[7]

Another innovation sponsored by Governor-General van Imhoff was intended to make men with European status conscious of a bond among them. This was a newspaper with the name *Bataviasche Nouvelles* (*Batavia News*). Its opening number was published on 7 August 1744 by J. E. Jordens, first adjunct clerk in the general secretariat. The venture met with "tolerable success," and Jordens was commissioned by the governor-general in Council to bring out a weekly edition of the paper for the next three years.[8] Thereafter the *Nouvelles* was published every Monday afternoon and distributed from the Castle. Its news was of shipping, of domestic events in the leading families of Batavia and Holland, and of arrivals and departures, and it carried advertisements, mainly announcements of household goods and staff for auction.

The weekly's life was short. Responsibility for the license had been taken by the Batavian authorities, who then informed their superiors in Amsterdam. The directors' response was contained in a letter dated 20 November 1745 ordering the paper's charter revoked forthwith. Their views were known in Batavia by the middle of the following year, and on 20 June 1746 permission to publish was duly cancelled.[9]

The paper merits more attention than its brief existence would imply. In the first place, its publication was an event without parallel in Indies history. True, there had been an attempt at producing an announcement sheet in 1668, and occasionally a leaflet of advertisements was circulated. What was novel about van Imhoff's paper was its intention to carry news of Europeans to a particular audience. The readership defines itself by the language of the *Nouvelles*, which was Dutch; it did not pretend to be a paper of all Batavians, but of the male immigrants and graduates of the city's two academies. The *Nouvelles* thus created a link between Dutch speakers while communicating news concerning only the readers' kind. And since the paper also printed news of events in Holland, it served to keep alive a tie, or at least an orientation, to Europe. Moreover, newspaper reading was a very Dutch habit.

Taken together, van Imhoff's reforms may be described as an attempt to promote in Holland's chief settlement in Asia a specifically Dutch urban culture. Company employees who were immigrants and free settlers would retain their cultural heritage through the link of newspaper, through new municipal amenities—for example, better health facilities, more taverns, a short-lived postal system, greater religious tolerance[10]—and through provision of exclusive schooling for sons of permanent settlers. The locally born would be made more European, eschewing the Asian and Mestizo tastes of their female kin.

Despite these deliberate efforts to transform Indies society, van Imhoff was unable to make any lasting change. In the first place, the governor-general failed to win his fellow councillors to his side, men with whom he had worked for almost two decades. Those reforms surviving the directors in Amsterdam were abolished in Batavia by his colleagues within a few years of his death. Governor-General Mossel saw the theological seminary and marine academy as "useless" and "too costly," and he ordered both closed in 1755. It was left to van der Parra to close down the hospital van Imhoff had built at Cipanas in order to allow VOC employees recuperation in a healthier climate and at mineral springs.[11] The main reason for the failure of van Imhoff's program, however, may be found in the strength of Mestizo culture, which proved able to withstand the deliberate attacks of a self-conscious crusader.

Van Imhoff's approach to government must also be considered a reason for the short-lived impact of his ideas, for the baron was thoroughly the Indies governor-general, autocratic and ruling by fiat. Moreover, despite all his aspirations for change, the inner conditions of colonial society were not to be tampered with; distinguished immigrants would still send their sons to Europe and make their marriage alliances locally. The ultimate aim of van Imhoff's colonial program was to foster among lower-class subjects an educated citizenry which knew its place, that of loyal subordinate and supporter of the senior officials who would, all of them, be native Dutchmen.

Van Imhoff was succeeded in office by Jacob Mossel of the sumptuary code and then by the Ceylonese-born van der Parra. It was not until Reynier de Klerk's accession in 1777 that another self-conscious reformer held the highest post in Batavia. De Klerk was then sixty-seven, however, and ill, and he was to die in office within three years. Nevertheless, during his brief term he attempted to make the city's inhabitants more Dutch by adding to the number of schools for the Asian group and by aiding private schools designed for children of the European community. Furthermore, de Klerk understood that it was not enough to keep Asians at a distance from efforts directed at turning Creoles and Eurasians into Dutchmen. Locally born girls, the bride pool for immigrants, must be made more European too. To accomplish this goal de Klerk's government requested the directors' permission to use a Company property for a young ladies' academy.[12]

VOC schools had always enrolled girls as well as boys, but there had never been a select school for girls comparable to the Latin schools of the mid-seventeenth century or to van Imhoff's seminary. What became of the request is unclear. We know that three private schools were opened by women for daughters of the communities centered on the Portuguese outer church, on the old Chinese-Eurasian neighborhood of the Spinhuisgracht, and on the Tijgersgracht, long the best address for Europeans in Batavia. The latter school was run by the widow of the Reverend J. Brandes and enrolled thirteen pupils. Most of the girls were part-Asian; all belonged to that elite group in which husbands and fathers were Dutch.

The names of some of them have come down to us by means of an award instituted for pupils of Batavia's private schools while de Klerk was still in office. The first school prize list was announced on May 1, 1778, the winners reading like a Who's Who of Batavia. Receiving awards from Widow Brandes's little school were Johanna and Constantia Alting, youngest daughters of then director-general W. A. Alting, as well as his step-daughter Maria Senn van

Basel; Christina Marci, who was to marry Councillor Wiese; Jacoba Maria Lodisio, future first wife of Governor-General P. G. van Overstraten and subsequently of A. H. Wiese when he was governor-general; Susanna Maria Janke, who married a member of the large and powerful Senn van Basel clan; and Johanna Everdina Maria van Blijdenberg, a Creole from Ambon who married Daniel van Son, first administrator of Batavia's warehouses.[13]

We can only guess at the nature of the education offered in a private girls' academy in Batavia in 1778 and its impact. The course of study certainly included Dutch, for Maria S. van Basel's prize was a volume in Dutch on manners and morals. Attendance was not lengthy. Maria, for instance, was eight when she received her prize; by thirteen she was a married woman. Her step-sisters were eleven and eight in 1778, and Christina Marci was also eight. The three were brides at fifteen.

Through other decisions in Council, de Klerk attempted to promote fluency in Dutch and a more thorough understanding of Dutch Calvinism among Batavia's Asian Christians, as well as to carry the Gospel to slaves on the private estates ringing Batavia. In these efforts the governor-general was less of an innovator, but to carrying out traditional policies of VOC governments he brought a new urgency and several novel methods. First, he reversed van Imhoff's decree requiring lay Christian leaders to learn Malay, and ordered Batavia's synod to instruct its "native teachers" in Dutch. He forbade its hiring any Indonesian as catechizer or sick-visitor who was not already proficient in Dutch. Then, in separate regulations for the schools, de Klerk designated the ministers Vermeer and Reinking to examine and coach all Asian teachers in Dutch and religion.[14] Next, de Klerk turned his attention to the pupils, for enrollment was low and attendance sporadic. His remedy was to institute a regular roll call and to cut off VOC rations to the parents of truants.

Further measures issued by de Klerk make it clear that the results of his educational reforms were disappointing. An order requiring—and reminding—school children to speak Dutch during recesses had to be passed in 1780.[15] Since Indonesian teachers were not attending language and catechism classes regularly, future absences were to be punished by a fine amounting to half their monthly salary. And finally, because graduates of the Company schools still seemed ill-fitted for employment, adult education for young men was instituted through evening classes held twice a week at the private school run by Isaac Boterkoper on the Rua Malacca.[16] Tuition was free; classes were conducted in Dutch and concentrated on the rudiments such as arithmetic.

It remained for Governor-General Alting to revoke most of de Klerk's education measures. In 1786 he withdrew the requirement that Dutch be the language of instruction in all VOC schools, of which there were then four. Henceforth, only classes in the poorhouse and orphanage must be conducted in

Dutch. Of the two other Company schools, Portuguese was to be used in one, Malay in the other, because the majority of pupils knew no Dutch and so could not follow lessons. The decree admitted that many of the children's parents had no command of the language of Batavia's rulers either. Two years later permission was granted the poorhouse schoolmaster to teach in Portuguese too. When the Company was dissolved in 1799, then, after one hundred and ninety-seven years in Asia, only one of its schools in Batavia could conduct classes in Dutch. Attempts at promoting Dutch through the Asian churches had also been renounced. After 1788, catechism classes for Indonesians were taught in Portuguese.[17]

The female elite of the colony proved as little receptive to endeavors to make it more European in thought and habit as the Asian Christian group. Nor, apparently, did the experiment in girls' formal schooling convince Batavians of its necessity. Widow Brandes's school closed after only six years, and it had no immediate successor. Nearly one hundred years were to pass before the appearance of government schools and private girls' schools which could last more than two or three years.

The assaults on Indies culture considered thus far had chiefly to do with attempts at making Asians, part-Asians, and Creoles feel a sense of loyalty and kinship to the Netherlands based on shared belief, tongue, knowledge (in the sense of shared curricula in the schools), and daily habits. Save the year-long newspaper and licensing of taverns, little had been done for male immigrants, who were evidently prone to absorption into Mestizo culture and who were unable to pass on their mother tongue to their own offspring. The Company had always recognized this tendency of its servants to assimilate into Mestizo culture, in repeatedly issuing regulations that limited posts above assistant to men born in Holland. Towards the end of the Company period, however, there lived in Batavia a few immigrants who attempted to establish conditions for themselves that would allow them to remain European and to follow the habits of the eighteenth-century ideal of the European gentleman. Because of the self-conscious nature of the group and its very public activities, this period has come to be known in Dutch colonial histories as the Indies Enlightenment.

It centered upon Jacobus Cornelis Mattheus Radermacher (1741–83), who founded the colony's first Masonic lodge and the Batavian Academy of Arts and Sciences, the first association for intellectual pursuits established in a tropical European settlement. Radermacher was the son of a prominent Dutch family. At sixteen he left Holland for Batavia as junior merchant. He rose to senior merchant, improving his connections through marriage to Margaretha Verijssel, daughter of the late director-general, Hugo Verijssel, and stepdaughter of Reynier de Klerk, who was then a councillor extraordinary. In 1762

Radermacher formed the lodge *La Choisie*. From 1763 to 1767 he was in the Netherlands studying law, and then returned to Batavia, where he engaged in the many activities of the public man.

The colonial government was unfailingly solicitous toward Radermacher. His father-in-law, who was then governor-general, encouraged all senior officials to join the Academy of Arts and Sciences by sending out a circular announcing its formation and accepting the post of chief director of the society when it was formed on 24 April 1778. There were 103 Batavians enrolled as members that first year, with an additional 77 resident in the colony's dependencies joining also, and there were several corresponding members in the Netherlands. The government also promoted the scientific interests of the society; it ordered all employees to submit written answers to questions put them by academicians and to collect animal, plant, and mineral specimens for its museum.[18]

The Academy's interests can be followed by looking at its most active members and the titles of their articles published in the society's *Transactions*.[19] Chief contributors to the first four volumes were members of Radermacher's coterie. The Reverend Josua van Iperen, during his single year's residence in Batavia, wrote essays on natural curiosities and on Javanese history and historiography. The Lutheran pastor Johannes Hooyman was a frequent contributor, writing on wheat and peanut cultivation on Java, cotton, and harvesting edible birds' nests. Hooyman also wrote a description of the Danish church's mission on India's Coromandel Coast. Many articles describing Indonesia's plant and animal life were contributed by the German immigrant Frederik baron von Wurmb, who was the Academy's first secretary. Tropical diseases, Batavia's sewage system, and the city's housing were subjects of articles by Jacobus van der Steege and the retired army lieutenant Jan Andries Duurkoop. Radermacher's many essays included anthropological and geographic descriptions, a glossary of plants, animals, and minerals, comparisons of calendrical systems, and suggestions for improvements to sea charts. He also contributed an article arguing for an end to the use of torture by courts and the abolition of capital punishment.

The Academy also served as a debating club for gentlemen who had been born into prosperous families in the Netherlands and educated there. It served as meeting place for them and social center, for in Batavia there were still no coffee houses or other places where upper class men could gather informally, as there were in Dutch cities. Before acquisition of a special building, Radermacher's gift to the Academy, the only place for men to congregate was the front veranda of private houses, and there formality reigned and Indies manners controlled all intercourse.

In attending a meeting at the Academy, members left the Indies world physically to enter a club dedicated to the pursuit of progress and where Dutch was the language of communication. For core members, who regarded a term in the Indies as but one stage in their careers, an important function of the Academy was to maintain their sense of being part of an intellectual community of Europeans. Radermacher, for instance, upon resigning from the Company in 1783, had no intention of retiring in the Indies, but planned to resume public life in the Netherlands. He was only forty-two when assassination during a mutiny at sea on the voyage home destroyed these ambitions.

This is not to say that there were no members prominent in the Academy who had not in some measure accommodated to the dominant Mestizo culture and committed themselves to long-term residence. Drs. Hooyman, for instance, carried out his agricultural researches on the properties he had acquired through marriage to the heiress Elisabeth Odilia Weijerman, India-born daughter of a commander of Malabar. Duurkoop was another. This former ship's mate and army man had also become a wealthy landowner through marriage, and he used his riches to support the studies of scholars like van Iperen. For such men the Academy helped preserve their sense of being European.

In the same way, membership in the Academy offered the Indies-born but Holland-educated a means of continuing interests learned in the Netherlands and of forming a social link with the immigrants. Consider the case of academician David Johannes Smith. He had been born in the eastern archipelago in 1740, but was sent at five to the Netherlands upon the formal request of his maternal grandmother and the mother-in-law of P. A. van der Parra, Ida Dudde. Smith returned in 1762—one year, that is, after his uncle by marriage had been made governor-general. Van der Parra was a generous supporter of family members, even those distantly connected. Smith profited, becoming councillor extraordinary at thirty-two and a full councillor at forty-one. To the Academy he was a liberal patron, donating money and a costly collection of manuscripts in eastern languages, maps, and paintings.

Approximately one-third of the first members were also Masons,[20] initiates of *La Choisie* or of the two lodges which replaced it. All three lodges were in Batavia. The first outside the capital was opened at Semarang in 1789, where Nicolaas Engelhard, son-in-law of Governor-General Alting was governor and the lodge's first worshipful master. Membership lists compiled by D. de Visser Smits[21] bear out the contention that Masons were among the colony's higher social ranks. There were the membership dues for one thing; but in the Netherlands Freemasonry had already established itself as the association of the prosperous and the distinguished.

Like the Academy, the Masonic lodge provided men with a place for social congregation. It appealed quite naturally to a society that was habitually segregated by sex, with the added intimacy of being a Dutch-speaking club in a non-Dutch world. Membership in a lodge, like a card in the Academy and professed concern with municipal welfare, horticultural experiments, and local history, are examples of the "very Hollandish" behavior that P. de Roo discerned in eighteenth-century Batavia.[22] Both institutions were the products of outsiders who were sufficiently wealthy and conscious of the European model to attempt to re-create in an alien environment the sociability remembered from the homeland.

But they could not totally exclude the world around them. Membership lists show Eurasians and Creoles alongside the expatriates. For the most part they were sons of rich men, for whom Masonic brotherhood was a mark of belonging to the European group, identification with its values, and outward rejection of Mestizo culture. For men like Jacobus Beijvanck, Creole son-in-law of the Mardijker Michiels, and the India-born Cornelis Andries Cantervisscher,[23] the Masonic movement was a guarantee against relegation to the fringes of colonial society.

It might be suggested that the rituals and secret practices of Masons were particularly attractive to the Indies-born as compared to the austere rites of Dutch Calvinism; but while the mystical aspects of Freemasonry may have been a source of appeal, the badge of European identity which lodge membership conferred was probably of greater importance, when one considers that many of the lodge members born in Asia were government servants. One looks in vain through lodge rolls for the names of van der Parra's descendants, for instance. Their wealth and connections could have opened membership to them; but it is likely that the purposes of lodge and Academy evoked little sympathy in them. Their lives were passed largely apart from the Company, their concerns were not those of immigrants. The importance of having a command of Dutch may be mentioned here too, as also a sense of belonging in a social gathering of men whose references were to a country the Indiesman's great-grandfather had left in his teens. For them that other attribute of lodge and Academy—opportunity for a personal acquaintance with those in positions of authority and the consequent jockeying for promotions—was irrelevant.

Both Indies Freemasonry and the Academy depended for survival in large measure on their founder. Within a few years of Radermacher's departure the Academy had almost ceased to function, while the lodges had a checkered career, dissolving, reforming, fusing. Their near-demise is instructive. Both institutions were formed by immigrants basically for immigrants, and their most active members were outsiders too. They had no links with the colony's past. Dr. de Haan has noted of the Academy, for instance, that it did not evolve from the Reverend J. M. Mohr's scientific interests in the 1760s, nor center on his observatory.[24] Indeed, the Academy made no use of it. After Mohr's death in 1775 the observatory he had built in 1768 was turned into a boarding house for bachelor clerks of the Company, and still later it was used as a barracks for troops. The Academy did not, then, build upon earlier activities of prominent

6. Observatory in Batavia. Painted by Johannes Rach. The observatory was built by the Reverend J. M. Mohr on land, near the Chinese section of Batavia, which he had acquired through marriage to the India-born Anna van 't Hof. Mohr was the Lutheran pastor in Batavia and first rector of Governor-General G. W. van Imhoff's theological seminary. (From F. de Haan, *Platenalbum*, plate K31.)

89

Batavians. Like the actions of Governor-General van Imhoff and of Mohr, Radermacher's were essentially isolated and discrete.

The debates and researches of academicians were, moreover, confined to a small clique of men. They held, in common, birth in the Netherlands or Germany, profession of Calvinism or Lutheranism, European education, Masonic brotherhood, and in Batavia, prosperity. Here is a further reason for the hesitant beginnings of lodge and Academy. The small number of European men of culture and learning, the irrelevance of both institutions to Indonesia generally, political upheavals in government, and the British interregnum of 1811–16, all hampered or interrupted their development. The real growth and importance of Indies lodges as a branch of international Freemasonry and of the Academy as a learned society came in the later-nineteenth-century colony. There were then far more immigrants, closer contact with Europe, and a government whose highest members eschewed cultural accommodation and were self-consciously European.

Lodge and Academy were formed by migrants asserting their own culture's ideals and as deliberate assaults on the Mestizo culture of Batavians with European status. In considering their failure to thrive in the last two decades of the eighteenth century one has, therefore, to reflect again on the strength of Indies colonial culture and its absorptive power. Radermacher and his colleagues failed, not only because their ideas took no natural root in Batavia and their activities were confined to a small clique but also because they had all of them in some measure become Indiesmen themselves. It is a striking but little remarked fact that all the men whose names are prominently linked with Batavia's Enlightenment were married to Mestizas and that they fully conformed to the colonial pattern by taking as brides young girls, often many years their juniors, who brought them connections and wealth but not necessarily sympathy for their ideals.

A description of the domestic arrangements of van Imhoff* must begin with the wife he selected in Batavia in 1727. She was Asian by birth, baptized Catharina Magdalena Huysman at Casimbazar in northeastern India. At the time of marriage, Catharina's father, Anthonij Huysman, was second only to the governor-general as director-general of trade. His early career and rise in the VOC hierarchy had been in India, where he was director of the Bengal trading settlement from 1709 to 1716. Huysman was a beneficiary of the father-son chain of command in the outer settlements, being the son of a director of Bengal (Marten Huysman), as well as son-in-law of another. A. Huysman had, moreover, been born in northern Ceylon at Jaffnapatnam. In the paternal line, then, Catharina Huysman's family had a long record of distinguished service in the Company's employ, while she belonged to the second generation of children born in Asia.

Her mother, Johanna Catharina Pelgrom, was in fact a Netherlander by birth, but had been taken to India at the age of two by her family and had been raised in Asia. Johanna Pelgrom had important connections on her own account. Her father as we have seen, had also been a director of Bengal (1701–05) and had then served as chief tax collector in Batavia. The Asia-born-and-bred Catharina van Imhoff-Huysman became first lady of all the Netherlands' Asian possessions in 1743. A year later she died in Batavia.

Van Imhoff gave no proof of a desire to replace Catharina with a wife who had a more direct knowledge of Europe and of Dutch culture, or to give Batavians a new first lady who could assist him in his crusade for reform. Rather, he consoled himself, during the six years that he continued in office after his bereavement, with the Celebes concubine whom he had had baptized as Helena Pieters. The mistress forms a direct link between the baron and Radermacher's coterie, for the wealth that she inherited from van Imhoff was put to supporting the researches of the latter group after her marriage to J. A. Duurkoop.

The Academy's first chief director, Reynier de Klerk,* was also married to a Mestiza whose relatives included many members of the colony's elite. She was Sophia Francina Westpalm (1722–85), who had been born at Batavia to Director-General Michiel Westpalm and to the Geertruida Goossens who was godmother to the Mossel children and first lady in her own right by her third marriage. On her father's side Sophia Westpalm was the daughter of an immigrant, but her mother had also been born in a VOC trading settlement and her mother before her, Sophia Fauconier, spent her life in Ceylon and Batavia. Sophia Westpalm was widow of the councillor Hugo Verijssel when she married de Klerk in Batavia in 1754. It was a daughter from this prior marriage to Verijssel who brought the Academy's organizing genius, Radermacher, into a family relationship with de Klerk.

Margaretha Radermacher-Verijssel died in Batavia in 1781. In Europe, many of the debates of the intellectual elite, the playreadings and theatricals, took place in salons run by educated women who used their social position and wealth to draw together the leading spirits of the day. Radermacher had no such role in mind for his second wife. He remarried the same year, again an Indieswoman or rather girl, for Anna Jacoba Bosch was only thirteen at the time (Radermacher was then forty). Anna Bosch's father was another Dutchman, her mother the Batavia-born Catharina Louisa Galles. By a later marriage, Catharina Galles became the third wife of Councillor David Smith and was thus considered a member of the family of van der Parra, in whose household Anna Bosch was briefly placed. In lineage and upbringing, then, both Radermacher's wives belonged to the Mestizo culture that had its roots in the seventeenth-century settlement.

The same could be said of the wives of Governor-General Alting, the Academy's second chief director and patron, since he married, successively, part-

Asian women who were raised in European households in Batavia. Nicolaas Engelhard, a leader of Indies Freemasonry, likewise was husband to a Mestiza, Maria Wilhelmina Senn van Basel, daughter of the Senn van Basel patriarch, Councillor Huybert S. van Basel, and granddaughter of the freed slave Susanna van Makassar. Maria Wilhelmina was one of Batavia's richest landowners. Hooyman's marriage to Elisabeth Weijerman has been recorded. There are also examples like that of Dirk van Hogendorp, governor of the North Coast of Java, critic of the VOC's principles of administration and crusader against domestic slavery, who married the thirteen-year-old Eurasian Elisabeth Bartlo, daughter of his army commander at Surabaya. Or take Mohr, whom van Imhoff selected to run his seminary. He was married to the Batavian heiress Anna Elisabeth van 't Hoff. Their only daughter was the fourth wife of Councillor Smith.[25]

In taking young Eurasian wives with whom they shared no cultural affinity nor language for weighty discourse, these men of the Enlightenment defeated their own purpose of promoting Dutch culture in Asia. Their decisions regarding their children had the same result, for they removed their offspring, at least their sons, from the Indies. Van Imhoff arranged for all his children to be sent to the Netherlands. Moreover, in settling property on Helena Pieters in Java, he clearly intended that she should not be reunited with them in the Netherlands. De Klerk had no legitimate issue. Of the children he recognized by slave mothers (named, without imagination, Willem Cornelis and Wilhelmina Cornelia), he sent the boy to Europe. Hooyman died in a shooting accident on his estate Pondokgedeh in 1789. His five-year-old son was removed from his mother's care and sent to Holland the same year, the widow remarrying by October 1789, and like Helena Pieters, remaining permanently in Batavia with her new husband, the Netherlander Godfried Christoffel Fetmenger. Radermacher's son Frans was sent to the Netherlands at twelve and was never to return. The Eurasian Smith was similarly an ambitious parent, sending the boys to Europe, keeping the girls by him in Batavia.

It has therefore often been argued that there is no continuity in Indies families before the nineteenth century. This conclusion is reached, first, by demonstrating that most European men in the settlements were soldiers, signed on for brief terms only and suffering high mortality rates, and second, by counting generations in the male line. Where distinguished men sent sons to Europe there was, of course, no growth of an Indies clan, no Radermachers for instance. There is continuity within the Indies-based group if one counts in the female line, however. By considering the daughters of these same servants of the Company, one may conclude that there was an Indies family system and that kin ties crisscrossed the top rungs of colonial society.

Consider Radermacher's first wife instead of his son. Margaretha Verijssel is the Batavia-born daughter of Sophia Westpalm, Batavia-born daughter of Geertruida Goossens, Batavia-born daughter of Sophia Fauconier. Sophia had married the Batavia-based merchant Johannes Goossens, and after his death, another Dutch immigrant in Gaspar van Mansdale. Her sister Judith Fauconier was the first wife of Abraham Douglas, councillor and later director-general of trade (1708–15). Beyond Sophia Fauconier the record is obscure, but she was the sole heiress of the Colombo-born and Holland-educated Frans Casteleyn, director of the Persia trade and then director-general of trade for all VOC Asia from 1715 to 1722. In marrying Sophia Fauconier's great-granddaughter, Radermacher was joining an Indies family whose female members belonged to Batavia's elite. His ties by marriage made him son-in-law of the governor-general and brother-in-law to the government secretary, Mr. Johan Hendrik van Panhuys. His marriage to Anna Bosch brought him Carel Joost baron van Neukirchen and Carel van Naerssen as brothers-in-law, second administrator of the warehouses on Onrust and head of the Grisek residency, respectively. Through his first marriage Radermacher was also connected to the dowager Thedens.

Thus in their own lives the self-styled reformers continued the very elements that had gone into the formation of Mestizo culture. They made marriages that gave them the necessary family connections, patronage, and wealth, but also partners who had no firsthand notion of European culture or of its currents. Immigrant men understood that their sons would never be Dutchmen if they remained within the Batavian household; consequently they sent them to Europe rather than urge on the Company directors a policy of support for good schools, libraries, and other institutions that would have helped to preserve Dutch culture and identity in a tropical setting.

By the last quarter of the eighteenth century, then, Batavia's elite, which Governor-General van Imhoff had hoped to reorient towards Europe, was more autonomous than before. Candidates for high office came from a pool of men who were connected by marriage to Indies women and who perceived their interests primarily as members of Batavian society rather than as subordinated to the interests of the VOC in Holland. Members of the most senior board of government, the Council of the Indies, were drawn from a very small circle. This fact is clearly illustrated by a review of membership of the Council as constituted under Governor-General van der Parra in 1775.

Links between councillors are detailed in appendix 3. In summary, there sat on the Council in 1775 uncle and nephew (van der Parra and Smith); father-in-law and son-in-law (de Klerk and Radermacher); men married successively to the same woman (Fockens and Smith); men whose children were to marry (van der Parra and Breton; van Riemsdijk and Craan); one whose nephew married a colleague's child (Alting and van Riemsdijk); brothers-in-law (Smith and Vos);

93

one married to a colleague's niece (Vos and van der Parra); one whose step-daughter married a colleague (Smith and Radermacher); a man and his son's guardian (van der Parra and Smith); and other more distant associations. In all cases the wife brought connections to men in high office, and in all cases the wives were born and raised in Asia alone. The circulation of spouses is clearly demonstrated, even within such a small sample as the Council in 1775. And it is no accident that the relatives are sometimes kin once removed; that is, uncle and nephew, where the nephew is actually the son of a half-sister; or father-in-law and son-in-law, where the son-in-law is connected through a daughter from an earlier marriage. Other ways can be devised to demonstrate the crisscrossing ties of office and family at many periods during the VOC centuries. The Council of the Indies, as the highest organ of government, neatly encapsulates the nature of Indies society.

On 31 December 1799, the Honorable Company was dissolved in the face of its huge indebtedness and of the political change in Europe following upon the French Revolution. Governors-general now acted in the name of the Batavian Republic under its Council of Asiatic Possessions, located in The Hague.

The Indonesian settlements became more isolated from Europe as English ships made the seas unsafe for Dutch vessels. In Batavia the ruling families settled ever more firmly into power. Alting's long term came to an end in 1797 when he retired to his country estate. His successor was his government secretary of many years, P. G. van Overstraten, husband to a former schoolmate of the Alting girls. Concentration of power within a small group became even more evident in the accession of Joannes Siberg following van Overstraten's death in office in 1801. Siberg was Alting's son-in-law as second husband of Pieternella, and it was over forty years since he had seen Europe. He, too, preferred retirement in the Indies to repatriation, and the man to whom he turned over the government, A. H. Wiese, was another old colonial hand, veteran of thirty-four years of unbroken residence in Batavia. Wiese's marriages with the Indies-born Christina Marci and then with Jacoba Lodisio, as we have seen, had enlarged his fortune and connected him to old Batavian families.

The expansion of the French Empire under Napoleon overtook these convenient arrangements made by Batavia's elite for dividing up the highest offices and gains among themselves. The Netherlands was annexed in 1806, and with Napoleon's selection of Marshal Herman Daendels, a new, self-conscious reformer stepped into the governor-generalship. When the marshal took up his post in 1808, he was the first governor-general in the two hundred years since Governor-General Laurens Reael (1616–19) who had had no Asian experience.

Daendels considered himself a son of the Revolution, and it was as repre-

94

sentative of the new spirit of the age that he took office. In his brief term he set about remaking Batavia. He did this by completing the move from the old city to the southern suburbs, laying out a great public park and promenade for the European citizenry, building the Harmonie as a clubhouse for a select group of men who would all be Europeans, and planning a palace which was to be the new residence of the governor-general. In 1809 he razed the Castle. More than any other deed, this symbolized the end of an era. For the Castle had represented the Company in the East, its system of monopolies, and the history of its servants in Asia.

Daendels had planned to alter the Company relationship with Indonesians, ending the old tributary relationships and cutting off the "feudal" aspects by prohibiting Europeans from using on their estates the unpaid corvée labor of the inhabitants. Lack of resources and the need to prepare Java's defenses against the expected British attack made him turn to pressed labor gangs as the means of building the Great Java Road, while his measures concerning domestic slavery were likewise directed to mitigating its most flagrant abuses rather than to abolishing the institution itself. Similarly, his hope of strengthening European identity among the elite was modified by the necessities of war.

Given the small numbers of immigrants, Daendels sought to increase the group he might count on in a showdown with British forces by promoting admission of part-Asians to the European community. In this, Daendels simply followed VOC traditions as expressed through rounding up abandoned Eurasian children for placement in the orphanage. Daendels' method was to make children legitimate upon formal acknowledgment by their fathers and payment of a sum set at 10 percent of the parent's salary.[26]

In expressing his policy on legitimation, Daendels noted that there were very few immigrants among the colony's women residents, and that even the most senior officials were married to illegitimate Mestizas or lived in concubinage with Asian women. A glance at the members of Daendels's Council of the Indies illustrates the accuracy of the observation, as well as revealing the ability of the Batavian clique to survive seemingly drastic changes of regime. His director-general, Wouter Hendrik van IJsseldijk, was married to Johanna Maria Magdalena Oland, acknowledged part-Asian daughter of the immigrant Pieter Oland. The senior Council member Willem V. H. van Riemsdijk was fifth-generation Indies-born on his mother's side. His wife, Catharina Margaretha Craan, was second-generation Indies-born on both father's and mother's side, and she had three half-brothers born to Indonesian women. In addition to their fourteen children, W. V. H. van Riemsdijk formally acknowledged six illegitimate children. Councillor Extraordinary Abraham Couperus was married to the Eurasian Catharina Johanna Koek of the Malacca Koek family. A final example is that of Councillor Extraordinary Willem Wardenaar, who had six children by a Javanese concubine. Wardenaar had her baptized Johanna Margaretha Filius and married her in 1800, thereby legitimizing the children. Several of them later served under Daendels as ensigns and low-level officers in his army.

Daendels was withdrawn from office in 1811 before he could have any lasting impact on colonial culture. The term of his successor, Jan Willem Janssens, was a matter of months only. Before the year was out, he had been forced to surrender to the English East India Company's forces headed by Lord Minto and his deputy, Lieutenant Governor Thomas Stamford Raffles.

The British officials who now took over the ruling of Batavia represent as self-consciously reforming a group as any set of Dutchmen in the eighteenth century. Their efforts constitute the second major assault on Indies culture as it had evolved in the VOC centuries. They were very different, however—outsiders with no ties to Batavia's past. During the years they controlled Indonesia, colonial culture was for the first time openly attacked by the entire ruling caste.

THE BRITISH INTERREGNUM (1811–16)

In several important respects this new ruling class differed from its VOC predecessors. It was an officers' caste, composed of younger sons and lesser branches of old English families, their commissions purchased in regiments with long traditions and with assiduously cultivated esprit de corps. Or they were civilian officials of Britain's East India Company, educated men, representing Britain and the Indian Empire at a time of its rising ascendancy, when confidence in British morals and manners was not yet shaken. They were disposed to look on all "foreigners" with sympathy and on Dutch colonials in particular with condescension. Some senior officials, moreover, civilian as well as military, were accompanied by their wives, who were not Anglo-Indians or Eurasians but Englishwomen of the same social status as their husbands who habitually mingled with gentlemen at public receptions and in drawing rooms. From their own imperial traditions the British inherited an identity as a ruling caste, a growing disdain for part-Asians, and a lively curiosity regarding Asian civilizations and peoples. In 1811, an influential minority was on the crest of an enthusiasm for abolishing slavery and bringing "progress" to the benighted wherever they found them.

And so officials of the English Company stand in marked contrast to the VOC Dutch. Although Indies marriage alliances bound senior officials together—indeed, one is hard put to discover a prominent Dutchman not tied to his colleagues by marriage—it is difficult to characterize leading families as composing a caste in quite the same sense as the British Company's officer corps. For one thing, the social, economic, and educational backgrounds of Dutch officials were too various; and since the Batavian ruling class had generally sent its boys to Europe for advancement, it did not pass on traditions of political and intellectual leadership to sons and sons' sons.

By Raffles's count, there were 376 European men in Batavia when the British arrived and 176 women. A further 706 men and 779 women were reckoned as descendants of Europeans, giving a total of 2,028 persons in Batavia with the status of Europeans in 1811. Alongside this group were the Asian residents, 45,189 of them in all, both slave and free.[27] All Europeans had been fairly cut off from the Netherlands during the two previous decades. This isolation had followed on the Company's inability to send out staff, owing to its economic troubles, to the Anglo-Dutch wars, and to the turmoil caused by the annexation of Holland to France. It is profitable to recall here too that of all the eighteenth century's first ladies, Elisabeth van Oosten alone had been born in Europe, and she had died a hundred years earlier in 1714.

Given this period of isolation imposed on Batavia's elite by upheavals in Europe, and considering the contrasting backgrounds of the two ruling groups, it is not surprising that there was shock on both sides at contact. Moreover, the British came suddenly and in such numbers that their differences could not go unnoticed. Not all of the 324 British officers and 5,144 noncommissioned officers and privates[28] were quartered in Batavia, of course, but most of them were, and many of the most senior, so that the composition of the city's European community was profoundly altered for the five years of British rule. Batavia was also the headquarters of government and center for the institutions introduced by the new rulers. For these reasons the Indies European community was inevitably caught up in the life of the British in Batavia and as the object of the victors' reforming zeal.

Batavia's Mestizos have left us no written record of their own for this time, but the British had much to say of the contact and how they felt about Indies life and people. In general, they found Batavia's Dutch quaint, backward, even downright vulgar. Their harshest strictures were directed against the women, who struck them as most alien in manners and culture. Many Britishers were particularly affronted by the mixed racial heritage of the wives of their Dutch colleagues and by the poverty of their education, as they saw it, which resulted in there being no common language through which they might communicate. Lord Minto, to whom Batavia's ladies with European status were presented at a ball given on the eve of his return to India, found nothing pleasing in their looks, manners, dress, opinions, or breeding. "The Dutch did not encourage, nor indeed allow freely, European women to go out to their colonies in India," he wrote his wife.

> The consequence has been, that the men lived with native women whose daughters, gradually borrowing something from the father's side, and becoming a mixed

breed, are now the wives and ladies of rank and fashion in Java. . . . They are attended from their cradles by numerous slaves, by whom they are trained in helplessness and laziness; and from such companions and governesses, you may conceive how much accomplishment and refinement in manner or opinions they are likely to acquire. . . .

An elderly Batavian lady's upper garment is a loose coarse white cotten jacket fastened nowhere but worn with the graceful negligence of pins and all other fastenings or constraints of a Scotch lass, an equally coarse petticoat, and the coarsest stockings, terminating in wide, thick-soled shoes; but by standing behind her you find out her nobility, for at the back of the head a little circle of hair is gathered into a small crown, and on this are deposited diamonds, rubies, and precious stones often of very great value. It is well with this if they can speak even Dutch, many knowing no language but Malay.[29]

Such sentiments of distaste produced in the British by Mestizas were not confined to the letters they wrote home or the memoirs they brought out in England years later. They were expressed directly at the time to all Batavians having European status, with the intention of assisting them to change. To follow this crusade we have to introduce its chief vehicle, which is at the same time one of the most illuminating records of Indies social life under the British.

This is the *Java Government Gazette*, a weekly newspaper published in Batavia. As the official organ of the administration, the *Gazette* announced new edicts and regulations, carried lists of appointments and transfers in government and army, and gave notice of taxes. It was conceived, too, as a news sheet of the English Company's Indian Empire, so that it also gave its readers news of England, reports on the struggle against Napoleon and on the war in America. It included news from India, announcements of marriages in Calcutta, for instance, and there were notes on the royal family and fashionable society in London. The *Gazette* carried news of Batavian social life too. Certain columns were open to the public. There were essays, letters, and a "Poet's Corner." English officers and their wives were thereby kept in touch with the fortunes of their homeland and deeds of their compatriots in India, Europe, and America, as well as given the opportunity to discuss the issues agitating them. An instinct for "Englishness" was thus maintained, as opposed to the "Indianization" that increased with isolation.

Though the paper was obviously very Indo-British, it was never intended for a British readership alone. Some government edicts were also printed in Dutch, as were parts of articles, and there were essays and commentaries directed specifically to the Indies Dutch. These dealt with facts of Batavian life that the British found peculiarly repellent, chief of which were the daily habits of elite women of the European group and the institution of household slavery. It is in articles of this type that the *Gazette*'s duty as instrument for civilizing Batavian society is revealed.

Editors of the *Gazette* urged Batavia's female elite to adopt European costume, for instance. Like Stavorinus, the British were forcibly struck by the modified Indonesian clothing habitually worn by women with European status, viewing the sarong as a petticoat and the kebaya as merely a chemise. Articles such as "Female Fashions for April" describing styles in gowns in vogue in Paris and London therefore found their place in the weekly's columns.[30]

Astonished as the British were by the sight of ladies going out in their "underwear," they were yet more struck by "the distinct separation" of the sexes at parties. "This must be changed," one British letter-writer declared in the *Gazette*'s letters' column, referring to the semisegregation which, in the VOC settlement, was a modification of Indonesian and Ibero-Asian upper-class behavior and one consequence of leaving the training in morals and manners of children with European status solely to Asians.[31]

Once they brought Batavian ladies into mixed company, however, it was immediately apparent to the British that their efforts at improving the "tone" of society were at nought unless their protégées were qualified to contribute. Consequently, the *Gazette*'s pages carried essays on female education and the need for girls' academies. Improvement of the female character was also expected to follow from the crusade to root out slavery.

The issue of slavery was a popular one with the British in the *Gazette*. In essay and letter, writers either appealed to the consciences of the Dutch or roundly castigated them; but invariably their starting point was Dutch obduracy before a new, enlightened stage in Western philosophy and practice. And the Batavian Dutch reacted. Slavery was one of the few issues that provoked Dutchmen to respond in the *Gazette*. Defenders of Dutch practice claimed an intimacy between owners and slave retainers that they contrasted with the cruel, degrading treatment handed down to "free" servants whom the British brought from India; or they sought hidden economic motives in the abolitionists' cause.[32]

As individuals, the British repeated their lessons to the Batavian Dutch. Olivia Mariamne Raffles, first wife of the lieutenant governor and principal female of Batavian society during the interregnum, ordered all cuspidors out of the governor's official residence, for instance, and refused to offer betel to ladies who waited on her at her fortnightly drawing rooms. In omitting the ceremonious offering of betel, she deliberately contravened Indies civilities. Nor did she conceal her displeasure at ladies calling on her in Indonesian costume.

In other ways, too, British newcomers of senior standing set examples of conduct they wished to see generally adopted by Batavia's elite. To their dinners, balls, and levees they invited the "chief, respectable Dutch inhabitants of the Settlement." At such occasions the van Riemsdijk, Senn van Basel, van IJsseldijk, Alting, and other leading ladies of Batavia would be expected to act according to British notions of civilized behavior, eating with knife and fork, sitting on chairs, and mixing with men in conversation and dance.

Balls and parties were not the only forums where Batavia's British and Dutch communities met socially and where British notions reigned. On 17 October 1814, the Military Bachelors' Theatre was opened in Weltevreden, the new southern suburb of Batavia, its announced purpose being "the amusement of the ladies" and provision of civilized diversion in the capital. The plays selected were chiefly comedies popular in England at the time. Again, the audience aimed at was not English alone but all Batavian society with European status. Announcements of coming productions in the *Gazette* were accompanied by a synopsis in Dutch, to encourage the widest possible audience.[33]

Standing back, one can see several direct consequences of the new social etiquette prevailing in the theater and at balls, as one can from the twin crusades concerning elite women and domestic slavery. In summoning Batavian ladies into mixed company, the British did more than require them to give up betel. They trampled notions of propriety in the relations between men and women that were fundamental to Mestizo society. For the first time, Indies manners were openly derided, not just in books for a readership in Europe, but directly, in Batavia. And since the British were at the head of local society, their manners became the standard for Batavia's "Europeans." Batavian women could neither avoid nor ignore them, for now social life revolved around Olivia Raffles and other senior ladies of the settlement like Flora Nightingall, wife of the army commander succeeding Gillespie. So from the interregnum there dates a tendency to confine Mestizo manners to the household while adopting European manners for public view.

The introduction of British etiquette and the newly awakening British horror at slavery had further consequences too. On the one hand, Batavian Dutch lost an important symbol of status when they could no longer be followed by slave attendants whose number and type of clothing all indicated the owner's rank and wealth. On the other, Batavian Dutch were deprived of their lifelong and daily companions. This separation was particularly important for women. European men had always moved between the twin worlds of the household, where the majority of members were Asian and enslaved, and the office, where there was a preponderance of men who were migrants from Europe. What the British period began was the introduction of that distinction more sharply into the lives of upper-class women who had European status.

This last point can best be illustrated by considering the theater and its implications for Indies life. Amateur theater was a European entertainment where performers were often the social equals of the audience and the plays were products of European culture. And so it was a very different form of diversion from that offered by Indies households: the slave orchestra, Indonesian dance troupe, and puppet theaters of Asia. These latter entertainments were staged in the household for the family and guests and were enjoyed, from a discreet distance, by their Asian retainers. The Military Bachelors' Theatre was the product of an alien culture, located physically outside the sphere of the house in a special building for the European group alone.

All these efforts directed at changing Mestizas apparently had some success. At least one English observer reported, with a certain smugness, "After the arrival of the English, the younger ladies, and those who mix much in society with them, adopted the fashionable habiliments of our fair countrywomen, and in their manner as well as dress they are improving wonderfully.[34]

But it was not enough to alter the women. Indies men also came under the reforming zeal of the new ruling caste. Many, of course, were employed by the British administration. At the same time, the British met with them socially, welcoming them into the associations, such as the Equestrian club, which they formed. The British sought also to involve Dutchmen in societies of a charitable nature that they founded in Java for goals to which they believed a gentleman ought to be committed. In 1814, for instance, the Java Auxiliary Bible Society was founded, and late in 1815, the Java Benevolent Institution was formed as an antislavery society, with the lieutenant governor presiding over both.

The desire to remake the Dutch extended to their personal habits of dress, cleanliness, and exercise too. Individual Britishers suggested through the *Gazette* how Dutchmen should change their ways. It began with a series of essays on causes of the old city's unhealthiness as compared to conditions in the new, southern suburbs. "Benevolus," a prolific letter writer, spoke of the narrow streets, small windows, cramped living quarters, and thickly curtained beds that prevented circulation of air, and argued that Dutchmen had only to change their habits for Batavia to be a safer place to live. Such opinions drew a derisive response from one Dutch inhabitant, who wrote that sea breezes and "noxious vapors" were the true causes of Batavia's high mortality rate.[35]

This apparent incongruity in Indies society—of women with European status wearing a form of Indonesian costume, speaking Malay, and eating Asian food, while married to men who refused to adapt to the Asian custom of frequent bathing or to modify their dress, consumption of alcohol, or working hours— may be explained by the key feature in that society. Women were Asia-born and bred but always married to men who were immigrants. It is one of the ironies of history that the *rijsttafel* (Dutch version of the Indonesian meal), the afternoon siesta, and the wearing of colonial whites are late-nineteenth- and early-twentieth-century adaptations to a tropical environment, introduced by Europeans who at the same time strove to maintain ties to their homeland. The immigrant of the seventeenth and eighteenth centuries, by contrast, clung to his Dutch habits in the isolation of his port city and country estate.

Other consequences of the demographic makeup of Indies society have already been noted: the semi-purdah of upper-class ladies, the lack of a gentry, and the absence of such institutions as schools. These considerations were not clear to newcomers at the time. William Thorn's remarks, for instance, were limited to noting the absence of schools, without seeking an explanation (beyond the implied barbarity of the Dutch), and we can suppose that his remarks accurately reflected British opinion of the time. "Public teachers of any note are not to be found in Batavia," he wrote, "and therefore the culture of the youthful mind of either sex is, at the present day, most shamefully neglected."[36]

It is only to be expected, then, that in addition to the theater, racing club, and charitable organizations, the British administration should encourage public education (though the administration did not open schools). Raffles's government imported English spellers, grammars, geography texts, the *Polite Preceptor*, copies of Aesop's fables, and French primers. A consignment of books for adults announced in the *Gazette* in 1814 included "new novels," essays on government and literature, prayer books, dictionaries, and "pamphlets, etc." Reading was not a habit of Mestizo society, and so the contrast with the British in this respect is strong. Individual Britishers had private libraries of their own too. In some cases the quantities of books were considerable. Raffles, for instance, on quitting Java in 1816, had a catalogue of titles in his library printed and sold 420 of the books.

By 1816 Batavia appeared altered. The number of Europeans educated and raised in Europe was much greater, to begin with; and the British among them had the power and the will to make changes. To cater to these Europeans and thus preserve a European identity, a network of institutions had been established. There were the weekly newspaper, the theater, clubs and societies, and all these were complemented by banquets and dances at which English rules of propriety reigned. English and French were the languages of polite society; Malay speech, costume, and habits were unwelcome in European elite circles, and slave-owning was increasingly regarded with contempt. The line between the worlds of Asian and European were drawn more sharply by British efforts to make Mestizas securely a part of a Western community. And finally, the men in highest office were all publicly committed to a belief in the superiority of Western civilization and to spreading its recently discovered truths and its most radical benefits to their Indies subjects. This was a very different concept of administration from that of the old VOC governors.

Given these pronounced differences in policy, convictions, background, and style, it might be expected that the British would shun contact with the Batavian Dutch altogether, leave Mestizas to their ways, and prefer their own kind, but they did not. The newcomers' idea of civilized society inspired them to bring Mestizas out of their partial confinement. One reason was simply that British entertainments required the presence of women as hostesses and company. Another compelling motive for their attention to Batavians with European status was political, the need to guarantee a degree of loyalty and cooperation of Dutchmen in the daily administration of the colony. A review of those Dutchmen employed in important posts by Raffles's administration and of those with whom the British mixed socially allows a deeper understanding of the period, while illustrating at the same time what prompted the British onslaught on colonial culture.

In 1811 the councillors of the Indies through whom Daendels and Janssens had governed were J. A. van Braam, H. W. Muntinghe, H. A. Parvé, P. T. Chassé, W. van Hoesen, J. J. Vogelaar, J. M. Baljée, F. J. Rothenbuhler, W. J. Cranssen, J. C. Romswinckel, and names already familiar here—W. H. van IJsseldijk, W. V. H. van Riemsdijk, C. A. Cantervisscher, W. A. Senn van Basel, N. Engelhard, and W. Wardenaar.

Raffles retained only one of these men for his own board of advisors. He was the Groninger Willem Jacob Cranssen,* who ranked third on the British Council. Cranssen's rise in the VOC hierarchy had occurred during the seventeen-year term of Governor-General Alting, culminating in the governorship of Ambon. His wealth in land and goods was accumulated in the usual way of position and marriage. His wife was Maria Eleonora Hartman, who was a first-generation Indies woman on her father's side but whose mother was similarly a Batavian by birth and daughter of a Dutchman. Cranssen's legitimate son Willem Leonard was raised in the Indies and married a cousin of a Makassar branch of his father's family, while his full sister, Rica Catharina, married Petrus Theodorus Couperus, eldest son of the former governor of Malacca. Cranssen also kept an Ambonese woman whom he had had baptized, forming her Christian names upon his own: Wilhelmina Jacoba, the feminine equivalents of Willem Jacob, and turning Cranssen backwards to form her surname Nessnarc. One of the children from this liaison whom Cranssen legally adopted was Wilhelmina Niclasina Cranssen, who became principal lady of the Indies through her second marriage to Mr. Pieter Merkus, governor-general from 1841 to 1844.

Raffles's chief justice was also a Netherlander, Herman Warner Muntinghe, but one who had been schooled in England. Unlike his Dutch colleagues, he had had no experience in the VOC's service; he had not come to Batavia until 1806. Muntinghe is best known as Raffles's close advisor and kindred spirit but also for his many papers debating colonial policy and propositions for reform. Nevertheless, he too was fully the Indiesman, having chosen for his bride Wilhelmina Adriana Senn van Basel, who was part-Asian and seventeen years his junior. She brought Muntinghe valuable connections as the daughter of the former councillor W. A. Senn van Basel by his first wife, Anna Maria Hooreman. Wilhelmina's mother was herself the daughter of a councillor, while her maternal grandmother had been born at Negapattinam. Through both sides Muntinghe's wife allied him to the powerful Indies clique of the van Riemsdijk, Engelhard, Alting, Wiese, and S. van Basel clans.

The advocate-fiscal during the interregnum was Jan Isaak van Sevenhoven, another Dutch immigrant who was a member of Indies families through marriage. His first wife was Catharina Arnoldina Mom, daughter of the councillor Mr. Arnoldus Constantijn Mom by Catharina Louysa van Riemsdijk, and granddaughter of W. V. H. van Riemsdijk and the Japara-born Catharina Craan.

The most powerful of the old Company officials—men like Joannes Siberg, Nicolaas Engelhard, and W. H. van IJsseldijk—were kept at a distance from the new administration. This is not to say that there was no contact at all. Nicolaas Engelhard was Raffles's vice-president of the Bible Society. Ordinary members included a few van Riemsdijken, Cantervisscher, and van Braam, and a Couperus, while on the committee were such old Indies names as Romswinckel, Coop à Groen, and Parvé.

We can profitably pause to consider the family history of Mr. Roelof Coop à Groen,* for he was also associated with Raffles as fellow committee member of the Academy, renamed the Batavia Literary Society during the interregnum. Coop à Groen's Indies antecedents stretched back to the seventeenth century, at which time his great-grandfather, Drs. B. Coop à Groen, emigrated to serve as minister in Malacca, Paliacutta, and then Batavia. His wife accompanied him to the East, bearing two children in Asia, both of whom made their careers there. The son, Bernardus, was born in Batavia around 1690, was reared there, and served the Dutch East Indies Company in various positions, ending up as senior merchant and chief of the Japara factory. He retired from active service in 1736 and died in Batavia four years later.

During his life this Coop à Groen married three times and had ten children. The two daughters surviving to adulthood were married to immigrants from the Netherlands. The sons were educated in Europe. One returned and was chief official of the VOC's settlements at Japara and Surabaya. The other, Mr. Willem Egidius C. à Groen, was born from his father's third marriage to Johanna Stul, daughter of a governor of Banda. He made his career in the Netherlands, but his son, Roelof, who was Raffles's colleague, emigrated to Indonesia. Roelof's European education allowed him to surpass his grandfather in the VOC hierarchy. By the time of the interregnum, Roelof C. à Groen was living in retirement in Batavia, after leaving the governorship of Banda and then of Ternate.

Van IJsseldijk and Cranssen regularly entertained Raffles, Major-General Nightingall, and other British dignitaries and their wives at dinners and receptions. The British were also entertained by members of Batavia's European community, who combined many of the characteristics (such as mixed ancestry, Asia-bred wives, concubinage) that the newcomers so disliked. Raffles and his entourage were principal guests at a ball given by Lieve Willem Meyer, for instance, in 1814. This Meyer was the son of Dr. Johannes Jacobus Meyer, a Eurasian from Ceylon sent by the VOC to Leiden University to study theology. Upon graduating, Meyer had returned to minister to Colombo and later to Batavia. Following charges against his character, he had been suspended and sent to the Netherlands, where Lieve Meyer was born. Lieve reached Batavia in 1791 in the role of ship's steward. In Batavia he was employed as a government clerk and there married a local woman of European status. Raffles used him as secretary and translator. One month after receiving the lieutenant governor and his suite in his Batavia house, Lieve Meyer legally adopted a child he had had by a Balinese woman.

Another Indies man admitted to Raffles's inner circle was Jan Andries van Braam. Born in India to a VOC naval captain, van Braam's rise to positions of power had come about after his marriage in 1800 to Ambrosina Wilhelmina van Rijck, daughter of the VOC commander at Pasuruan. Orphaned early, she had been raised in the household of Councillor Extraordinary Anthonij Barkeij. Van Braam's brother-in-law, Gerardus Carolus van Rijck, was married to a van Riemsdijk. Van Braam received special favor from Daendels, being designated governor-general *ad interim,* although this honor was rightfully van IJsseldijk's as second-in-command. During the interregnum van Braam was in Bengal and the Netherlands, but spent 1814 in Batavia and returned again late in the following year. While resident in Batavia he was frequently host to all the distinguished British at what the *Gazette* described as his "superb mansion."

Only at gatherings of the Benevolent Institution was there little contact between Dutch and British. The group represented by van IJsseldijk, van Sevenhoven, Muntinghe, van Braam, Cantervisscher, P. T. Couperus, W. A. Senn van Basel, and N. Engelhard, who all rejoined the Literary Society, visited the Harmonie, subscribed to the Bible Society, and so on, stayed away from Raffles's anti-slavery association. So did former governor-general Siberg. The three Dutchmen listed as founding members of the Benevolent Institution were aides-de-camp and under-clerks.

Only one representative of Batavia's leading families was persuaded to become a member, and that was Cranssen. He joined in 1816 in the society's last months when the membership totalled seventy. The number of Dutch participants had only climbed to ten. The distinctly anti-Dutch tone of many of the antislavery proponents accounts for the distance, as well as the underlying threat to the fortune and status of Batavia's elite. Nicolaas Engelhard, for instance, had reckoned his wealth in slaves at 20,942 rix dollars, nearly equal to his wealth in gold and jewels, estimated at 28,941 rix dollars and far exceeding his property in carriages and horses (2,500 rix dollars).[37]

In their abstention from the antislavery movement, which was one of the chief crusades of Raffles and his circle, Batavia's Dutch showed a sense of group identity. The examples given above of high-ranking Dutchmen in the British administration and of Dutchmen who mixed socially with the British are representative of the Batavian European community at the beginning of the nineteenth century. That is to say, members were linked by marriage, by partnerships in the old VOC hierarchy, by long residence in Asia, by family histories reaching back generations in the maternal line, and by assimilation of Mestizo cultural values and habits. What the British found, as Daendels and Janssens had before them, was a closed society, fully functioning through all the changes in government brought about by political events in Europe, and continuing to absorb immigrants and transform them. This strength and inner cohesion is an important consideration in assessing the impact of the interregnum and in understanding the history of the first fifty years of the nineteenth century, when the colony passed directly under the control of the Netherlands monarchy.

In describing the British period in Batavia it is not intended to suggest that the new rulers were interested only in their own world and in transforming the city's "European" elite. They had a curiosity about Indonesia's islands that expressed itself in mountain-climbing expeditions and in parties to excavate old temples. Some collected plants, animals, and mineral specimens and made maps of various localities. There were others interested principally in the indigenous inhabitants of the islands. John Crawfurd, who assumed the position of resident, or European administrative head, of Solo, for instance, gathered ethnographic data for his three-volume *History of the Indian Archipelago*.

The government promoted such researches. Raffles's part in the excavation of Borobudur is perhaps best known, but his interests were more extensive than that. The lieutenant governor joined expeditions, promoted collection of information which was later summarized in his two-volume *History of Java*, and aided in the dissemination of such knowledge. His addresses to the Academy discussed the work of the American botanist and naturalist Thomas Horsfield, and he was a generous patron of the naturalist, orientalist, and antiquarian Sir Colin Mackenzie. In addition to advancing the researches of others, Raffles found time for the study of Javanese texts. In September 1813 his secretary, Thomas Travers, recorded: "At the moment of my now writing, the Governor is translating a poem termed the "Brata Yudha" or "Holy War," which would have been an ornament to the works of the Grecian, Italian, or even [!] English bards of old."[38] British contributions to the Academy's *Transactions* during the interregnum included transcriptions of old Kawi texts and suggestions for their interpretation, a report on the Prambanan temples, descriptions of the geography of various regions, chemical analyses of certain fruits, and an essay on the principles of Malay spelling.

Nevertheless, where there was a will to discover and describe the Indonesian world there was equally the wish to change and reform it. One part of Raffles's attack on Mestizo culture was an attempt to alter the Dutch style of dealing with their Asian subjects and to impart British ideals of conduct to those Asian subjects too. These motives are behind Raffles's efforts to introduce the land-rent system in the areas of Java that had been ruled directly by the VOC. The lieutenant governor saw as part of his mission bearing this message of change to the very heart of Javanese civilization itself. He thus undertook what no Dutch governor-general save van Imhoff ever did, and that was to tour Java extensively and enter into personal relations with the rulers of Solo (also called Surakarta) and Yogyakarta. Such considerations of civilizing duty may have prompted him to include Olivia in his entourage, not just as companion of his travels but as first lady with ceremonial roles in her own right.

The extraordinary results can be followed in the *Gazette*.[39] Late in 1813 we read that Raffles's party traveled by boat to Semarang and then overland to Solo. They were met by civilian and military representatives of the *susuhunan* (ruler), Pakubuwono IV, and by the assistant resident, Lieutenant J. Eckford. A nineteen-gun salute was fired and then the entire party traveled to "Clutchoo," country seat of the susuhunan, where the ceremonies of meeting were to take place. The *Gazette* reports:

> On alighting from their carriage, the Hon. the Lt. Governor and Lady Governess conducted by the Emperor *and Empress* proceeded to seats prepared for them in a commodious apartment, where the suite of the Hon. the Lt. Governor and the Officers of his Staff and Escort arranged themselves on one side, whilst the Crown Prince with the Sons of the Emperor, the prime minister and other Officers of the Court occupied the other side of the room. A table was laid in the centre covered with refreshments which were handed round by female slaves. After mutual congratulations and a few complimentary toasts, his Highness the Emperor conducted the Lt. Governor to the state coach (Kia Doodoo), the Empress having handed the Lady Governess to another state coach immediately preceding the Emperor's. [Emphasis added.]

All then proceeded to the *kraton* or palace of Surakarta, "the wife of the Resident [Hugh Hope] or chief European lady of Solo" joining the company in her own carriage. The principals were then seated in the audience hall of the palace, where toasts were proposed as the "gomblongs" (gamelan) played. At the conclusion of ceremonies Raffles and Olivia withdrew to the residency, where "all the Civil and Military Servants as well as the European Ladies and Gentlemen residing at Solo were assembled."[40]

The evening of December 6 included staging of a "Javanese comedy" at the residency and the reception of the susuhunan and his consort. All the local Europeans attended the evening's festivities, at which there were a fireworks display, a conjuring demonstration, and an exhibition of dancing by palace women who had been transported to the residency in enclosed palanquins. Supper ended with toasts to "Mrs. Raffles" proposed by the susuhunan and to "Her Highness the Empress," "Souracarta and prosperity to it," and "the Ladies of Java" proposed by the guests. "These and some other toasts having been drunk," the report continues, "the party adjourned to the Ballroom, where his Highness the Emperor led off a country dance with the Lady Governess. *The Hon. the Lt. Governor danced a few couple with the Empress.* Reels concluded the festivities of the evening." [Emphasis added.]

The seventh opened with tiger fights staged by the Javanese and attended by Raffles, Olivia, and the susuhunan. From there, all moved into the kraton. "The Emperor and Empress then conducted the Lt. Governor, with his Lady and their Suite, to an interior chamber of the Palace, where the Daughters and other female relatives of their Highnesses were presented in form." The day following, Raffles and his party went on to Yogyakarta, where similar ceremonies and entertainments were staged. Here, too, the sultan's chief wife, the "Ratoo-Kanchono" (*Ratu Kencana*), took part in greeting Olivia and visited the residency to drink toasts. As at Solo, "the Lt. Governor and his Lady were conducted by the Sultan and the Ratoo into the interior of the Palace where they were introduced to his Highness' mother and to the Princesses of the Court."[41]

It is outside the scope of this discussion to explore the political intrigues and uneasy relations between the sultans and the new rulers of the Indies which prompted Raffles's journey into Central Java. What is important to an understanding of Mestizo society and culture is the form which these official meetings took and which will now be examined more closely. In taking Olivia with him on these visits of state, Raffles obliged his hosts to produce a counterpart from among their wives to partner her. In this, Raffles had no precedent, for representatives of the British government in India never attempted to meet elite women, while his knowledge of the Malay world told him that upper-class ladies were generally also maintained in seclusion. In this way, Raffles established a new trend in relations between Batavia-based European and Asian, for his style of social intercourse with the Javanese nobility was not to be a singular event. Speaking of Pakubuwono IV, Thorn had this to say of the susuhunan's relations with Calcutta's Solo-based representative: "The Emperor, who is about fifty years of age, is courteous in his manners; and in his visits to the British Resident, he is generally accompanied by his favourite wife."[42]

Before the interregnum, relations between European men and Asian women had generally been confined to the coastal settlements and had been those of superior and inferior, of owner and slave-concubine. The Asian woman in European households was liable to abuse, abandonment, or sale. Now some European government officials were publically trying to deal with certain Asian women outside the colonial enclaves as their social equals. It is worth noting the details of this contact and their consequences. Not only was a secluded lady

108

required to greet foreigners; when the susuhunan's consort danced a few steps with Raffles, she was obliged to enter into a degree of physical contact with a strange man that was forbidden by religion as by custom, and to do so before the entire court. Then there is the unprecedented admission of European men into the susuhunan's and sultan's inner apartments for introductions to "other female relatives."

The demands of religion were also contravened by the drinking of wine. It is clear, from the accounts of contemporary observers,[43] that this was not a new, sudden break with the law. Raffles remarks: "the ceremonies and state of the native courts have lost much of their genuine character, from the admission of European customs, introduced by the Dutch after the last Javan War [1755]."[44] He attributes the taking of alcohol to the new familiarity with European ways, and adds this interesting detail on the overlaying of foreign manners with Javanese notions of correct behavior: "When the Susuhunan drinks wine with the Governor, the rest of the company are offered white wine, while they alone drink red, and a flourish of trumpets sounds as the glass approaches their lips."[45]

It is useful to compare the *Gazette*'s account of the 1813 visit with the second, which was made in January 1816 and described in the diary of Thomas Travers. In most respects little was outwardly different. There were the receptions, the ceremonious compliments, the dances, tiger fights, and parties. What was different was the role of the chief Javanese ladies. Olivia had died the previous year, and in her absence the part played by the susuhunan's wife at Solo was subtly altered. Having no counterpart in the lieutenant governor's wife, she was not brought forward. Thus, neither at the ceremonies where wine was handed round in the palace nor at the ball given in the Solo residency did the chief wife appear. It is not to be supposed that all contact had ceased, however. Travers states: "After partaking of refreshment and wine, the Governor was led by the Emperor to the harem and presented to the Empress, after which the different gentlemen present were introduced and shook hands; without sitting we all returned to the hall of audience, and took our seats as before."[46] European men, senior in government, then, still entered the women's quarters. There was physical contact in the European form of greeting, the handshake, but now the meeting was momentary.

The entry of upper-class Indonesian ladies into the public arena was to be dependent upon a profound change in the demographic composition of colonial society. Only when there was a greater proportion of European women in the colony and of recognized families among the Dutch did this take place. So long as Dutch colonial policy restricted the immigration of European women, Asian notions of decorum prevailed and men from Europe conformed to them, keeping their concubines and wives largely out of sight, as did a Javanese official his secondary wives and consort.

The situation we are describing was especially true for the Batavia-based Europeans, whose ruling elite was Dutch and who had limited opportunities for contact with upper-class Javanese. In the subsidiary settlements and port cities where an Asian elite ruled, the behavior of the Dutch was different, regulated according to the dictates and personality of the local ruler. Even so, if travelers such as Cornelis de Bruijn are to be believed, senior Dutch officials and their wives seldom met publicly with the women of the elite, and his admission to the presence of the sultan of Bantam's consort was a singular event.[47]

Once the sex and race ratio altered, Java's elite modified its behavior to conform with European ideas. Here lies the ultimate significance of the British interregnum for Mestizo culture: it opened up new relations between Europeans on the one hand and Asians and part-Asians on the other. Mestizos and Indonesians alike were required to change and adjust in order to meet British ideas of civilized social intercourse, and the changes made involved in each case deliberate breach of tradition, religious sentiment, and custom. This is not to deny any modifications on the British side. On the whole, however, British-style manners dominated during the interregnum because power lay with the newcomers and because they brought with them their wives and a determination to impose their own codes on public behavior.

The British interregnum lasted five years. In April of 1816 the commissioners-general for the Kingdom of the Netherlands arrived in Batavia, and they formally accepted transfer of the government from Lieutenant Governor John Fendall (Raffles's successor) on August 19 of that year. The British, in writing of this period, have always dwelled on the land-rent system. So, too, have Dutch historians, although with the rather different object of modifying the former's claims and disputing the extent and success of the so-called reform. Change in terms of the altered social relations that this section describes has received little or no attention, and yet the British had attempted to transform Dutch colonial culture radically. As part of this goal they had required their Dutch counterparts to introduce their Eurasian and Creole wives into society.

Such changes in the accustomed social role of women could not leave the Batavia Dutchman unaffected. The British crusade against the semi-purdah of Indies society obliged him to accept a more public role for women, to modify his own behavior accordingly, and consciously to follow northern European styles in dealing with them. This change in the Indies Dutchman is illustrated by the habit of announcing family affairs through the columns of the newspaper. Van Sevenhoven, W. A. Senn van Basel, and Willem Nicolaas Servatius, for instance, announced the death of their wives—Catharina Mom, Dorothea Jacoba van Riemsdijk, and Sara Catharina Senn van Basel respectively—in the *Gazette,* and had notices printed extolling their "amiable qualities."[48]

The point here is more than to note the regular appearance of a newspaper in Batavia with personals columns. The placement of notices concerning wives, marriage of daughters, and the like signals a new attitude of Batavian men towards Indies women: to mention them by name and description in a public paper effectively brought them out of the semi-seclusion hitherto characteristic of the Indies lady, and suggests changing views of the role of women with European status in colonial society.

Similarly, dancing in the European style became an established part of Mestizo culture during the interregnum and remained a permanent feature thereafter, though adapted to Indies notions of decorum in that the sexes continued to sit in separate rooms between dances. The frivolity of this cultural borrowing should not obscure its significance. From the interregnum dates the ascendancy of a European-style of entertainment, while the slave orchestra and ronggeng troupe declined in popularity. Furthermore, this pastime of dancing marked the entrance into society of ladies with European status, and it ensured them a permanent, visible place in it. At the same time, it was a break from their slave women.

The impact of the British was therefore immediate and visible in the related issues of the role of women and the institution of slavery. Their impact was also strongly felt by Batavia's Europeans in a broader sense. A whole generation of Indies people had grown up in the last years of the eighteenth century and early years of the nineteenth quite cut off from Europe. In the four years of Governor-General Wiese's term (1808–11), for instance, not one ship had arrived from the Netherlands. Local government had been left without new employees and the infusion of new migrants whose habits and loyalties had not yet been reworked by life in the colony. The recurring reminders of Dutch ways were absent. Consequently, more Creoles and Eurasians were taken into government employ, while the upper class was left to make and remake family alliances and to promote locally born men and rule in its own way, without interference or checks from overseas.

The British victory of 1811 admitted hundreds of Europeans to Batavia of a sudden. Indies society was wrenched out of its isolation by their very numbers as by their sense of mission. The British victory also lifted the blockade on supplies of goods from Europe, the absence of which had rendered life particularly bleak for the upper class. Stores of wine and oil, for instance, had been so depleted that Daendels and Janssens had prohibited illumination of private houses and the staging of large parties.[49] Since the new rulers immediately threw balls to honor Lord Minto and others of their heroes and invited the principal Dutch to them, there was generated a new excitement in Batavian life. It is probably not an exaggeration to assume that the newcomers particularly gratified Batavian familes, dependent as they were on immigrant males for husbands to their daughters. The first Dutch-British match, between Jacoba

Maria Goldman and William Barrett, was celebrated before the first year of the interregnum was out and reported in the *Gazette* in terms of its promise of happy relations between the two European communities.[50]

Some Batavian Dutch were enthusiastic admirers of the Britons and expressed their sentiments in extravagant epithets in public speeches. The most outrageous demonstration (and evidence) of Anglophilia was a penchant for baptizing children with the names of the new heroes. P. T. Couperus, for instance, seized the opportunity in the birth of a son to christen him Willem Jacob Thomas Raffles Couperus (the first set of names honoring the boy's maternal grandfather, W. J. Cranssen). Couperus's brother-in-law named a daughter born in September 1813 Olivia Mariamne Timmerman Thyssen.[51] Outdoing them all in zeal, Raffles's comptroller had his daughter baptized Olivia Mariamne Stamford Raffles Villeneuve!

The five years of British rule did not succeed, however, in wresting Indies life out of its established patterns, for three basic reasons. In the first place, the contact was too fleeting. Five years were not sufficient to undo a culture that had been two hundred years in the making. By the time British rule was into its third year, it was known that it would be an interregnum only and that the Dutch would reclaim the seat of power. Consequently, those with an eye to the future could not be excessively tied to a caretaker regime. And there were always leading Batavians who were never much touched by British rule but deliberately held themselves aloof.

A second reason lay with the character of the British rulers themselves. They, too, were cultural hybrids, coming to Java not directly from England but via India and from an "Indianized" culture that had developed over two centuries. Thus while Raffles and his reform-minded officials fulminated against the barbarities of slave-owning, the *Java Government Gazette* continued throughout the interregnum to print lists of slaves for sale. Nor were individual Britishers without slaves in their households. The following notice, for instance, appeared in the *Gazette* about the time of Major-General Gillespie's return to India: "His Slaves, not mentioned in the former advertisement [a list of household goods], will also be sold on the same day, of which a separate list and description will be circulated previous to the sale."[52] Travers, Raffles's secretary and confidant, also had slaves on his household staff.[53]

Furthermore, many Britons lived openly with Asian concubines. The William Robinson who is recorded by the *Gazette* feting Olivia Raffles on her birthday, for instance, had fathered three children by an Asian woman while in Penang. They were baptized with his surname in Batavia some nine months after his death in 1815. And it is one of the ironies of history that the liaisons between Asian women and European men that have passed into novels and to the stage date precisely from the interregnum and involved Englishmen. The first example is of Alexander Hare, Raffles's political commissioner for the

Native states of Borneo and resident of Banjermasin, whose use of Javanese slave labor on his properties in southern Borneo brought scandal to the British administration. Hare's notoriety as lord of a harem has been made the subject of a recent novel.[54] Another example illustrating the case for the Englishman as "India-man" is the liaison between Edward Williams and a Sundanese woman, immortalized in Mestizo stories and theater (the *Komedie Stamboel*) as *Njai Dasima*.[55]

The third cause of the immediate failure of the British crusade lies in Mestizo culture itself. The Dutchmen who flocked around Raffles—Muntinghe, Cranssen, Couperus, van Braam, and the rest—were all Batavians in habit and mentality. The old clan system was stronger and further-reaching than ever, and could not be undone by five years of hectoring on manners and morals. Only a complete replacement of Indiesmen with immigrants in high positions could break the political power and cultural influence of Batavia's elite. Raffles did not have the necessary numbers of British officials at his command and was forced to rely on the heirs to the VOC system and society. As the first all-encompassing cultural attack on Mestizo society, then, the British interregnum revealed that society's strengths.

In 1816, when the British returned control of Java to the Dutch, the old family system in the capital was still intact and able to dominate Batavia's governing councils a little longer. For this reason the nineteenth century, which opens with the appearance of dramatic change, saw a slow flowing back into the ways of the Company, in methods of rule and administration as in individual taste and habits. Thus was Mestizo culture afforded the opportunity of expansion into the interior of Java, which process continued in the second half of that century at the same time that it was under the assault of organized Dutch culture. These contrary trends and the tensions between them compose the subject of the final chapters.

5

The Destruction of VOC Society
and the Creation of the New Colonial

THE THIRD IN THE SERIES of assaults launched on Mestizo society by outsiders began in 1816 when the British transferred the Indies government to commissioners-general of the Netherlands monarch. This assault was to succeed in destroying the Company's legacy, for it was political as well as cultural. Neither van Imhoff nor Radermacher and his friends had ever seriously considered altering the Batavian ruling system that had raised them to their positions of power and wealth. They limited their activities to efforts at transplanting European habits and civilities, whereas the commissioners deliberately attacked the political strength of the local elite. One consequence was that the Indies clan rapidly diminished in political importance; the upper-class Mestiza could no longer offer ties to inner circles and was replaced as social model by immigrant Dutch titled ladies.

Raffles and his two immediate predecessors had been moving in the same direction. Lack of time and manpower, and withdrawal of backing from home, had prevented their accomplishing much. Raffles, for instance, had been obliged to use Indiesmen in his administration because he had too few Englishmen at his disposal, but he had selected them for their talents and loyalty, not for their family connections. The same is true of the regimes of Daendels and Janssens. A. H. Wiese was the last governor-general to appoint and promote men because of their membership in the Indies family network. Viewed in this light, it is apparent that the political power of the Batavian elite ended forever in 1808. The fact that men bearing the surnames Senn van Basel, Engelhard, and Cranssen continued awhile to figure among senior appointments conceals this political reality.

Newcomers serving the Dutch Crown tended to return to Europe upon completion of a tour of duty in the Indies. The matrilineal character of Indies society was thus broken. For hitherto, Mestizas had married immigrants whose lives were spent in the Indies, and the family line had continued through the daughters of these unions who in their turn married immigrant men. Mestizas who now married Hollanders disappeared from Indies history by retiring to Europe with their husbands when these resumed careers in Europe. Continuity in the Indies family now passed to the male line. The colonial family, thus reoriented, reformed on the fringes of European society as its male members were displaced from the administration by civil service requirements of birth and education in the Netherlands.

The appointment of outsiders to senior positions in Indies government, beginning with Daendels, also had another very important effect: it prevented realization of a trend just discernible in Indies society for sons of the political elite to climb the Batavian hierarchy rather than being detached and sent to Europe. As previously noted, Governors-General van der Parra and van Riemsdijk seem to have hoped to found dynasties, and the careers of Councillors W. A. Senn van Basel and David Smith seem to confirm that the ruling elite was developing a patriarchal cast as Batavia became more isolated from Europe.

Under political attack, however, Mestizo culture retreated into the private domain, and this development was frozen. The group designated European changed considerably in composition and economic occupation during the nineteenth century, and one segment became self-consciously a group apart. At the same time, a new colonial type was born from the interaction of newcomers with their environment. Many of the political changes were wrought overnight. Cultural change always follows more slowly, the old order lingering on, disguising the reality of the new. It was not until the catastrophes of war, occupation, and revolution in the twentieth century that the political and cultural came suddenly together, resulting in the disappearance of the Mestizos as a special community.

The Dutch who moved into Java in 1816 looked very much like their British predecessors. For one thing, they were all men born and educated in Holland and their most senior officers were members of prominent Netherlands families, titled, drawn away from careers in Europe for limited terms in Indonesia. These newcomers had received their posts from the new Dutch monarch on the basis of their birth and educational qualifications, and in their promotion there was no supporting or confirming voice from Batavia's leading families. As officers of a newly independent kingdom, they were united in a nationalism directed towards the homeland, sharing the mission of administering the colony for the benefit of the Netherlands middle and upper classes rather than the old Batavian cliques. And, finally, like their British predecessors, the chief authorities were accompanied by wives who were themselves titled ladies, convinced of their worth and the righteousness of their values and manners.

Immediate signs that Indonesia's new rulers were direct heirs of the British rather than of the VOC regime were the bookshops, libraries, schools, sporting and theatrical societies, and weekly newspaper that were soon established in Batavia. As under the British, their function was to keep alive a sense of identity, forge a bond of origin across class and religious denomination, and protect migrants from absorption into local traditions and cultures. Thus among the multitude of edicts and official pronouncements carried in early issues of the *Bataviasche Courant*[1] were directives to churches requiring prayers for the Dutch royal family at all services, an insistence on use of Dutch in the newly created government school system, and a revival of Raffles's Bible Society and of clubs for European pursuits. Like the *Gazette*, the *Courant* announced events designed for the European group alone and occasionally opened its columns to poems and essays from readers. The paper reveals, too, another aspect in which the new Dutch resembled the British, and that is in the crusade against Mestizo manners and the celebration of European habits of sociability.

Again, the shock of contact is described wholly from the immigrants' side. Many of the new Dutch officials felt the same revulsion as the British in their dealings with leading ladies of Batavia's European community. There is, for instance, Ver Huell's account of the morning call he paid on Johanna van IJsseldijk-Oland, whom he found sitting, "in sarong and kebaya, her hair hanging down, on a mat, on the floor, ringed by a number of women slaves, each one occupied with some kind of work, while the lady of the house was cleaning vegetables. Close by her ladyship stood a great silver cuspidor, into which she spat whole streams of blood-red spittle every now and then. She addressed me in Dutch, and then appeared to be describing me briefly to her chief slave in Malay; and I heard the words "baroe datang," that means a newcomer or one who has just arrived. . . . All now looked on me with greater interest, and I was extremely relieved when I had acquitted myself of this first call on an East-Indian lady."[2]

Highly placed individuals, including baroness van Tuyll van Serooskerken, wife of Governor-General G.A.G.P. van der Capellen, and jonkvrouw Theodora de Salve de Bruneton, who was wife to Governor-General D. J. de Eerens, took up the task of civilizing this segment of colonial society with all the zest of the late Olivia Raffles. "Mevrouw de Eerens," according to the traveler J. B. J. van Doren, "spares no pains from her side to persuade the ladies to adopt a more suitable and less bizarre costume, and as a result the manner of paying calls and receiving visitors has undergone a considerable change."[3]

Such reactions and crusades point to the fact that Batavia's culture was still predominantly Mestizo, even under exacting lady governesses like mevrouwen van der Capellen and de Eerens. If they forbade sarong and kebaya in their reception rooms, it was because Batavian ladies habitually wore that modified Indonesian costume at home and on outings. Five years of insults from the British had not sufficed to make Johanna van IJsseldijk conceal her Mestizo manners from Ver Huell's horrified gaze. She remained on her mat, occupied with her betel. Confidence in her world had not yet evaporated, even though its underpinnings were being swept away.

The new Dutch authorities showed from the first that they had learned the lessons of the past. In place of the old joint stock company was the newly created ministry of colonies responsible for selecting the governor-general and for all senior appointments. The VOC's directors had also reserved to themselves the power of appointment, confirmation, and dismissal; but since 1639 their role had often been that of approving appointments long since made by the men in Asia. The nineteenth-century governor-general arrived to serve a limited term and depart, his future career in Europe depending on performance acceptable to his patrons at home. None was to choose Indonesia for retirement. The chief official came without debts, for Batavians no longer elected him; and he came, too, without entrée into their inner circles. Consequently, he relied on the men he brought in his suite and had no use for all the brothers-in-law who had formerly divided up the spoils of office.

Nowhere is the new policy better illustrated than in decisions of the ministry of colonies in 1840 and in 1844 following the death in office of the ruling governors-general. Senior Councillor Carel Sirardus Willem graaf van Hogendorp took over as acting governor-general upon the passing of Dominique Jacques de Eerens, which was standard practice from Company days, when councillors chose one of their number, usually the most senior, and sent the nomination to Holland for approval. This councillor was uniquely qualified for permanent appointment, being the son of the reformer and ex-governor of the East Hook (East Java), Dirk van Hogendorp. C. S. W. van Hogendorp had been born in Bengal to the Eurasian Elisabeth Bartlo and been raised in Java, but had completed his higher education in the Netherlands and had married there a native Dutchwoman. He returned to Indonesia in the wake of the commissioners-general and began his colonial career in the important position of resident of Bogor. From 1837 he sat on the Council. Despite these credentials, van Hogendorp was passed over by the minister of colonies, and he stepped down in 1841 with the arrival of the new chief from Holland.

The jonkheer Joan Cornelis Reynst's Indies career had been built up over thirty-one years when he became acting governor-general upon Mr. Pieter Merkus's death in office in 1844. Reynst had emigrated to Java at eighteen and had served the colonial government in such posts as resident of Palembang (1823–26) and councillor (1836). Once again, in place of experience, preference was given to a man who had not seen Indonesia before his arrival there in 1845 to take up his new duties.

At the same time that the post of governor-general was altered and a new type of officer selected, the Netherlands monarchy, through the ministry of colonies, struck at that other seat of Indies power, the Council. Acting upon instructions, the commissioners had decreed in 1818 that councillors must be Dutch, legitimate, and recorded in the civil registers of their birthplaces. Furthermore, Council members might not be related to each other by blood or law within four degrees of kin.[4] Constitutional Law Number 48 of 1836 sealed the Council's fate by reducing it from its former position as co-legislative body to an advisory board to the governor-general.[5]

The laws most effectively excluding members of Indies families from politically influential posts in government, however, were those on the selection of civil servants. After 1825 all positions were reserved to men born and educated in the Netherlands.[6] It is true that in the VOC centuries, senior positions had only rarely been held by Creoles and Eurasians who had not been schooled in Europe; yet the native Dutch office-holders were often men like Goens and Joan van Hoorn who had left Europe at nine and te careers had developed in the Mestizo society of Batavia and its o the new educational qualifications this pattern was broken. Eleve the highest posts to which Creole and part-Asian men might aspir out: commissary and inspector third class.[7] Again, in 1849, gover tions decreed that, with few exceptions, all posts in the civi reserved to those educated entirely in Europe.[8] Eurasian and Cr cated solely in Indonesia were thenceforth confined to low-l paying employment. They became a class of petty clerks who tated that they live more according to Asian ways and on European neighborhoods in the cheaper housing. The impove was to become the subject of government enquiry late in the nin

All these decrees had announced specific qualifications in matter and standard of excellence, and in 1842 a school had be Netherlands with a curriculum designed for career officers service. This was former governor-general Jean-Chrétien Ba emy, called into being specifically to serve the needs of the C and closed in 1864 when that system of agricultural production was running down. In its brief twenty-two years, however, the Delft Academy started a tradition of teaching aspiring Indies officers to look upon Indonesians as children needing protection rather than as subjects with rights and duties. This had typified the attitude of the commissioners too. With the notions of "child-like" and the associated benevolence having to do with "uplift," "moral duty," and protection of the indigenous population from the harsh modern world came a greater debasement of Indonesians than before.

In addition to its influence on attitudes and expectations of the nineteenth-century colonial servant, the Delft Academy concentrated colonial service training in Holland. The damage to the livelihood and prospects of Creoles and Eurasians lacking the means to acquire the expensive Delft diploma was quickly advertised and protested in May 1848.[9] The authorities were unmoved, compelling the group's leader, the Reverend Wolter Robert baron van Hoevell (1812–79) to repatriate, and entrance requirements for the civil service remained unchanged until 1864.

118

Thereafter, eligibility for posts in the Indies civil service was freed of requirements of origin and place. Instead of the Delft diploma, two qualifying examinations were instituted, the *grootambtenaarsexamen* that admitted successful candidates to senior posts and that could be taken either in Leiden or Batavia, and the *kleinambtenaarsexamen* for junior levels and given exclusively in Indonesia.[10] Preparation for the senior officials' test in Indonesia could be had through private tuition or secondary school. Indonesia's first high school opened only in 1860, however, and for a long time had no successor. Prestigious and powerful positions continued in the hands of immigrant Dutchmen, with only the exceptional locally educated man rising beyond the lower rungs of government.

It is true that two of the nineteenth-century governors-general were actually born in Indonesia. Mr. Pieter Mijer, forty-eighth to take office since Governor-General Both, was a Batavian, but was sent at the age of eight to the Netherlands for schooling. Upon return, he spent twenty-two years in government service as a lawyer and was responsible for framing many of the colony's regulations. Later, he resigned to take up a political career in the Netherlands Lower House. He twice served briefly as minister of colonies before returning to Indonesia as governor-general in 1866. When he left office he retired, not in his native land but in Holland, where he was to write on colonial history entirely from the Dutch imperialist point of view.

Similarly, jonkheer Carel Herman Aart van der Wijck, although born in Ambon (1840), was educated in the Netherlands. He returned, with his Delft diploma, for a career of twenty-seven years which included the posts of assistant resident and resident in Solo, Tegal, and Surabaya. He, too, sought the Netherlands for retirement, but returned to Indonesia for business reasons and was later installed as governor-general in 1893. In 1899 he settled permanently in the Netherlands. It is safe to say of both men that although Creoles they were spiritually Dutch. Years of schooling in Europe and the changed conditions of the nineteenth century lifted such men socially and economically far above the Creole/Eurasian male fringes of the colony.

A review of the history of a well-established colonial family, the van Riemsdijken,[11] demonstrates concretely this sudden demise in political importance of the Indies clan. In Chapter 4 I traced the family from its founder, the Utrecht native Jeremias van Riemsdijk, who emigrated as an enlisted man to Batavia in 1735 and rose to be governor-general forty years later. His son Willem Vincent Helvetius van Riemsdijk* (1752–1818) was the last of the clan to hold prestigious appointments in the colony. By nineteen he had been on the VOC payroll ten years and ranked as merchant, with the lucrative post of first administrator of the Company's warehouses on Onrust. Two years later, in 1773, he was promoted to senior merchant and harbor master of Batavia. Then, while his father was governor-general, W. V. H. van Riemsdijk held the posts of commissioner for native affairs, hospital regent, and member of the dike reeves' commission. Later he was made councillor extraordinary (1793), chief customs officer, postmaster general, and in 1799, full councillor.

It was largely owing to his father's influence that W. V. H. van Riemsdijk, a Batavian by birth and education, rose so high. Jeremias van Riemsdijk had, after all, been second in command since 1764 and governor-general in 1775. W. V. H. van Riemsdijk's position had also been strengthened by his marriage in 1763 to Catharina Margaretha Craan. She brought an Indies history of her own, born as she was fifteen years earlier in Japara to Johanna Henriette Breekpot, a Japara woman in her turn, and to Jacobus Johannes Craan, a Creole born in Ambon in 1728 to a Dutch minister. The dominie had been expelled from the VOC's possessions upon accusations of "scandalous behavior" and had left Jacobus Craan behind in Batavia. Craan had subsequently defied discrimination against Creoles or been part of new trends in Batavian political life of the eighteenth century, for he held posts normally reserved for men born or educated in Europe, such as chief administrator of Makassar and, after removal to Batavia, councillor extraordinary (1772). He also held the lucrative directorship of the opium monopoly. He died in Batavia in 1780, the year that he became full councillor. Craan was also related to the director-general, Hendrik Breton. It might be noted in passing that Catharina's three half-brothers, born to Indonesian women in Craan's household, were all sent to the Netherlands for schooling, a privilege not extended to legitimate daughters because unnecessary for their social advancement.

Given the connections leading into Batavia's most prominent families from this van Riemsdijk/Craan alliance, it might be expected that the next generation would contribute sons to high posts in the inner circles of government, in line with the new trends, and would bestow its daughters as brides on councillors. On the contrary, not one van Riemsdijk son so figures; neither did the daughters make splendid matches. Already the process of withdrawal from public life had begun with W. V. H. van Riemsdijk. After the fall of the family-style government of Wiese, the senior van Riemsdijk devoted himself to the management of his estates and sugar mills and to the affairs of his numerous offspring. Perhaps he recognized the changing times and the declining ability of the old Batavian clique to further its members' interests in government. He directed the sons to private landownership and to plantation agriculture. W. V. H. van Riemsdijk stands as a forerunner to those Creole and Eurasian men who in the nineteenth century became a class divorced from government.

Consider, now, W. V. H. van Riemsdijk's provisions for his children. He recognized twenty-one in all, fourteen from his marriage to Catharina Craan, six by freed Indonesian women in his employ, and one adopted, the child of a sea captain by an Indonesian woman. Fifteen lived more than twenty years,

7. Dina Cornelia van Riemsdijk (c. 1807–77). Portrait of the eldest daughter of Daniel Cornelis van Riemsdijk and of Mea (later known by her baptismal name Christina Simans). Dina was the great-granddaughter of the eighteenth-century governor-general Jeremias van Riemsdijk, and could trace her female kin in the paternal line back to the late seventeenth century. The portrait dates from 1851. (From Victor Ido van de Wall, *Oude Hollandsche buitenplaatsen van Batavia*, vol. 1, plate 31. Print courtesy W. van Hoeve Publishers.)

some into their sixties and beyond. It is not possible here to give accounts of all. For our purposes of establishing the development of a landowning gentry among the Indies-born with European status in the nineteenth century, it is sufficient to concentrate on only two. Suffice it to say of the rest that none of the sons was sent to Europe for school and that all the adult daughters married either immigrants or Creoles, who were outside government service.

The two selected here are Daniel Helvetius van Riemsdijk (1783–1860) and Scipio Isebrandus Helvetius van Riemsdijk (1785–1827). Both were legitimate and passed their entire lives on Java. Taking Daniel first, he had three daughters by the Javanese woman Mea, and gave them Christian names and his own surname. A fourth child died in infancy. About the time he came to marry off the oldest daughter, Dina Cornelia, Daniel applied for letters of legitimation for the three girls, and this application was granted in 1827. Dina married the immigrant Tjalling Ament, becoming through this marriage the founder of a large Indies clan in her own right.[12] Both Ament and the husband of the second daughter, Sophia Wilhelmina, were to rise in the service of the Indies government, Ament becoming resident of Cirebon in 1843, and Sophia's husband, Carel Marinus Visser, rising to governor of the Moluccas. Perhaps the importance of his daughters' connections inclined Daniel van Riemsdijk, now in his sixties, to regularize his relationship with their mother. Accordingly, in 1844, Mea was transformed into a Dutchwoman under the baptismal name Christina Simans. That same year Daniel married her and again officially acknowledged his daughters. The fortunes of the youngest are intertwined with the family of Scipio I. H. van Riemsdijk, to whom we may now turn.

Scipio also preferred concubinage and the company of Asians to the unknown Dutchwomen who started immigrating in his lifetime. From his union with the free, non-Christian Bamie he had one daughter, baptized Maria Susanna van Riemsdijk in 1808. His six other children were born to the free, non-Christian Manies van Bali. Scipio had them baptized, thus formally recognizing an obligation to rear them as Europeans in his own house, rather than have them raised by Indonesian relatives in a *kampung* (village). Unlike Daniel, however, Scipio did not marry Manies; nor did he give her children his own surname. Rather, he adopted an expedient that his father and Cranssen had used, turning his own name backwards and calling them Kijdsmeir. His children were still illegitimate. To strengthen their social position, Scipio formally adopted them once they had survived babyhood. An important distinction between his solution and his brother's was in the status of the Asian mothers. In Daniel's case, marriage meant that Mea/Christina might now appear publicly with him, and she was, on her death, buried at his side in the European graveyard. None of these honors, so important in colonial society, was conferred on either of the mothers of Scipio's offspring.

The fortunes of the children surviving to adulthood in the two families are subtly different. Daniel's two eldest daughters married men with distinguished careers in the new officialdom. Three of Scipio's daughters married Netherlanders too, but none was prominent in government circles. Of his two sons who reached their majority, one had a Chinese concubine named Bibiet. The other, Willem Martinus, joined the two families in marrying his cousin Catharina Petronella. From this union of cousins and surnames, Kijdsmeir-Riemsdijk, were born eight children, of whom it may confidently be said that the Indonesian side of their heritage was predominant and immediate, through their half-Indonesian parents, their Indonesian kin, and their family retainers.

Within three or four generations, then, we see descendants of Jeremias van Riemsdijk moving easily towards the Indonesian, not in defiance, like Pieter Erberveld, the eighteenth-century Eurasian rebel-turned-Muslim, but naturally, by reason of remoteness from European culture and of daily contact with the Indonesian. By then the chief distinction from Javanese of the same economic standing lay more in name, boasts of ancestry, and occupation than in real differences in way of life. And there are examples of Eurasians who were proud of their Asian ancestry, claiming descent not from patrician European families but from Oriental princesses. The linguist H. N. van der Tuuk was one, insisting that the Koek family of Malacca were Eastern grandees.

In the van Riemsdijk family history, then, can be traced the larger history of Mestizo society. Starting in the eighteenth century with the immigration of Jeremias van Riemsdijk, the family acquires power and wealth through senior positions in the VOC hierarchy and marriage into Batavian clans with long roots stretching, on the female side, into the seventeenth century. With the advent of government officials inimical to the aspirations of Indies cliques, wealthy Indiesmen such as the van Riemsdijken withdraw from government and turn to plantation agriculture as their source of income and occupation.

This shift in orientation coincides with a shift in residential patterns from cities of the north coast into the interior of Java. The divorce from government position and its prestige prevents members of Indies families from marrying upward in colonial terms. Van Riemsdijk sons continue to seek Creoles and Eurasians as brides if they marry, the women to take immigrants as husbands, but their partners are similarly often outside government circles. Now their family alliances are with other landholders of similar descent too, and unions appear in the marriage registers with men surnamed Arnold, van Motman, Ament, even Michiels. Legal marriage in the European style ceases to be sought by the men, and the family completes its return to one part of its heritage with the full assimilation of descendants into Indonesian communities.

While the political power of the Indies clan was quickly disposed of, cultural changes followed several steps behind, and VOC Mestizo influence lingered on well into the middle of the century. Clear evidence of the Mestizo world comes

8. Tobacco Planter and Family, Central Java around 1865. Note the classical backdrop, with Greek temples attached to bamboo poles. The mother appears Indonesian; she and the children are in European clothing. The youngest children are being held, Javanese style in carrying shawls, by the Javanese nursemaids. (From the photographic collection of the Koninklijk Instituut voor Taal-, Land- en Volkenkunde, Leiden. Print courtesy the archivist.)

from that very example of "Europeanness," the *Javasche Courant*. There is, first of all, the language. It was Dutch, but certain Malay words are habitually used in the *Courant*'s columns, words (such as *toko* for "shop") that would be immediately understood by the readers. Sarongs are offered European ladies in lists of stock in hand, along with shawls and frocks. And then there are the advertisements for slaves.

The Constitutional Law of 1818 forbade international commerce in slaves; that is, it prohibited import of slaves for sale to Indies households. It did not outlaw the sale of slaves within Indonesia itself until 1855.[13] Typical would be this notice placed by Catharina ten Cate- van Riemsdijk in the *Courant* in 1840, announcing the sale of several servants: "For sale from the estate of F. J. ten Cate: Lafleur, cook's apprentice; Julia, seamstress and personal maid, with her three children, the oldest of whom is four; Juria, seamstress, personal maid, and hairdresser, with her eight-month-old child; and Augusta, seamstress and personal attendant, aged eighteen years."[14]

Another indication of the multiracial character of colonial society and of the ambivalence as to lines and barriers is a notice periodically placed in the *Courant* by government officials and directed to "all Europeans and *gelijkstandige*" (those of the same status). Usually such notices had to do with regulations for registering births, with visitors to a residency, and the like, and the persons so identified were Europeans by birth and all those grouped in the European category: Creoles, Mestizos, recognized illegitimate children, and Asian wives.

Now all this was a normal part of daily life to the old-timer. Newcomers like Ver Huell were struck by the continuing force of the old Mestizo culture, as in his recollection of wedding festivities for a "wealthy Ambonese Jufvrouw": "Towards evening we betook ourselves to the bride's house, and were received by a procession of young men decked out with sprays of flowers on their chests. . . . They escorted us into an apartment where the bride, splendidly gowned and glittering with jewels sat on a throne. . . . Like a queen, she was ringed by a suite of young girls. . . . With my officers I approached the steps of the throne and made my humble compliments in Malay, to which the lovely bride responded with a proud bow. The ball was opened by the young pair."[15] Ver Huell notes that most of the young ladies preferred to tackle Western dancing in their bare feet.

In the passage just quoted and many others of Ver Huell's *Memoirs* there is the tone of the amused observer, one who does not forget to regale his Dutch readers of the 1830s with scenes of Eurasians barefoot at a ball. He touches on what European immigrants perceived as outlandish and tasteless, hints that Eurasian pride in family and social position is without justification, and altogether puts forward a view of this group as barely civilized. Through this point of view one can appreciate the European visitor's first sensations, but the effect

125

is to make scenes of everyday life bizarre. All sense of proportion is thereby lost, for Ver Huell was observing the daily norms of an affluent sector within the European group.

The influence of Oriental civilizations was present in all levels of the nineteenth-century colonial settlements. The wives of Governors-General Baud (1833–36), Merkus (1841–44), and J. J. Rochussen (1845–51) were Mestizas whose surnames recalled the heyday of Indies family alliances and isolation from Europe. J.-C. Baud,* to take him first, was no stranger to the Indies world when he took up the duties of governor-general. He had first journeyed to Batavia in 1810 as Governor-General Janssen's secretary and then joined the new Indies civil service with the rank of second-level officer. He survived the transfer to British rule, acting as translator and head of Raffles's secretariat. Under the commissioners Baud became government secretary and later general secretary to Governor-General van der Capellen. Upon return to Holland he guided the new Netherlands Trading Company, became director of East Indian Affairs in the ministry of colonies, and then went to Indonesia in 1833 as governor-general.

Baud's rise up the colonial ladder was swift. He had established himself with the Batavian elite by marrying Wilhelmina Henrietta Senn van Basel in 1815. The surname Senn van Basel by now evokes old Company families with links running to all the rich and powerful in immigrant and female Eurasian circles. To particularize, this Wilhelmina was daughter to the Indies-born, Holland-educated councillor Willem Adriaan S. van Basel, whose stepsister was wife to Nicolaas Engelhard. Her mother was Theodora van Riemsdijk, a granddaughter of the governor-general in the legitimate line. Her stepsister Wilhelmina Adriana was wife to Muntinghe, and her full sisters brought into the clan Servatius and Mr. Simon Hendrik Rose, resident of Cirebon. Her stepmother (W. A. Senn van Basel's third wife) was one of the Wiese family. It would be tedious to enumerate further the links to the powerful and prestigious that this marriage brought Baud. Suffice it to say that it opened doors to the old VOC elite by bringing him into intimate union with families with long-established Asian roots. In his bride was a woman whose Creole ancestress in the maternal line had been born in Japara in 1738.[16]

Wilhelmina Baud-Senn van Basel had been born in Batavia in 1798 and was raised by an Indies-bred mother and Asian slaves. It is safe to assume that she spoke Malay more fluently than Dutch, and that her manners resembled those of Johanna Oland more than those of the baroness van Tuyll. Little from her Indies background can have prepared Wilhelmina for life in the Netherlands, where she spent her last years. Four of her nine children were born in Indonesia. Only the two Batavia-born sons made their lives there, whilst the daughters were established in Holland. The trend of events noted for the nineteenth century Mestizo community is further reflected here in that neither son of a former governor-general made a name for himself in government. Both were landowners and died on their estates in Java.

Baud *père* had made brevity of term in Indonesia a condition of his accepting the post of governor-general. It might be expected that in remarrying he would choose a woman eager to retire in Holland. As it turned out, he waited until his return to Batavia before choosing his second wife. The man who had seen his first marriage smooth his way was to follow the same sage course again. His choice fell on Ursula Susanna van Braam, Batavia-born daughter of J. A. van Braam, Raffles's old associate and councillor under Governor-General van der Capellen. In Ursula's mother there was also an Asian background and links to the van Riemsdijk, Barkeij, and Engelhard families.

Mr. Pieter Merkus generally enters colonial histories as an opponent of Governor-General Johannes van den Bosch and is sometimes credited with giving Indonesia its first divorced woman as chief lady. It is not usually noted that mevrouw Merkus was also a recognized daughter born out of wedlock to a freed Ambonese slave. She was Wilhelmina Niclasina Cranssen, illegitimate daughter of the councillor and of Wilhelmina Nessnarc, born in Ambon and eighteen years Merkus's junior. Together with her own children, Wilhelmina Merkus-Cranssen raised one Henriette Elisabeth Merkus, who had been born to a Christian Ambonese woman while Merkus was governor of the Moluccas. One week before his marriage, Merkus had Henriette legitimized. After his death, Wilhelmina took this stepdaughter to the Netherlands. There she was to marry a former first lieutenant in the colonial army, and later, after a divorce, this part-Ambonese stepdaughter entered the Dutch nobility through her marriage to Mr. René Frederik Willem baron Sloet tot Toutenborgh. In the case of Wilhelmina Merkus-Cranssen, again we see the nineteenth-century pattern of removal of Mestizas from the Indies as a consequence of their marriages to immigrants and the disappearance from Batavia of Indies families in which descent is traced in the female line.

Of Rochussen it may be quickly said that governor-generalship of the Indies was merely a six-year interlude in a diplomatic career centered in Europe. He returned to the Netherlands to resume his former interests and only renewed his Asian connections to serve as minister of colonies from 1858 to 1861. He was already forty-eight and a widower when he reached Batavia. There he was to marry the twenty-one-year-old Elisabeth Charlotte Vincent, who had been born in Padang to the secretary of the residency. She was connected to the prominent and racially mixed Indies families Dupuy, Janke, Engelhard, and Senn van Basel, while her brother was married to Anthoinette Pahud, daughter of the future governor-general and whose mother and grandmother had been born in India.[17]

After Elisabeth Vincent, the wives of ruling governors-general were all

Dutchwomen save one,[18] and so were those of senior officials. The standards they set as acceptable were of Dutch, not Asian, inspiration. Their efforts at reproducing Dutch bourgeois society in Indonesia were reinforced by the sheer numbers of Europeans moving into Java's cities during the nineteenth century.

When the British took over Java, they estimated the number of inhabitants with European status at about 4,000. A half-century later (1852) the figure for Europeans, excluding the military, was reckoned as 17,285 on Java and 4,832 scattered among other islands. In 1870, restrictions on immigration from Europe were lifted entirely with the passage of agriculture laws abolishing the Culture System and opening Indonesia to private entrepreneurs.[19] Population figures reveal these changes to the economic system and to the demographic structure of the European group. In 1872 the number of Europeans in Indonesia was 36,467. In 1882 it was 43,738, and it had reached 58,806 a decade later. By 1900 those with European status in Indonesia totalled 75,833, with privately employed individuals far outstripping government employees in number.

Part of the growth of the European group—from 4,000 in 1812 to 76,000 in 1900—was the result of natural increase, with many persons part-Asian. But after 1870 there was heavy immigration, with some 10,000 new migrants entering Indonesia in the decade 1870–80 alone. Had the European immigrants been dispersed evenly to all areas of the archipelago, the influx would have been barely noticed. As it was, most people with European status were concentrated in a few key spots, with 62,477 of them on Java and only 13,356 in all the rest of Indonesia.[20]

Women were part of the new wave of immigrants. The majority came as wives and daughters of government employees and private entrepreneurs, but some few, discernible through the advertisements they placed in Java's newspapers, entered the Indies on their own to earn a living.[21] Women migrants were always far fewer than men, and it was not until the 1930s that the sex ratio among new arrivals was approximately equal. Over the period 1900–30 the proportion of Europe-born women to Europe-born men in Indonesia rose from 471:1000 to 884:1000. In actual numbers this meant an increase from about 4,000 Dutchwomen at the turn of the century to around 26,000 in 1930. As late as 1930, however, 70 percent of all persons legally classified as Europeans in Indonesia had been born there.[22]

Most immigrants lived in cities, Batavia foremost, then Semarang, Surabaya, and Medan. As such, living in European residential quarters, they created a culture of their own. It was for this immigrant group, as well as for the exploitation of Indonesia's resources, that the communications grid was expanded in the second half of the nineteenth century. Innovations in the fields of medicine, the telegraph, publishing, and transport networks affected the daily life of migrants in important ways. First of all, immigrant men trained for the civil service and coached to view Indonesians as inferior to themselves could now have a degree of contact with each other—by sheer numbers in the cities, and by train, tram, and telegraph—not possible before. The Dutch-speaking club had expanded. Secondly, contact with the Netherlands through telegraph and fast ship meant that there was no longer a sense of total isolation from the homeland. Through imported newspapers and periodicals, the new Dutch in Indonesia could follow developments in European theater and the arts; they could even keep abreast of the races.

The introduction of the furlough system gave government and military officials paid leave of two years' duration in Europe, and more generous pensions permitted retirement there. Furlough meant more than just a chance for physical recuperation. It offered the opportunity for intellectual and spiritual renewal at the source. It was a break in Indies employment to be anticipated and planned for. The attitude thus engendered was far different, then, from that of one such as Johannes Thedens, acting governor-general from 1741 to 1743, who at sixteen enrolled in the VOC's army with slight expectancy of ever seeing Europe again in a life that was to run another forty-odd years.

Boat, letter service, rail, and telegraph all brought contact with one's own kind. Goods and ideas passed along these channels too. From the columns of newspapers it is clear that shops catering exclusively to immigrants were opened in the second half of the century. In their way they assisted in keeping the newcomers European and minimizing the dependence on local products and hence local ideas. Tinned biscuits and chocolates could now replace Indonesian snacks, and Christmas could be made more like home with purchases of Saint Nicolaas gifts and gingerbread. Children's toys from Holland and picture books might counteract the influence of the Indonesian nursemaid, and there were now novels and essays available in bookstores for adults. Evidence of the influx of European women comes from advertisements too, such as those for medicines and for Dutch-language pamphlets on the proper rearing of children in the tropics. Like innoculation against smallpox, which had been introduced in 1803, these were to stand consciously against Indonesian and Mestizo cures that combined medical and spiritual or magical knowledge in remedies.

Notices of property auctions, numerous in all Indies papers, also convey an idea of the immigrants' housekeeping. It is worth comparing these notices with those from the first half of the century. The latter always included slaves, described by name, type of employment, sometimes by age. After 1854 such advertisements disappeared; the cessation of trading in Asian lives was one more indication of an increasingly authentic Dutch style of living in Indonesia.

Greater numbers of immigrants and larger concentrations meant that there were more local branches of Masonic lodges, associations for sports and music, and men's clubs, too. Club life has a long history in nineteenth-century Indonesia.[23] It stretches back to the time of Daendels, who established the Harmonie in Batavia and promoted it by obliging all civilian and military officials to join. Clubs spread to other cities, wherever there were numbers of European men. Yogyakarta's club, *De Vereeniging* dates, therefore, from as early as 1822, but there is no clubhouse at Surabaya before 1843 and none at Bandung until 1895.

Serving a similar purpose of marking off and identifying were the amateur groups devoted to music and drama and the learned societies. By 1840, Batavia's Europeans were offered a weekly play or opera in French by the resident Théâtre Français. The *Courant* announced "grand vocal and instrumental concerts" and "*soirées musicales*" from time to time. Then there were public lectures sponsored by the Academy, and a brief-lived magazine, *Lakschmi*, devoted to verse. After 1850, a male immigrant might meet his fellows to discuss the capital's cultural events in the newly established coffee houses.

All these resources—theaters, libraries, clubs, shops selling pianos, and so forth—obviated dependence on local entertainments. Immigrants amused themselves as they had done in Europe, and so preserved tastes based on childhood upbringing in another hemisphere. The attitude they now displayed towards Indonesians was one of scientific interest when it was not one of humorous contempt. Whatever the attitude, European immigrants to Indonesia were deeply conscious of living in an alien land. Their understanding of it and accommodations to it were defined by the colonial culture, which in the nineteenth century expanded far beyond its territories of origin, the port enclaves and immediate environs of Batavia.

Indies culture in the nineteenth century grew away from its VOC heritage. For one thing, its key components were now altered. At the conclusion of the Napoleonic Wars in Europe, Britain had returned to the Dutch only their territories in the Indonesian archipelago. Gone forever were their settlements at the Cape and in India, Ceylon, and Malaya. While these political deals meant little at first to many archipelago peoples, the impact on that legal category of persons known as Europeans was immediate and permanent. For them, the policy decisions taken in London and The Hague signified not only the need to adjust to another political regime but also the need to reorder both their inner lives and their relationship to Indonesia.

Neither Java, nor yet Indonesia, had been the total VOC domain. Company employees were linked by occupation, family ties, sometimes birth, to a number of Dutch settlements in Asia and Africa. The early eighteenth-century governor-general Abraham van Riebeeck, for instance, was born in southern Africa; he spent a part of his childhood in Holland and his adult life in Batavia. His mother died in Malaya. His father's second marriage brought into the family a woman who had lived in Japan and west Sumatra. The marriages of his sisters and daughters removed them to Batavia, Ambon, and Ceylon. He was buried in Java.

After 1816 ties were cut with Africa, India, and Ceylon, and after 1824, with Malaya. Only the link to Japan was left, but the settlement at Deshima declined greatly in its economic importance to the colonial exchequer and hence in the social consequence the post of local chief could confer on colonial officials. Attention was thereafter focused on Indonesia. The archipelago became the natural habitat for settlement, transfer, posting of sons, and bestowing of daughters in marriage. It was the archipelago that was the arena for the expansion of Mestizo culture. Henceforth only Indonesian peoples and immigrants direct from Europe contributed to its development. Quite naturally Malay triumphed over Portuguese as the language of intergroup communication and of the immigrant male's household. Nor did any of the old avenues of contact with the coasts of India and Burma remain: import and sale of slaves from outside the islands ceased completely in 1818, and no longer did families removing from, say, Jaffnapatnam bring local slaves in their suite.

With this change in colonial boundaries also came a change in residential patterns for the group with European status. At the start of the nineteenth century members of the group were predominantly urban dwellers esconced in port cities along the coasts. By the end of the century a greater variety of settlement could be discerned, comprising a movement out of the cities and also into the other islands. Land was taken up by private settlers and entrepreneurs. The chief expansion followed on the Agriculture Law of 1870.

Well before that time, however, some individuals had purchased or enlarged their private estates. Sale of land on Java had begun in 1808 under Daendels, who was seeking added sources of revenue. Raffles continued this expedient for adding to the treasury, setting up commissions to sell land east of Batavia and coffee estates in Priangan. During the same period, individuals with European status acquired large estates in the Solo and Yogyakarta principalities. By 1854 8 percent of Java was owned privately, and after 1863 long-term leases brought Europeans to east Sumatra too.[24]

In Java's interior, in isolation, the evolution of a Mestizo culture began anew, or rather continued in new locations. Immigrant whites, coming into contact with Indonesians, especially from the lower classes, and detached from church and white society, borrowed from the Javanese, and discarded parts of their own culture. A Mestizo style was established in small towns and on estates, even though the prime actors were not actual descendants of VOC Eurasians themselves.

Consider the following description of an immigrant planter and landowner near Semarang, as set down by van Doren and relating to the year 1840: "Manuel entertained his habitués in a truly oriental manner, especially when it was his own or one of his children's birthday, at which occasions things sometimes went beyond all bounds, and yet with due deference to the fair sex, for apart from a Chinese Nyai [mistress] with whom he had been married in the Eastern way, beneath a coconut tree between heaven and earth, he maintained a small harem for his pleasure."[25] In short, Manuel was not so different in his mode of living and values from one of the van Riemsdijken. And he, too, later married his Chinese mistress in order to legitimize his daughters and make good matches for them.

To generalize, the key elements needed for the evolution and continuation of the Mestizo style on Java were white men, Indonesian mistresses, Eurasian wives. Then there were the distant, competing models of upper-class European and Javanese aristocracy to be reverenced, imitated in some form where possible. There were the part-European, part-Asian children, some entering the Dutch group, others raised as Indonesians. There was the awareness of the colonial caste system that judged living as an Indonesian and being accepted as such to be a degradation to the part-European. There was the distance from concentrations of Europeans and their culture, and there was the immediacy of the Indonesian. There was the lack of reading materials with the tie of thought and language. In their place was the emphasis on the oral and visual arts. There were the numerous slaves, thinly disguised after 1860 as free servants. There was the daily intercourse in Malay or Javanese. There was the distance from church and its social functions of sanctifying marriages and blessing the dying. In its place were local values, sayings, reliance on divining good and evil days. In the absence of European doctors there was the trust in Indonesian magical and herbal forms of medicine. There was the cooler Indonesian costume and Indonesian food. There was the seigneurial style of living for the wealthy that European status and exploitation of local peoples made possible. Mestizo, too, were the practices concerning women: the Indonesian mistress remained hidden from public view; the partially confined Eurasian wife was surrounded by women attendants; the daughter was married off when barely in her teens.

This was the reality of the nineteenth-century colony, the context for Europeans in Indonesia. In describing a similar process, the absorption of immigrant Chinese into an Indonesian-Chinese culture, G. W. Skinner has spoken of "intermediate society."[26] The concept is useful here. Newcomers did not adjust to an Indonesian style of life, whether variants of Sundanese, Javanese, Ambonese, or whatever. Their adaptations were conditioned, molded and guided, by all the years of earlier responses that had resulted in a Mestizo culture which had taken on a life of its own. All Europeans participated in it to some extent, from ardent devotees of the opera to the great-grandchildren of immigrants and Asian women. Similarly, Indonesians who had any contact with Europeans participated in it too. This was as true for the upper class whose

9. Childhood In Java. This may have been one of the groups of ronggeng dancers who visited the houses of Europeans, as well as Javanese, for performances. European children grew up in what R. Nieuwenhuys has called "the other world," the world of Indonesians. (From E. Breton de Nijs [R. Nieuwenhuys], *Tempo Doeloe*, p. 93. Print courtesy of R. Nieuwenhuys.)

members could afford pianofortes as it was for the women entering the white man's household as mistresses and domestic servants.

Mestizo culture was pervasive. "Mestizo" refers to a style, and like the term "Eurasian," is not always a label of biological identity. W. F. Wertheim has pointed out that Mestizo culture might embrace not only the physically mixed but also the Creole and the European migrant who chose the Indies over Holland as a permanent home.[27] The latter was also called a *blijver* (expatriate). It is common to contrast the blijver with the *trekker*, the person planning on only a limited stay in Indonesia with the ambition of permanent settlement in Europe. Associated with the term *trekker*, therefore, is the idea of shunning Indies manners, abhorring "Indianization." And yet the trekker was inevitably altered. In a tropical colony where immigrants were a decided minority, though a privileged one, there was no escaping adjustment.

Thus the old VOC culture and type were destroyed in the nineteenth century and a new Indies colonial character formed. Nineteenth-century colonials differed from their VOC predecessors in one other respect not yet discussed: they described their life patterns through newspaper advertisements and they wrote down their experiences in a volume that had never before existed in colonial literature. The final chapter will take this written record as its subject, for it gives an inner view of the last stage of Mestizo culture, as genealogical data does for the VOC centuries. The chapter concludes with an outline of the Indonesian response that was to destroy that culture forever.

6

The Inner Life of Late Colonial Society

UNLIKE THE COMPANY PERIOD, the nineteenth century is rich in personal records that have survived from members of the rapidly expanding Indies-based European group. No longer was the capturing of experience left to the traveler. Now the new settlers from various levels of colonial society felt compelled to commit their opinions to paper. Many of the writers were struck by the fact that Netherlanders were not able to maintain in Indonesia the coherence and integrity of their own culture, even for a few decades. I have tried, in preceding chapters, to show that this was so partly because demonstration and maintenance of status required adoption of Mestizo values and manners. And in addition, there was the onslaught of a colonial, polyglot society.

Nineteenth-century immigrants surveying the colonial culture described in chapter 5 sought reasons for the sudden changes in their culture elsewhere. From Johannes Hennus to Bas Veth, they pour out a constant stream of criticism of prevailing conditions of Indies life and of what they saw as the degeneracy of Dutch settlers there.[1] Their explanations for cultural change range from the alleged refusal of immigrants to respect class privilege and birthright to miscegenation and the supposed "pull of the blood." Concubinage with Indonesian women was sometimes said to cause the loss of Dutch values, to undermine home life, and to result in the abandonment of many part-European children who grew into adults dangerous to law and order.

Other critics blamed the sudden alteration in living styles and beliefs on white women, whom they perceived as idle, arrogant, and worldly, once transplanted to the Indies. Others railed against a supposed loss of piety, and characterized immigrants as obsessed with money, rank, and precedence. It became fashionable with critics to deride the reading habits of Indies Europeans as lacking direction and serious purpose. Or they would attribute cultural change to daily contact with part-Indonesians and urge parents to send their children to Holland for schooling. They wrote with shock of Europeans who visited Javanese *wayang* (shadow puppet theater) performances and took delight in other forms of Indonesian arts.

The greatest contempt was reserved for those European migrants who took to living as Indonesians. Such "horror stories" were traded in all accounts of Indies life. Their cautionary note reminds us that in colonial society outer badges of identification carried many implications. Alteration in costume meant also alteration in the way people earned a living, dictated which legal system ruled their conduct, described different sets of privileges and obligations, raised or lowered status within separate groups.

At a later date another set of writers extolled virtues and habits they perceived as specifically Indies.[2] These writers spoke of "our Indies hospitality," which was a liberality of purse towards friends and relatives and a graciousness towards house-guests, who were entertained royally and suffered to stay for lengthy visits. They discerned an elegance to life in the slow pace of daily affairs, the long hours of conversation outdoors in the evening, the carriage rides and balls. They found a warmth and eagerness to help each other among the Europeans where the critics saw only backbiting and hypocrisy. They waxed eloquent over the Indies rituals of morning coffee, midday sleep, and ceremonious exchange of visits. Against those who complained of a lack of intellectual stimulation in the colony, they spoke of a broadening of mind and a new generosity of thought. And there were some who sang praises to the faithful *nyai* (Indonesian mistress) who stuck by her master and who revealed to him the "mysteries of the Orient." Still others immortalized their Javanese cooks or nursemaids in their writings.

These writers gloried in Indies habits that characterized the colony in the second half of the nineteenth century, particularly the costume, bathing, and rijsttafel. As noted earlier, it was precisely when immigrants were able to keep in close touch with the homeland, by furlough, telegraph, libraries, and so forth, that they ostentatiously adopted Indonesian practices. The VOC male immigrant who would probably never revisit his home country stuck to his layers of clothing and his wig, shunned bathing and frequent changes of linen, and worked steadily throughout the afternoon. But, starting from the late nineteenth century, the Dutch civil servant wore colonial whites, left the office at two in the afternoon, and donned batik pyjamas after a siesta and an Indonesian meal.

So it is odd that yet others should characterize their sojourn in Indonesia as basically the same as their life in Holland.[3] C. W. Wormser, for instance, only remembers mixing with European immigrants, and the intimacy of the family circle which revolved around mother and housewife, its members devoted to the virtues of hard work and thrift. It is easiest to pull apart that kind of record, to note a blindness that made Indonesians invisible, without even the faithful nyais of the devotees or the inscrutable, menacing hordes of the detractors. By the turn of the century that Wormser was recalling, the modest Dutch household was maintained by a staff of four to six Indonesian servants who lived, according to Indies practice, in the home compound with their spouses and

10. Mevrouw van Kloppenburg-Versteegh, in the costume typical for the nineteenth-century Indies lady. Her books on Indonesian herbal medicines were widely used by the European community. (From the photographic collection of the Koninklijk Instituut voor Taal-, Land- en Volkenkunde, Leiden. Print courtesy the archivist.)

137

children. The average Hollander, therefore, lived among at least a dozen Indonesians.

The many photographs preserved from the last quarter of the century show European immigrants at their ease, the women in sarong and kebaya, the men in batik pants and collarless jackets. They posed for the photographer with their servants cross-legged on the floor in Indonesian style. At the office and court room one sees the European seated on the grandest chair, dignitaries of the Indonesian and Chinese communities on stools to left and right, the lowest Asians in attendance on the floor.[4] As late as 1900, Augusta de Wit observed that it was customary for lower-class Indonesians to squat in the streets, hands clasped, before passing Europeans, giving them the deference due a Javanese of rank, whilst even Western-educated Indonesian members of the colonial civil service were expected to sit on the floor before the junior Dutch officials to whom they reported.[5]

These are but a few examples taken from colonial life which dispose of the versions of the "isolationists" such as Wormser. Similarly, the prejudices of the critics can be readily answered. More elusive, because more charming, are the glorifications of Indies life. Every memory of liberal hospitality and generosity must be countered by statistics on the growing impoverishment of the majority of Java's inhabitants or the corruption based on the all-pervasive racial categories. In seeking to gain a just appreciation of colonial life, one has to turn away from such carefully contrived narratives to other sources, first of all to the newspaper and principally to its personals columns: the advertisements, letters to the editor, and essays submitted by readers.

The printed advertisement can be viewed as a source for the candid opinions of members of the European community and as almost the sole such source available. There has been occasion to remark on the censorship exercised by colonial authorities on all forms of private and public utterance. Correspondence with acquaintance in Europe had to be submitted to official inspection in the VOC period, and there were forced delays to publication of such works as Valentijn's *Oud en nieuw Oost-Indiën*, or outright bans, as in the case of Governor-General van Imhoff's *Nouvelles*. Nineteenth-century governments kept strict surveillance of the press, and would not tolerate even mild protests such as van Hoevell's in 1848. It is well to emphasize again that all the frank characterizations of Indies life and people quoted in preceding chapters were published in Holland, not Indonesia.

The printed advertisement deserves study for reasons beyond its value as a vehicle for the unfettered expression of opinion, however. It was the repository of attitudes, not of the published author or person of affairs but of the average resident. It was here that those whose opinions ordinarily are not recorded

138

voiced their preferences, described what they took to be their strong points, unselfconsciously stated their prejudices. In this respect, a newspaper reflects a living society, garners the experience of the entire European community—immigrants, Creoles, and Eurasians alike. Viewed in this light, the newspaper is superior, as a source, to the books listed above and to such scholarly expositions as Colijn's *Neerlands Indië*. In that carefully organized compendium, the realities of colonial society are concealed both through omission and through the separating out of groups for special consideration as "problems."[6] There is no such self-censorship evident in subscribers to regional newspapers, nor tailoring of views to create an impression. Semarang's *Locomotief* will be the chief source here, for it is representative of newspapers of the European communities that in the nineteenth century were expanding in Java's provincial and district capitals.

Advertisements have already been introduced as evidence of the influx of Europeans and of organizations catering to them exclusively. Turning now to their content, the following examples are typical of advertisements for governesses: "Wanted: a governess, aged between thirty and forty, of the Reformed faith, to teach young girls in the inland"; and "Wanted: a Governess for two girls aged twelve and nine, to teach French, Dutch and music."[7] Note that there is no requirement that the applicants have teaching diplomas. Indeed, it is uncommon to find such a stipulation. Qualified teachers were scarce outside Batavia, but it is also true that to the majority of parents, conversational powers and accomplishments were more important than a grounding in arithmetic, for example, and formal qualifications in the teacher. Far from being merely implied, this preference might be stated quite explicitly, as in this notice: "Needed: a refined European lady, not a certificated Governess, to teach two young children."[8]

It is the statement of qualifications that makes this and many other advertisements so valuable as records of colonial society. There is evidence that by 1885 people no longer saw a Christian name, frock, and hat as sufficient indication of status and communal identity. Piano and French had replaced betel box and slave retinue as symbols of status in the late-nineteenth-century colony, a status now most forcefully pressed on the growing European community. No longer were Java's upper classes the point of reference; nor did Indonesian opinions seem important as compared with the immigrants'.

With the stress on European languages we return to a theme first discerned in the early decades of Batavia's history. Young children did not grow up fluent in Dutch; that still had to be acquired. Stress on Dutch in advertisements for governesses signals that competence in that language was now becoming a necessity for girls hoping to strengthen their claims to European status, as it had always been a prerequisite for boys aspiring to a position in government.

Reports of nearly every Netherlander traveling to Indonesia in the nineteenth century include cruel humor at the oddly accented Dutch of the locally born and their transposition of certain consonants.

To counter these gibes, parents no longer left the entire care of their children to Indonesian servants, but sought out nannies and teachers who could speak a European language. A family would advertise for "a Nursemaid, speaking good Dutch or German, to take care of a child of two," or there would be a notice for an assistant teacher having a "refined pronunciation of the Dutch language."[9] Applicants, aware of this criterion, would describe themselves as "fresh from Holland," "European," or "Netherlander by birth." The same promise of proper speech regardless of actual birthplace is contained in this notice: "A young Lady, having been educated in Europe from her childhood, offers herself to a family to give young children lessons in the four languages and music."[10] For some households, being educated in Europe was insufficient; birth in Europe was also a desired qualification in the employee, so that one frequently sees this type of notice: "Wanted: a Nanny, preferably European, for two young children."[11]

Expressions of preference concerning race and birthplace were by no means confined to advertisements for governesses, nor can they simply be interpreted as signs of concern for good speech habits. Considerations of race permeated colonial life. Just as Governor-General Mossel's sumptuary laws had reflected honor on the highest officeholders by reserving the employment of native Europeans as domestic servants to them alone, so too did the nineteenth-century Dutch associate race with station in life. Advertisements for male tutors, clerks, sales assistants, and the like would often carry the requirement of "European" or "Hollander by birth," the desirable quality in the urban office employee or the mentor of sons. On the plantation, it was another matter. Here owners looked for men capable of directing large numbers of Indonesian laborers, and would ask of applicants that they be an *inlandsch kind* (native child, literally, meaning, in this context, Eurasian or Creole) and able to speak Dutch as well as Javanese.[12] If European applicants were sought, then a fresh attribute would be attached: that they be bachelors.[13]

Single status was a common requirement in the hiring of white men throughout Indonesia's colonial history, from VOC to state rule. But there were motives behind this demand by planters that differed from such reasons as the supposed expense of a European wife and her unsuitability as a settler. First of all, landowners were often married to Eurasian women, or like the planter Manuel, maintained several Asian consorts. A white woman as wife to a junior employee would complicate the hierarchy on an estate, since her origins would seem to dictate that she be ranked above the owner's chief lady. In the second place, there was the notion that white women established a distance between the employee and his Indonesian subordinates.

140

Such a conviction was based on the belief that easy relations with Indonesians in general were primarily achieved through the white male/Indonesian mistress relationship, and there was no conclusion that friendship between men of the two races might substitute for the sexual union when a European wife was introduced to the estate. The conviction probably arose from the awkwardness that white men long absent from European drawing rooms felt in their rare dealings with immigrant women, as much as from the attitudes of the incoming wives themselves towards Indonesians.

Thus identification of preferred racial category in candidates for positions indicates more than a colonial system which assigned occupation by ethnic group. It also shows with whom the advertisers felt most comfortable. Such is the interpretation to be made of the following notice of a housekeeping position vacant in 1885: "Wanted: a middle-aged Lady (preferably *Indische*), knowing, and able to oversee, the preparation of Indies as well as Dutch dishes"; or of this advertisement for a nursemaid: "European girl wanted to look after ditto children."[14]

It was only natural that people so accustomed to associating personality and race should have definite preferences about the race of their spouses too. These biases made their way into advertisements for marriage partners. A European announcing his quest for a bride would state his preferences this way: "An engineer wishes to make the acquaintance of a Young Widow (European) to enter into a legal marriage."[15]

Some of the most remarkable and informative statements on the nature of colonial society were made by way of advertisements for housekeepers in families where there was often no legal wife. Placed by women seeking such posts as well as by prospective employers, they shed light on everyday realities and commonplace attitudes to race, sex, and family. Consider this sampling of notices which appeared in the *Locomotief* during 1885: "A middle-aged lady, fully acquainted with Indies housekeeping, seeks a position as housekeeper to a widower or unmarried man;" "A young bachelor is seeking an Indies lady [*Indische dame*] to keep house"; "A Dutch lady seeks a position with a married family looking after children. . . ."; "A Juffrouw needs employment helping with cooking and housekeeping for a married family in the inland"; "A refined Dutch lady is seeking a job housekeeping for a gentleman with or without children."[16]

Precision as to racial category within the European group is again a common feature in these notices. What obtrudes here is the qualification as to the household. There is the novel formulation of "married family," and of gentleman, not widower, "with or without children." Some are thinly disguised marriage advertisements placed by women whose sense of delicacy forbade them from describing their wishes baldly. Yet all acknowledge in their notices an awareness that many men requiring housekeepers did have illegitimate children in the house and perhaps their Indonesian mother as well. This almost offhand acceptance demonstrates the existence of intergroup relations with greater immediacy than statistics drawn from the Civil Registers, and counters the dominant impression of separation by race and social distance given by many writers on the nineteenth-century colony.

A generation later the hints, implications, and tastes of the 1880s advertisements are translated into concrete detail. Thus, 1904 issues of the *Locomotief* yield the following: "Wanted: Refined European lady, about thirty to forty years old, to raise a little girl and take over the housekeeping for an unmarried man"; "A young lady wishes a position keeping house for a bachelor, preferably full-blooded European and in a government job"; "Needed in the inland: a nursemaid, speaking pure Dutch; only those making no objection to the presence in the house of the Native mother will be considered."[17]

It would be inaccurate to assume that the realities of Indies domestic life were not laid bare until the twentieth century, however. The *Locomotief*'s readers had been fully acquainted with the so-called hidden details of Indies life for years. Since its first issues in the 1860s, the paper had published birth records from the Civil Register monthly under such headings as "Acknowledged Natural Children" and "Born out of Wedlock." And the facts of colonial life were sometimes announced forthrightly, as in these samples from the *Javasche Courant*: "Married: J. F. Thierbach to the Mother of his children. Semarang, 18 April 1850"; and, less graciously, "Married, in order to legitimize his children, George Weijnschenk, Jogja, 7 September 1850."[18] The same matter-of-fact acceptance of a polyglot world, so different from the homogeneous society of nineteenth-century Holland, is evident in the many notices directed at "Europeans and those on the same footing." All bore on the daily reader the constant message that for many, their position in society was tenuous, maintained only by choice and effort.

Occasionally that message was conveyed stridently, as in the *Locomotief*'s report on the recovery of a seventeen-year-old girl, Henriette Meeng, who had been feared abducted from her home in the European quarter of Surabaya. "Fortunately," the story continued, "the sheriff van Ham was able to discover her yesterday in one of the *kampungs* [villages, Indonesian residential quarters], in the company of the Native Kardi. The girl had dressed herself in Javanese clothes and had represented herself as named Sadinem."[19]

One does not need to rely on sensational items or the job vacancy column in the *Locomotief* to conclude this argument concerning the inner nature of colonial life. The newspaper is a mirror of living society. On every page are stamped its characteristics. Not only did Europeans purchase "finely embroidered kebayas" as well as Western bridal frocks, or read advertisements for furniture in the Indonesian language; they also sprinkled their notices with such

11. Lady and Foodseller. Photographed this century in Batavia. European women still wore a modified form of Indonesian costume at home before the Second World War. The photograph shows the adaptation of Europeans to Indonesian codes of politeness governing body posture between superior and inferior. (From Hein Buitenweg [H. Chr. Meijer], *De laatste tempo doeloe*, p. 153, from the Shell Foto [B.P.M.] Rotterdam Collection. Print courtesy Servire Publishers.)

Malay words as *obat* (medicine) and *laki* (male), and even described Dutch manners, customs, and laws by their Malay term as "our *adat*."

Thoughtful members of the immigrant community might confront the realities of "colonial adat" and offer solutions. Here is the contribution of one who joined a debate being conducted among *Locomotief* readers on the reasons for the poor quality of education in the Indies. While conceding to earlier writers that ill-qualified teachers and the low level of school certificate examinations were contributing factors, he gave as the chief cause the fact that children of the European group were being taught in Dutch. "Are not the children here," he asked, "if not speaking in Malay, always thinking in Malay—barring exceptions? And is it not then irresponsible—I almost said insane—that people should address such children in Dutch, teach them in Dutch from the beginning, whether they understand or not?" His solution was to use Malay in teaching children with European status in their first school years, introducing Dutch as one of the subjects for study before using it as the medium of instruction at higher levels. [20]

This seemingly sensible suggestion drew protests from readers who felt Malay was an "unworthy" vehicle for a Western education. One of the more moderate respondents could still aver: "I give as my decided opinion that schools for children of Europeans in the Netherlands Indies ought to be good schools, where the Dutch language reigns, where classes are taught in Dutch. . . . European parents, he ended, must give up the "inexpressibly perverse habit" of turning their children over to Asians to raise. [21]

Though he might not have suspected it, this writer was defending a point of view that has its origin in letters Joan Maetsuyker sent the Company's directors as long past as the 1640s. There exists in the colonial history of the Dutch in Indonesia an unbroken tradition of promoting the Dutch language and of attributing defects of character to the habit of leaving child-rearing to Asian subordinates. Almost as unalterable as the judgments themselves is the very custom of employing Asians as nursemaids and guardians. The hostility expressed by European commentators is testimony to the enduring influence of Asians and their steady contribution to colonial culture. Nevertheless, a command of Dutch continued to be prime in conferring European status. It remained the sole language of instruction in schools for all classified as European, even though a survey of 1,476 beginning pupils classified as European, conducted in 1900, showed that only 433, or 29.3 percent, understood a little Dutch, in comparison with their command of an Indonesian language, while 621, or 41.5 percent, knew no Dutch at all. [22]

If the facts of colonial life thus proven caused no upheaval or reconsideration in education policy, they did become the subject of analysis and of reforms proposed by a group of thinkers proceeding in quite a different manner. In the last quarter of the nineteenth century a score of novels written by Dutchwomen were published whose chief subject was the evils of the colonial society of their day. In commentaries on the nineteenth-century colony, these now-forgotten authors are sometimes mentioned in remarks introducing discussions of E. F. E. Douwes Dekker, P. A. Daum, and Louis Couperus, whose Indies novels have had a lasting appeal.[23] In such treatments the works of the women are characterized as "boarding school literature" or "women's books."[24] It is not difficult to understand the origin of this disparagement. It lies in the effusive sentimentality of the authors, the grotesqueries of plot, the abundant coincidences and infelicities of style. Twentieth-century tastes have caused scholars to overlook the descriptions of colonial society which these novels contain and to concentrate on the male novelists.

The livelier narrative of Daum and Couperus came in part from the substitution of storytelling for the moralizing of the female authors, whose sense of outrage forced plots to fit the lesson. In so doing, however, the women reveal of a sudden a wholly new point of view in and on colonial society. We are dealing with crusaders whose sympathies are engaged for the Indonesian and part-Indonesian, perceived as victims of the authors' own class and kind.

It must immediately be said that there is, in the novels by these women authors, no call to the barricades in the cause of an altered relationship between Indonesia and the Netherlands. Their writings do not have the breadth of the twentieth-century novelist Madelon Lulofs, for instance, whose subject was the plantation economy of Sumatra.[25] Nor are there to be found the large-scale descriptions of the colonial regime that form the core of Daum's *How He Became Councillor of the Indies*. The subject matter of their books is circumscribed, particular, for they wrote about what they knew. And that, for the nineteenth-century lady, was the domestic circle.

Reading the books of Marie Vanger-Frank, Françoise IJzerman-Junius, Mina Kruseman, Thérèse Hoven, and Nicolina Marie Sloot, we discover what constituted the daily life of the colonial in Indonesia: the complicated racial relationships, the intricacies of status, the pressures of an alien environment, and the threats to continued home life from colonial wars, attacks by Indonesians, frequent transfers, and distance from kin in Holland. The constant themes of these novels are the problems of concubinage, the relationship between the immigrant bride and her husband's children from previous alliances with Indonesian women, tensions between legitimate and illegitimate children of a white father, marriages of convenience, loneliness and isolation, the role of the housewife in Indonesia, the obsession of many Europeans with promotion and money, and the personal feelings of Europeans towards Indonesians.

The titles of their works reflect the intimacy and circumscription of the subject matter. For example, there is *A Natural Child and Other Netherlands-Indies Tales* from Marie Frank under her pen name Katja-Mata, and *Indies*

145

Marriages, a collection of stories by Françoise Junius, who published all her works under the name Annie Foore. Mina Kruseman's *A Marriage in the Indies* manages to cover the ill-fated match between a Creole and an immigrant, the neglect of illegitimate, part-European children, impoverishment and helplessness of abandoned mistresses, a crusade against animal sports and an appeal to end war. Thérèse Hoven's *In Sarong and Kabaya* is a collection of sixteen Indies sketches which mostly give the viewpoint of the immigrant woman newly arrived, while the theme of *Estranged* and the title story of *Nonnie and Other Tales* is the impact of sneers and insults by Europeans on the personality of Eurasians. This is also a chief subject of Marie Sloot's *The Resident's Family*, which she wrote using the name Melati van Java.[26]

Marie Sloot breaks out of the narrow domestic world of her colleagues in her historical novel, *Soerapati*. For she moves away from a contemporary setting to make as chief character of her fiction a hero of the Javanese. It is true that there is little of the Indonesian in her portrait of the eighteenth-century opponent of the VOC. Surapati is, in her hands, "the noble savage," attracted instinctively by all that is finest in European civilization and repulsed by the coarseness, racism, and arrogance of its bearers.[27] A far more successful portrayal of an Indonesian was later to be undertaken by Marie van Zeggelen in her biography *Kartini, A Pioneer for Her People*,[28] for she attempted to enter the world of an upper-class Javanese family and show this social reformer on her own terms.

Empathy of this quality was a late development in the lives of the writers themselves and in the unfolding of character in their stories, as it was a late development in colonial sentiment and then shared by a very few. Turning to a closer examination of the novels, we see that as newcomers, Hoven, Junius, and Frank had experienced markedly different reactions. Sentiments of distaste and fear had arisen from the strangeness of the country, from ignorance, and from the absence of relations between the immigrants and the Indonesians and Eurasians as peers. The initial impression of being alone in a sea of hostile or callously indifferent Indonesians is conveyed in Françoise Junius's *Bogoriana*, for example. Here a newly arrived bride is alone on her first day in Bogor, supervising the unpacking of furniture: "She sees the half-naked men, the brutal brown faces, distorted further by the wad of tobacco all have tucked in their mouths; she hears the rough noises which sound more like the grunts of beasts than men's voices, especially when one understands not a single word of the language, and . . . she becomes terribly afraid."[29]

And there it was that the knowledge of many immigrants rested. Such entrapment in ignorance is presented in story form by Marie Frank. The occasion is a visit of condolence paid by an immigrant woman to the home of a Eurasian widow. From her outsider's point of view there are "swarms" of relatives, "ostentatious" displays of grief succeeded by apparent indifference on the part of the mourners, "pagan" pieties of burning incense by the body and placing rice and dishes of food close by. All these details are laid side by side until the visitor thankfully escapes with her own thoughts: "To each his own; but no matter how I sympathised with the bereaved, everything struck me as ludicrous and excessive, rather than imposing or tragic. The dignified composure, the quiet that prevails *among us* in a home where there's been a death I find more appropriate in such solemn hours than all that hubbub. Can you believe that all that grief is genuine! And eating and drinking by a dead body!" [Emphasis added] [30]

Confronted by such evidences of a colonial culture quite distinct from Holland's, many newcomers simply accepted racially based myths of the blood affinities linking Asian and part-Asian. They attributed all that was foreign and puzzling to the "Oriental inscrutability" that so bedevilled Couperus and to the alien force that he descried smoldering in every Easterner. Frank and Junius had shown how surely distaste could arise. Their explanation for the immigrants' sentiments—as growing out of ignorance—was grounded in the rational, and is therefore more informative than Couperus's perspective on colonial life. The same impulse led these women authors to look beyond first impressions and to examine and interpret everyday realities of colonial life. Preeminent among those realities was the widespread practice of concubinage.

The situation with respect to concubines had already changed considerably by the time our novelists begin their chronicle of colonial society. In the VOC centuries men had made free with the Asian slave women of their households. After 1860, however, there was no more domestic slavery. Men living in concubinage now sought their companions among the free population of the Indonesian villages. The woman selected assumed management of the European's household and staff, a position that gave rise to the common colonial euphemism for concubine, "housekeeper." It became customary for the concubine to exchange her colored or indigo kebaya for a white one and to wear slippers, the clothing symbolizing her new status and passage from the Indonesian to the halfway world of a bachelor-centered Indies society.

It seems that government officials and plantation staff were urged by their superiors to take a housekeeper. (Soldiers had always been encouraged to find local women to cook for them and tend their needs. Until early in the twentieth century, when a new colonial morality preferred prostitution to regular union, concubines were permitted to live in the barracks with the troops.) The reason commonly advanced was that a concubine would charge herself with the care of her man's health, food, and clothing. She would promote a more orderly life by keeping her master from causing trouble roaming the Indonesian residential quarters at night. And she would teach him the region's dialect and customs. [31]

Colonial values dictated that the housekeeper be unseen, retiring to the back part of the house after serving European guests. Such invisibility gave currency to extravagant notions about the mistress. The Indonesian nyai swiftly entered myth in the nineteenth century, the subject of fantasies as seducer of hapless European men by means of potions and magic, and popularly suspect as poisoner of the rival or bride who replaced her. Newspapers carried stories of alleged murders by nyais, and a novelist like Daum helped create the image of the concubine possessed by evil and cunning.

Once a man had reached a rank and income that could support a woman with European status, he was expected to dismiss his concubine and to marry. Discarding an Indonesian mistress for a legally wed European caused grave social problems, for the rejected woman lost her means of support, and young children might be suddenly bereft of paternal care or left to the uncertain welcome of an immigrant stepmother.

The license colonial society allowed European men was an immediate problem that forced itself upon every immigrant bride, and so it is not surprising that the nyai should play a central role in the novels of the female writers. Upon occasion, the plot might include the systematic poisoning of a European master by his housekeeper. This is the point of action in a tale from Françoise Junius.[32] It occurs, however, not out of any innate malevolence in the woman. Marie is part Dutch, but had not been acknowledged by her father and so is Indonesian in status and stands in relation to the European immigrant Henri as concubine rather than wife. When he proposes separation after a relationship of some twenty years and taking their teenaged daughters with him to Holland, Marie seizes on poison as her only weapon against him. This was not, in fact, so very fanciful. Articles 40 and 354 of the Civil Code of 1848 had settled that mothers with Indonesian status had no rights over children recognized by a white man. Nor might they lay claim to guardianship of minor children in the event of the father's death.[33] In this light, the Marie of Junius's story is a mother struggling to keep her children by her.

Marie is by no means elevated to sainthood, but is portrayed as jealous and unprincipled. All the same, Junius attempts to explain her character's motives through the injustice of concubinage and assumption of racial superiority by whites. She shows, too, how far-reaching the consequences could be: a pact is struck whereby in return for marriage, Marie agrees not to use poison again. Marriage obliges Henri to permit his wife to appear in public. After years of modest withdrawal, Marie now presides in her own home, receiving guests instead of serving them. While she must endure slights, nothing can take from her the Dutch title *mevrouw*, (reserved for married ladies of the middle classes), her Western dress, and her appearances in public.

Other women writers took up the defense of the concubine unequivocally. In so doing they created a new stereotype in the eternally faithful, greatly wronged housekeeper. From Marie Frank there is a vignette in this vein under the title "The Englishman's Error."[34] An Englishman in his seventies boasts of the

Indonesian mistress with whom he has been living for the greater part of his life yet disdains to marry. The woman leaves him, following a grievous insult. Faced with a dirty house, meals never on time, and unmanageable servants, the old man attempts to woo her back and eventually pays her price, which is a lawful marriage. Through this story the author suggests that there is a common humanity and moral code between Europeans and Asians. In her hands, the mistress wants marriage, not in order to give herself the privileges of a legal European, but to satisfy her yearning for a social respectability that race prejudice had long denied her.

Despite the slightness of the tale, Marie Frank was able to show a moral truth that had been wanting in Indies belles-lettres ever since the diatribes of Tavernier and de Graaff in the seventeenth century. In the hands of Thérèse Hoven, the contrasts of character and situation were driven to extremes, reducing the human truth but making the points more explicit. Such a story is that of Sima, the illegitimate daughter of a Chinese man and a Javanese woman. Her fate of servitude commences at the age of twelve, when she becomes nursemaid to a Chinese girl. Soon, however, she is forced to flee to avoid becoming her employer's concubine. Alone, she is made wretched by poverty, and finally makes her way to the quarters of bachelor European army officers. There she is taken in as mistress by a young Dutch lieutenant, and dons the uniform white kebaya along with the sarongs and jewels he gives her. Sima has become a concubine, the fate she had sought to avoid. But in surrendering to the demand of poverty, she avoids a further loss of status, in colonial terms, by concubinage with a European rather than a fellow Asian.

As the story continues, Sima learns to love her officer and follows him to war in Achin in northern Sumatra. There she searches the battlefield, finds her wounded man, and nurses him back to life. Her devotion is later rewarded with dismissal, for the lieutenant becomes engaged to an immigrant Dutchwoman. Sima returns to the Indonesian quarter of the city which occasions this aside from Hoven: "Sima would no longer be able to wear white blouses, as that was not allowed the wife of a Native." Married to a Javanese, she again falls victim when her Muslim husband decides to take a second wife. Our heroine's moral outrage forces her out, and having nowhere to go she wanders by the house of her former officer, who is sitting on the front veranda, ringed by his wife and children. This is the final blow. Sima dies in the backyard, clasping a lock of his hair. No one takes much notice, since in the words of the story's title "it was just a nursemaid."[35]

In Mina Kruseman's treatment of the long-suffering mistress, attention is focused on the poverty and distress arising from abandonment.[36] Representatives of this sad lot are two women, one Indonesian, one Creole. Their lives are linked by their relationship with a Dutch immigrant, Stevens van Langendijk. The Indonesian Mina is his housekeeper, acquired during his days as inspector and by whom he has two sons. Louise is the Creole he takes as wife upon his promotion to resident, chief European official in the area, and after banishing Mina and the boys to the kampung. In time, Stevens divorces Louise. She is taken in by another Dutchman and cares for his household as his mistress. Bereft of any protection from the state, both women suffer tragic fates. Mina dies as a result of a brutal beating from Stevens. Upon his death, Louise is thrown out of her lover's house, along with their child, and is left penniless because he had made no provision in his will for her.

The sympathies of readers of colonial novels by female authors were often enlisted in behalf of children born to concubines. From Marie Frank comes the "autobiography" of Fransie, who is the "natural child" of the title story of her collected Indies tales.[37] Oppression is seen as handed down from generation to generation in the group of outcasts. Fransie's mother is similarly a natural child, daughter of an Indonesian mother and a Dutch official. Following the father's death, Fransie's mother had been taken into the local resident's employ as household help and had in time become the resident's mistress and borne him children, amongst whom was Fransie. After the death of the resident's wife, Fransie's mother had presided over the house and had been like a wife in all respects "save that she neither paid nor received visits; in the eyes of the world my father lived as a widower, but at home everything was subject to the will of my mother."[38] Fransie had been raised with the resident's legitimate daughters, had shared their tutor, learnt French and music, while her brothers had been sent to boarding school in Europe.

Once the resident died, however, Fransie and her mother were immediately evicted by the legitimate children and left to fend for themselves. At once all worldly relations had altered. The resident's daughter, for all her French and piano, was now a Javanese. Accordingly, her fiancé of yesterday would take Fransie only as his mistress. By the time Fransie was pregnant, he was ready to shed her and take as his lawful wife a legitimate Creole, Fransie's own stepsister.

A different approach was taken by Françoise Junius in the short story "Willie's Mama".[39] The Willie of the title is about three years old when this sermon begins. He is the son of Otto Dorman by his Javanese housekeeper, who had died in giving birth. Dorman is now eager to marry the legitimate European Cécile Haakstra, but meets opposition when admitting his "problem" to the girl's father. At first it is a matter-of-fact "naturally you'll pack the kid off to the kampung?" soon replaced by an enraged "throw the ape out!" Dorman protests that Willie is his own flesh and blood, but finds no sympathy in his fiancée either. Eventually Dorman comes to a compromise: he will have the boy raised out of sight in the kampung; in return Cécile will agree that Dorman should make regular payments for Willie's upkeep.

Over the next three years Dorman pays furtive visits to his son, who, without proper acknowledgment as a European, is being mistreated. When Cécile finally has a child of her own, she comes to understand what Willie, his race and birth forgotten, meant to his father. This new perception of Willie as a human being causes Cécile to seek him out and bring him into her own home to be raised as her son. Cécile's entreaty to her father to accept Willie allows Junius many paragraphs of elaboration on her call to conscience, which is that Dutchwomen should seek out their husbands' offspring by Indonesian women and wipe out the "stain" of their birth by raising them as Europeans and Christians.

This is not a principle that finds favor now, but in 1887, when "Willie's Mama" first appeared in print, it was without parallel in commentaries on the colonial and racial relationship between Dutch and Indonesian. Being aimed at a female, politically nonexistent audience, Junius's little homily attracted no public attention. In those receptive to her pleas on behalf of the innocent offspring of unregistered unions, however, there must have been nurtured a disposition to accept the need for greater efforts towards improving the welfare of Indonesians and part-Indonesians. Women writers, then, were creating a sentiment in favor of change and "uplift" a decade and more before such public figures as Pieter Brooshoeft and C. T. van Deventer openly joined in this cause.[40]

Against the conviction of racial superiority implicit in the benevolence of a Françoise Junius are seeming instances of its opposite in the work of Marie Sloot: a belief in the innate moral superiority of the Indonesian and part-Indonesian over Europeans. There is her portrayal of Surapati, for instance. The same perception of the "untouched native" shapes her *Resident's Family*. In this novel, she puts into the mouth of Dr. Gordès a description of those Javanese still "unspoilt" by contact with Europeans as being "good, simple, and willing."

We may take this characterization as part of Sloot's campaign against the racial attitudes of her contemporaries. In itself it brought the reader no closer to perceiving Indonesians as fellow human beings. Her characterization is noteworthy, however, in presenting a notion wholly contrary to the image of Indonesians as liars, layabouts, and fanatics, an image often purveyed in the travel books of visiting Dutchmen. In inclining all her Indonesians instinctively towards the Europeans' culture, Sloot, of course, betrayed her own faith in the supremacy of Western civilization. This is one part of her message in *Family*.

The heroine bearing out this truth is Constance, recognized daughter of van Welven by a Javanese housekeeper. Most of her girlhood is spent in boarding school in Holland. The action of the novel commences after her return to Java to make her home with her father, who now holds the post of resident, and with her European stepmother. The situation allows the author many opportunities to show the bigotry of Europeans. The stepmother, for instance, attaches impor-

151

tance only to Constance's skin color and disregards the girl's learning and attainments.

One of the many melodramatic scenes of the novel has an Indonesian running amuck, a favorite subject for Daum and Couperus meant to exemplify the uncontrollable passions of the Oriental. In Sloot's book there is a rational explanation for the sudden upsurge of grief and rage. Its place in the novel is to allow Constance the role of nurse and sympathetic friend to Indonesians. Dr. Gordès finds her in the kampung, binding the wounds of the injured, and expresses his amazement at such an act by a woman with European status. The exchange that follows carries Sloot's appeal to Eurasians obsessively insistent on their Dutch status: Constance says to Dr. Gordès, "The Javanese are just as much my compatriots as the Hollanders," to which he replies, "Are you proud of that?" "No," Constance answers, "but I'm not ashamed of it either. I never forget that my mother belonged to their people."[41] Gordès thereupon decides to marry Constance, discovering in her the partner who would assist him in his mission to "uplift" the Javanese. Later he must defend her against the insults of full Europeans. Sloot puts her conviction of Eurasian superiority into the doctor's defense of Constance: "My experiences have taught me this much, that an Indies woman with a brush of civilization stands far above the Dutch woman, however much polish she has."[42]

It comes as no surprise to learn that Sloot was born on Java. It is rare to find her point of view voiced publicly before the twentieth century, rarer still that it should come from a victim of prejudice. All the same, she muted sentiments of anger and resentment in her novelistic treatment of relations between Indonesian, part-Indonesian, and European. Hurt, bewildered surprise at ill-treatment is the extent of her response.

The passion of feeling was there in some Indies novels. Thérèse Hoven caught it. In *Estranged* she shows a hatred for whites that was also a form of self-hatred, poisoning the lives of Eurasians. In the central character, Reewald, there is no warmth for the Indonesian mother who gave him his darker skin and Asian features. He sees the Indonesian part of his heritage as a blot to be erased, and he does this by marrying an immigrant. "Mr. Reewald was in love with her of course," Hoven remarks,

> but for him it had also been a sort of promotion, in a certain sense an improvement to his social standing, to be married to a full-blood European.
> Also he thought that through this mingling his family would make progress—in a few more generations, by degrees, the dark blood would dwindle away. This Mr. Reewald was a *Sinjo* with strongly pronounced anti-Sinjo sentiments and prejudices. He hoped that the children, begotten of a blond, white woman, would take after their mother and depart from the *Indo* type.[43]

All these complex sentiments between Indonesians and the native Dutch were bound to end up in the associations of the second decade of this century

152

which emphasized the special interests of the Eurasian under such mottoes as ''the Indies for those who make their home there.''[44] It has no echo in the novels. As I noted at the outset, there is no revolutionary impulse in the writings of these women. They appeal for reform of discrete, immediate evils, for legislative protection for children, a change in attitudes concerning color, and so on. Only in Sloot's work is there a vision of something entirely different. It comes early in her historical romance and is vouchsafed to Surapati:

> No future more beautiful could dawn on Java, he mused, than if the two peoples fused together, just as once Islam had gathered up the old Hindu ways of worship into itself. More glorious yet would the victory be, then only would Java be mighty, mighty and one in the material and spiritual matters of state and of religion.
>
> There would be no more rulers, neither ruled anymore; the frightful arbitrary power of the native courts, the mindless oppression, the needless greed would be checked and, lovely as the morrow, would break the shining, splendid future over Java, which he would help build through his loyal help and assistance offered the Hollanders.[45]

Such a vision was doomed from the beginning since the Dutch were the flawed partners. This was made plain in the novel and was of course obvious from the events which had passed between the period of Sloot's story and her reader's own present.

It is not in blueprints for the future that the value of these novels and short stories lies, however, but in the facts of colonial life they reveal and the attitudes they bring to light. As the authors tell their tales, they impart an extraordinary wealth of detail about colonial society in the last quarter of the nineteenth century. In Junius's novel *The van Sons* it was entirely conscious. Here the author takes her newly arrived couple, Dora and Emile van Sons, on a round of formal visits to leading inhabitants of a small town in the inland of Java. Principal among them are the Javanese *bupati* (administrative head of a district under a Dutch resident) and his *raden ayu,* or chief wife. This visit gives the reader an unusual glimpse into the household of a Javanese aristocrat of the period:

> The Regent [Dutch term for the bupati] is already coming forward to his guests, and escorts them—with the great courtesy that is peculiar to the upper-class of Javanese—to an inner apartment furnished entirely in European fashion.
>
> The Rhaden-ajoe and the three daughters who are present (another eight women and about fifty children live in the *dalem* [palace, or women's quarters in the palace]) are typical of the Javanese nobility.
>
> The girls offer bouquets, good port wine, and delicious cakes. Fortunate that they understand Dutch, although they don't dare speak it, so that Dora does not have to make mistakes in Malay. Emile speaks Javanese with the Regent and has little trouble making himself understood. Both are very glad when the visit is over without any major clumsiness or grave transgressions against the Javanese adat.[46]

153

A much easier visit is that paid the *patih*, or Indonesian second-in-command in the district, and his wife Fatimah, who is also the bupati's eldest daughter. She has been reared by Dutch governesses, so that she is "European in all her wishes and thought" and living proof of "the modest simplicity of the Eastern woman paired with the cultivation and talents of the Western."[47] She had fallen in love with a young Dutch official, but the colonial government had intervened to forbid the marriage. Dora can readily sympathize with love thwarted, and the two become genuinely friendly. In contrast is Fatimah's old-style husband; he will not open up to the alien, and limits his conversation to conventional expressions of subservience.

Dr. Broks follows in the local hierarchy. His wife is a Eurasian, her language full of Indonesian words. She had made Broks give his illegitimate, half-Indonesian son a proper education by sending him to the Netherlands. Unable to bear children herself, she has sought out a fair-skinned little girl in the kampung, the abandoned daughter "of a great man," to raise as her own. Mrs. Broks keeps this child at home, fearing to send her to school lest she be called "Indo bastard" by the other pupils, and engages instead a European governess to make a Dutch lady of her.

Another little tragedy is glimpsed in the visit to the town's notary and his wife:

> The notary was married to "the mother of his children." She must have been a beautiful Javanese woman once, but little was left of her looks now. Half-ashamed, she sat hunched up in a corner of the sofa where she motioned Dora to sit. She said very little, and then so diffidently and in such bad Dutch that she was difficult to understand.
>
> It wasn't much that she told, drawn out by the friendly look of her lady visitor. Her sons were in Holland, all four; her only girl was in the Indies, but she was allowed to see her only infrequently lest the girl become too native. The notary was repatriating to Europe in two years and she would have to go with him! . . . and the great black eyes expressed so much fear, so much sorrow, that the visitors, to their amazement, began to feel sympathy for the ex-housekeeper.[48]

One more character in *The van Sons* deserves mentioning. He is known simply as Oom Jan, or Uncle John, and is manager on a tobacco plantation. He had taken in the daughter of a deceased friend and the Javanese mother, Kamisah. In time Jan had discovered the refining influence of a child and the benefit to a household stemming from a good mother. He had formally adopted the girl and given her a Western education. Emile van Sons is astonished to learn that the Javanese mother is still with Jan. "What sort of a man do you think I am, Emile?" is the reply, "that I would toss Kamisah out when she stood by me faithfully in bad times, now that things are going well? No, dear boy, I married her as soon as it was at all possible, and we live together as happily and contentedly as it's possible for anyone on this earth!"[49]

154

The reader of this Indies romance cannot fail to be impressed by the characters thus marshalled, the combination of partners, the circumstances and private histories. It makes statistics on mixed marriages, legitimations, and "equalizing at law" come alive. It gives credence and substance to all those newspaper advertisements placed by governesses requesting positions with "married families," or posted by parents asking for refined pronunciation in nanny and schoolmistress. It gives meaning to aloof government reports on the declining welfare of Indonesians and Eurasians. It is a window on a society that was extremely mixed and that by the turn of the century was breaking down under constant assault from outside.

In her Indies novels and short stories Junius records these facts, but as incidentals to her main interest: the delivery of a sermon through a love story. In the same way another key point about colonial society is made incidentally in the novels of Sloot, Frank, and Kruseman: that women could sometimes pass between ethnic communities, cross lines drawn by color and caste, and enter slots for which they had no birthright, depending on their alliances with men. A second look at the convoluted plot of "A Natural Child" will illustrate this point.

It will be recalled that Fransie had been raised with her father's legitimate daughters until his death, when she and her Dutch-Javanese mother had been evicted. Without money to rent a house in the European quarter and without the patronage of a man of European status, they are obliged to live in the town's Indonesian neighborhood and therefore to act as Indonesians. It is now that the Dutch fiancé alters his proposal to match Fransie's new, Javanese, status. He installs her in his house as mistress, not wife. Now Fransie wears the white kebaya of the concubine. She no longer attends social functions for Europeans but remains invisible, immured in his house. All old ties and acquaintance are lost.

When Karel marries, he takes a bride from the European group to which Fransie had once belonged. Dismissed, Fransie can only return to her mother, shedding the symbols of concubine status for the Javanese again. Later she meets a Frenchman who asks for a legal marriage. This relationship has the effect of making Fransie a European once more, entitled to be addressed as "mevrouw," to wear frocks and hats, and to mix with Europeans socially. After a number of misfortunes, Fransie turns to her old nurse in the kampung. Our repentant heroine now takes on her final identity as a Javanese. She goes to work for a European household as a seamstress, where once she had been entertained as a guest. Here Fransie remains identified as a Javanese by her occupation, her clothing, her seat on the floor, and the Indonesian terms used to address her.

When Eurasian men with European status assumed Indonesian clothing for public outings, it was always a furtive act and was a way whereby a man who kept his position in the European world might yet enjoy the Indonesian part of his cultural heritage. For Indonesian clothing was not a badge for the status of the woman to whom he was attached. Indonesian clothing was assumed when Eurasian men visited the kampungs to attend Javanese theater performances and to spend their evenings with ronggengs; it facilitated easy relations with Indonesians. Women had no such avenue for fusing two worlds. Indonesian costume on a woman of European parentage meant a usually irreversible step down the colonial social ladder.

The little melodrama of Fransie reveals the nature of colonial society. In general, Asians were born into their respective ethnic groups, which governed their dress, the type of formal schooling they received, their mode of occupation, the law regulating their daily lives, and so on. For most Asians there was no escape from destiny, save for the very few men, in the areas of heavy European settlement, who might consciously seek to stamp out their Asian past and be made European under the law. From the Dutch point of view that was to move upwards. The contrary movement, of men with European status becoming assimilated with Indonesians, was never the result of application at law. It was more apt to be involuntary, the result of loss of employment in an occupation reserved for persons with European status and impoverishment. It was perceived by the immigrant Dutch as a degrading, downwards course.

The movement by men between compartments was slight enough to allow for the development of a theory defining the early twentieth-century Indies as a plural society, one in which groups of diverse cultural and racial heritage lived "side by side, yet without mingling, in one political unit."[50] Introducing women into consideration overturns this orderly hypothesis, for their nationality had always been, in the Dutch settlements, inherently unstable, dependent upon the man to whom they were attached. Thus it was possible for one and the same person to be now Indonesian, now European, now Mestiza, according to circumstances. What were plural and separate were the laws regulating each group. The separate legal system was most elaborate in the second and third decades of the twentieth century, obscuring actuality by creating the impression of cultural separation.

Eurasian children who were born out of wedlock similarly introduce a disorderly element to definitions of pluralism. Their status, like women's, depended entirely on their white fathers. When they were acknowledged, such offspring were Europeans; when not, they were Indonesians. To be accepted as European required, generally, Christian baptism with a Dutch name, Dutch schooling, and Dutch costume. What only the novels make clear, however, is an additional condition: permanent residence in a European household until adulthood. Once claim to European status was lost by a Eurasian man, there was slight opportunity for retrieving it. Women, on the other hand, could sometimes shed their Indonesian status by their ability to marry white men.

True pluralism requires a natural sex ratio within the ruling group. In Indonesia this was never the case (although the immigrant European community in large cities was moving closer to a balance by the 1930s). Hence there were many individuals who spanned groups. As shown earlier, when immigrants from Europe were predominantly male, they were absorbed into a society whose stable element was the local woman and her European kin. The route to power, wealth, and prestige lay through acceptance into a Mestizo clan. In the nineteenth century, however, monopoly of high-level positions passed to those educated in Europe. And in the last quarter of the century a new path to wealth was created for migrants, that of private enterprise in business or in plantation agriculture. At the same time, the demographic pattern began to alter as more women were among the new arrivals. In areas of heavy European settlement these women were able to transplant their home culture, albeit necessarily altered.

Thus the means to power and wealth and the moral reference point were wrenched from local Mestizo society and anchored firmly in the Netherlands. When once that happened, Eurasians and Creoles became dependent for social acceptance upon the immigrants. Since the key to prestige lay in being reckoned European, Mestizo society broke up. It left as the record of its existence in Indonesia only a curious medley of cultural elements in the upper class of Indonesians.

Mestizo culture lived on intact for a little longer inland than in the coastal cities, but with its members now divorced from European government service, it showed all the signs of imminent collapse, or rather of reabsorption into the Indonesian world. The great Indies landowning families, distantly descended from immigrant men, are shown in P. A. Daum's Indies novels, especially his *"Ups" en "Downs" in het Indische leven*. In his treatment, the Indies family is still shown as based upon ties between female kin and their relations traced through their mothers. Writing of the Lugtens family, Daum shows us the home compound in the European residential section of town: the large house for the Dutch immigrant and his Eurasian wife and, in the servants' quarters to the side, the Indonesian mother of the lady of the house. She is maintained there by the daughter, who has gained permanent footing in European society for herself because her tie to a white is that of marriage, not concubinage.

All that was fascinating by its oddity or that called for reform became, in the novels of Eurasian authors, parts of a natural whole, a fusion of worlds and civilizations that was the Mestizo culture of colonial Indonesia. The tone of the memoirs of Nieuwenhuys's *Yellowed Portraits* and of Maria Dermoût's *The Ten Thousand Things* and *Yesterday*[51] was neither moral outrage nor titillating gossip, but tender recollection, a rendering of a beloved Mestizo world. They wrote when that culture had dissolved, separated back into its original elements of Indonesian and Dutch. It was not possible before. Mestizo culture, by its nature, did not produce a written literature. To write about themselves, Eurasians had to be drawn into one or other of the literary heritages and languages, and that was possible only after the creation late in the nineteenth century of extensive, formal education systems in Indonesia. That, however, inducted the individual irrevocably into the Dutch or the Indonesian, and in the process transformed the pupils. Nieuwenhuys and Dermoût both wrote of Mestizo culture from Holland after political events had brought the colony to an end. Those events—the increasingly plural character of the law codes, education systems, and employment slots; the Indonesian nationalist movement; world war and occupation—all forced individuals to take sides, to choose loyalties, and to obliterate ambiguities. With worldwide acceptance of Indonesia's independence in 1949, Indies society was ended forever. In the renamed capital Jakarta the development of a national culture proceeds, one that fuses the many cultures of Indonesia, the colonial past, and elements of Western or "international" culture.

Epilogue

TO RECOUNT IN DETAIL the final dissolution of Mestizo culture and of colonial society as a whole entails quite a different study from this one, which has focused on the Dutch of Indonesia as a distinct community with values and folkways of its own. It requires an examination of the Asian communities of the archipelago on their own terms and the introduction of new sets of actors, such as segments of the Javanese aristocracy and representatives of Indonesia's other ethnic groups who came to Batavia to study and stayed to lead the country to independence. The first response of these groups to the Dutch came about as a result of the expanding communications grid and of increased contact with the Dutch as European communities spilled out of their coastal enclaves and into the interior. That first response was to adopt parts of the colonial culture, so that the bupati families on Java, for instance, appeared to be blending into Mestizo society. In this light they added to the composition of Mestizo society an ingredient hitherto missing, an upper class of Indonesians who mixed more nearly as social equals with the colonial ruling elite. Upper-class Indonesians had not had to deal regularly face to face with the Dutch elite of VOC Batavia. But in the nineteenth century ritualized contacts with Holland's new representatives, as distinct from the old VOC embassies to their courts, became customary for upper-class Indonesians and an established part of colonial culture.

This apparent fusion partially obscured the opposition of interest between Indonesian and Dutch. As traditional leaders on Java, bupatis and lesser officials in the Indonesian arm of the colonial civil service were the first to come into close contact with the Dutch and their culture. Some bupatis came to see in it, and particularly in a Dutch education, a means to revive their social standing and to reassert over the populace that political authority which they had lost to the European administration during the first half of the nineteenth century. Such a definition of interest was too narrow to satisfy some of the junior officials and the Indonesians representing communities in other parts of the archipelago. They were to deny the privileges of tradition and to claim leadership not over Java alone but over the entire territory of the Netherlands East Indies by virtue of a new political vision.

159

It is possible here only to sketch the early responses to the Dutch in which lie antecedents to the nationalist movement that was to destroy the old colonial society. Without them the story of Mestizo culture and society is incomplete, and the impression is given that changes within the European community alone were key to political developments in the twentieth century.

Some members of Java's upper classes deliberately sought close contact with the Dutch during the course of the nineteenth century. They were no longer preoccupied solely with their own civilization and past, but now wished to understand the culture of the colonial rulers and were attracted by parts of it. In most cases, their contact with the European heritage was filtered through the Mestizo culture that predominated in areas of European settlement. Few of their number actually saw European culture firsthand in Europe, at least before the 1920s. Therefore the shock of contact was lessened, the new easy to grasp by reason of its assimilation by generations of people who were part-European and part-Indonesian.

This interest in the European dates approximately from the mid-nineteenth century. By that time the Dutch were supreme on Java, and their senior officials were men who were Europe-born and who intended to repatriate. Some among them entertained notions of "moral duty" and "uplift" towards Indonesians. Translated into colonial practice, this meant the beginning of a school system for upper-class Indonesians that would make the Dutch language their tongue. For the first time in colonial history there would be a language for communication, in the sense that both parties would be able to speak it well and could engage in conversation as peers, rather than using the highly stratified Javanese or the insulting coarseness of colonial Malay.

A. W. P. Weitzel had observed in 1858 that the reason for the absence of intercourse between cultivated Indonesians and "respectable" Dutch was the lack of a tongue in common.[1] The majority of contacts were between Dutch employers and Indonesian subordinates, carried on in a coarse Malay or pidgin Javanese and chiefly concerned with giving and taking orders. This lack of cross-racial contacts between peers is particularly noticeable in the novels of colonial life. Only Françoise Junius, of the novelists surveyed, speaks of visiting a bupati's residence, the kabupaten, and this may be explained by the fact that she was the wife of a senior government official. As such, she had formalized and ritualistic contacts with distinguished Javanese. Still, she does not devote much attention to those encounters, offers no description of the interior of the kabupaten, and says little abouts its inhabitants.

We know from other accounts of Indies society from this period—the records of travel books and photographs[2]—that European and Javanese dignitaries and their respective spouses met regularly on state occasions. While there was little intimacy of contact, both groups altered their behavior to meet the

other's expectations and codes of politeness. This became fixed colonial practice by the last quarter of the nineteenth century. Before that time, isolated
individuals among the Javanese had learnt Dutch, interested themselves in
European arts and hobbies, and mixed in European circles.

Raden Saleh is the best known of this group.[3] His long life spanned the
nineteenth century and compressed within it the experiences of several generations of distinguished Indonesians. He was born in 1814 in Semarang, at an
early age came into contact with Europeans in the Directorate of Agriculture,
Arts, and Sciences, and was sent to Holland at sixteen as a protégé of
Governor-General van der Capellen to study Western painting and lithography.
His sojourn in Europe stretched to twenty-one years, during which time he
became a celebrity in the courts of Germany, Belgium, and the Netherlands and
his paintings—in grand empire style—were hung in the major galleries of
Europe.

After returning to Java, Saleh was able to impose his reputation upon the
colonial Dutch and was feted in Batavia and Bogor, where he mixed with the
upper levels of the European community. He was an honorary member of the
Batavian Academy of Arts and Sciences and curator of the State Portrait Collection. Saleh set a precedent for a later generation of Indonesians who studied
in Holland by marrying a woman with European status upon his return to
Indonesia. She was a wealthy Eurasian who owned extensive property in the
Weltevreden district of Batavia. By 1867 his marriage to juffrouw Winkelman
had ended in divorce, and Raden Saleh then married a woman belonging to the
ruling family of Yogyakarta. She entered the world of the European with him,
under the title Raden Ayu Danoediredjo, and accompanied him to Europe in
1875. By February 1879 Raden Saleh was back in Bogor, and he died there in
the following year.

In Raden Saleh we are dealing with the extraordinary. More usual were the
contacts between Dutch and Javanese officials that became the practice following Olivia Raffles's entry into the women's quarters of the Solo and Yogyakarta
ruling families. Ver Huell made an extensive tour of Java in 1818 and has left
us a record of these encounters. Early in the year he was a guest of the sultan of
Madura. His party, which included several Dutch gentlemen, two of them
accompanied by their wives, was met by the sultan himself to the strains of
gamelan music. "His Highness," says Ver Huell, "offered his arm to one of
our ladies and led her to a sofa under a Pandoppang [pendopo, the reception
pavilion]. A great number of crystal chandeliers, mirrors, English engravings
in gilt frames, and other items of furniture filled this airy apartment. All the
mighty in the kingdom and courtiers came to greet us, after having bowed low
before the Sultan."[4]

In this meeting the seemingly trifling circumstance of the sultan's offering
his arm should be noted. It was a public transgression of an Islamic sense of

propriety concerning contact between the sexes, as it was a departure from Javanese etiquette, which forbade any touching of the sultan's person on formal occasions. It was, furthermore, the adoption of an infidel courtesy, and pushed to special prominence not a male, but a woman, in an audience hall where no Indonesian lady was present.

Later, Ver Huell was to visit the bupati of Lamongan in northeast Java. "What really amazed me," he writes of this call on Adi Arjo Negoro, "was that we were received by the Radinaio [raden ayu], wife of the Adi Patti, and her daughter-in-law, since in general, women of consequence in these regions never leave the harem. . . . This Regent, who seems to be more polished than other Native Princes, insists that his wives, contrary to custom, appear in company with foreigners."[5]

To prepare themselves and their family members for these encounters, Java's bupatis undertook to learn the intricacies of Dutch manners by appointing Netherlanders as tutors and governesses to their children, and they sometimes included their wives in such instruction. Pangeran Ario Tjondro Negoro, bupati of Demak, is the most famous Javanese aristocrat to take this step. His choice, C. E. van Kesteren, was to become known for his role as mentor to the father and uncles of Raden Ajeng Kartini, and for his later activities as an Indies schoolmaster and as editor of such influential newspapers as *de Indische Gids* (*Indies Guide*). From the mid-1860s, a number of Javanese government officials sought tutors through the now-familiar route of newspaper advertisements, of which the two following are examples: "Needed: In a Javanese family in Japara Residency: a Dutch man, unmarried, capable of giving instruction in the Dutch language and basic arithmetic," and "Sought by the Regent of Brebes, a European lady, middle-aged, to give conversation lessons in Dutch to the Radenajoe and daughters."[6] Bupatis used the weight of rank to press for admission of their sons into the primary schools reserved for Europeans, and they placed the boys as lodgers in Dutch households, that they might acquire an intimate knowledge of Dutch language and manners.

The newspapers yield evidence of increasing social contact between the immigrant and Javanese elites. Thus a notice from the Semarang subcommittee for the Arts and Crafts Exhibition that was held in Batavia in 1865 publicly thanks, "above all, Radhen Mas Trengono, son of the Pangeran of Demak, who deserves special credit, both for contributing numerous Items and for his services to the Subcommittee."[7] Furthermore, Western-educated Javanese were now ready to offer their opinions abroad. One describing himself in a letter to the *Locomotief* as a "Dutch-minded (*Hollandsch-gezind*) Javanese in the Principalities" wrote of the abuses of feudal corvée rights, and urged the colonial government to interfere in the affairs of the sultanates to alleviate the general exploitation.[8] In much the same vein, a fellow Javanese addressed the

Locomotief's readers the following year, distinguishing himself by signing his own name, Tommowiegono.[9]

Criticism of the susuhunan of Solo and the sultan of Yogyakarta as backward and oppressive rulers of the Javanese had become common among Dutch liberals in the second half of the nineteenth century. It was to be a theme, too, in those bupati circles whose members were acquiring, along with their Western schooling, an ambition to become leaders of the Javanese liberated from both the European administrator and the descendants of the former rulers of Mataram. Such interests were expressed in the second and third decades of this century through the *Regentenbond,* an association of bupatis. They pointed to their Western schooling, their fluency in Dutch, their adaptations in dress and behavior, and their efforts to improve popular welfare as evidence of their fitness to rule. And as proofs to the Dutch of their genuine assimilation of European cultural values, they were willing to extend a Western schooling to their daughters and to relax the etiquette that had regulated the lives of upper class Javanese ladies.

What did the immigrants think of Javanese who were showing such interest in their manners and learning? Some expressed approval and satisfaction, for example in obituaries that appeared in newspapers following the death in 1885 of the bupati of Brebes. They spoke of the "purity" of his Dutch and lauded him as a promoter of popular welfare. He was depicted as "enlightened," "dependable," and abhorring "creeping servility." One writer concluded his remarks with the hope that the Tjondro Negoro family would "continue to bring forth many such fine descendants who will be a blessing to Java."[10]

This wish was soon to be fulfilled by the deceased's niece, Raden Ajeng Kartini (1879–1904). Possibly because it was difficult to find a suitable person for governess in the small town of Japara, her father had taken the unprecedented step, around 1885, of enrolling Kartini and her younger sisters in the local primary school for Europeans. But it was a step in keeping with the response of Java's upper classes to the nineteenth-century Dutch. They were the daughters of the bupati class, however, and so represented elite values to the Javanese and had to conform, to a degree, to the demands of tradition. Accordingly, Kartini's father withdrew his daughters from school as they became teenaged, for the seclusion from society that was expected of girls before marriage, whilst he sent his sons to Semarang to continue their studies in a European high school. In his plan, the girls should reenter society as consorts to fellow bupatis, trained in Javanese traditions but also equipped by their fluency in Dutch and familiarity with Dutch manners to take their place in colonial society.

To accomplish his purpose, and as a result of his daughters' ardent response to their brief acquaintance with the culture of the Dutch, Kartini's father modified their seclusion in important ways. Javanese custom covered a Javanese

12. Daughter of a bupati. By the twentieth century, members of this class, male and female, were receiving a Western education in the Dutch language. (From E. Breton de Nijs, *Tempo Doeloe*, p. 112. Print courtesy R. Nieuwenhuys.)

world only; its prescriptions did not comprehend the Mestizo society that was coming to absorb the upper class. While Kartini and her sisters might not enter their own society before marriage, they were permitted to meet Dutch people, those men as well as women whose social position in the colonial elite gave them access to the kabupaten. They were also permitted to leave the kabupaten on several occasions to attend special events in the colonial world. They attended the dedication of a church, for instance, and a performance by a Dutch orator in a Semarang theater. They appeared in 1898 at a ball honoring the coronation of Holland's Queen Wilhelmina, and as recognition of their becoming spokeswomen for Western education for Javanese girls of their class, Kartini and her sisters were invited to spend a week meeting officials in Batavia and Bogor to discuss their own further study.

In addition to these formal contacts, Kartini maintained the acquaintance of several Dutch people through private meetings and through a large correspondence. The experience of intellectual exchange as between equals, as opposed to the ritual contacts of colonial society, was a powerful influence in shaping the ideas for which Kartini was to become famous: ideas concerning polygyny, marriage practices, divorce, vocational and professional training for Javanese women and men, advocacy of Dutch as the lingua franca, revival of Javanese arts and crafts, reform of administrative practices in promotion and prerogatives, changes in the role and status of women at all social levels, removal of race and color prejudice, and association between high-ranking Dutch and Javanese to raise the standard of living of the rural majority of Java.

Kartini's reflections on colonial society, radical and original for her class and time, were expressed in many forums, including meetings and correspondence with such Dutchmen as J. H. Abendanon, director of education, cottage industry, and religion from 1899 to 1905, and H. H. van Kol, a member of the Netherlands Lower House. There were also her occasional essays printed in Indies magazines (Yogyakarta's *de Echo*, for instance), in the *Bijdragen tot de Taal-, Land- en Volkenkunde* (*Contributions to Linguistic, Geographical, and Anthropological Studies*), then published in The Hague, in *The Dutch Lily*, a feminist journal published in the Netherlands, and in a memorial to the Dutch government.[11] The best-known expression of her thoughts is contained in the collection of her letters to Dutch friends first printed in the Netherlands in 1911.[12]

W. F. Wertheim has said that in 1911 Kartini exploded on a colonial Dutch public that was totally unprepared for a Javanese woman using a fluent Dutch to argue for reforms in Indies society.[13] But she was already a well-known, controversial figure on Java in her own lifetime, at least in circles reading Dutch-language newspapers. The *Java Bode*, for instance, printed a long article on Kartini and her sisters Roekmini and Kardinah in 1904. A hint of the quality of Dutch approval for Indonesians who adopted their learning and ways can be taken from this same article's description of the teaching methods employed in the school for Javanese girls which the sisters had established in 1903. Kartini's sisters, the reader is informed, squatted down, Javanese style, beside their pupils. "They want European culture and learning, but they remain Javanese. . . . They are one with their own people! A lesson for many." [14]

Nevertheless, the adoption of Dutch manners, the habit of speaking Dutch, and the growing acquaintance with Dutch learning on the part of the Javanese aristocracy drew hostility and opposition from some quarters in the immigrant community. P. A. A. Djajadiningrat, who was one of the first Indonesians to complete his secondary education in a school for Europeans in Batavia, has left in his Memoirs[15] a record of slights and prejudices experienced as members of his class mixed more with the Dutch. In 1896, the year he entered the senior grade of primary school in Batavia, attendance by an Indonesian was still quite new. The school's headmaster, fearing opposition from parents of the pupils, devised a solution peculiar to the society we have been studying: Achmad Djajadiningrat, scion of an old and honorable Sundanese family, could only be acceptable in the guise of an illegitimate but acknowledged Eurasian, for that is the implication of the name under which he was enrolled, Willem van Bantam (William of [or from] Bantam). Kartini encountered race prejudice too, in the Japara school as well as in the drawing rooms of Europeans, and spoke of it often in her letters.[16] The experience led her to stress the need in the colony's schools for moral training and character development, along with regular subject matter.

Stages in the adoption of Dutch practices can be followed through a perusal of announcements concerning their domestic affairs placed by high-ranking Javanese. It was already transgressing Javanese propriety to bring one's wife forward for public notice, as instanced in the following advertisement, even though the lady's own names are not disclosed: "Given birth to two Daughters: the Wife of Radhen Toemenggoeng Danoe Koesoemo, Regent of Malang" (1866). Established decorum was again renounced in the desire to conform to Dutch practice in this announcement: "On the 17th of this month died suddenly, after giving birth to a healthy daughter, my beloved Wife, the Raden Ajoe. Hadiningrat, Regent of Demak" (1885). In time, women's names came to be included in the personals placed by their male kin. For example, a death notice is inserted in 1904 for "my beloved mother, the Raden Ajoe Pangeran Hario Gondosiwojo," and the age of the deceased is also given. The next step was for announcements to be issued jointly by husband and wife. In heavy type comes, "The Regent of Toemenggoeng, R. M. T. Tjokro Adi Koesoemo and Raden Ajoe announce the birth of a daughter" (1904). In a later issue, the Regent of Magelang and Raden Ayu announce the approaching marriage of their daughter, whom they mark by name, Raden Ajeng Patemah. And finally, in announcing the death of Kartini, her parents described her by both her marriage title and the single names under which she had become a public figure: "The under-

166

signed beg to express their thanks for the great sympathy they have been shown on the loss of their daughter, R. Ajoe Adipatie Djojo Adiningrat (Raden Ajeng Kartini), Sosroningrat and Raden Ajoe, Japara'' (1904).[17]

Bupatis' families also adopted the habit of sending good wishes for the New Year to the public at large, their names joining those of local notables of the European and Chinese communities on the front page of regional newspapers. They began setting reception days, which they also announced through their daily papers. The rooms into which European guests were conducted were furnished as Mestizo parlors, showing a combination of elements: heavily carved Javanese furniture and screens; velvet draperies and carpets from Europe; stuffed animals; collections of Javanese *krises* (daggers) alongside Chinese porcelain; Japanese lacquer work; and portraits of members of the House of Orange on the walls.[18]

In illustration of increasing social exchange between the upper classes of European and Javanese communities is the solicitation of the local bupati or the sultan and their consorts as patrons of clubs for the Dutch. There were also the contributions from the Indonesian side to Dutch charitable causes. For instance, a fancy fair in aid of impoverished Eurasians was organized by the bupati of Semarang in August 1904. A string orchestra played pieces by Verdi and Rubinstein. The players, according to the *Locomotief,* were all members of the royal family of Solo and proved that Indonesians had aptitude for ''the musical conceptions of European composers.''[19] This local report suggests the extent and scope of deliberate borrowing on the part of Java's upper classes. Such borrowing from the customs of the colonials made them appear to be like their counterparts in Eurasian society.

Opposition to these trends, and anxiety, was the response of Europeans concerned about ''white status.'' They had always expressed themselves through the newspapers on the need to inculcate the virtue of hard work in Javanese laborers, whom they predictably saw as slothful. When it came to the upper classes, Dutch responses took a different turn. They knew enough of Javanese social codes and etiquette to introduce a variation of their own: addressing a Western-educated Javanese in Dutch, but permitting responses only in Malay or High Javanese. In the matter of social contacts, it was natural that such enemies of the Javanese should first object to encounters between Indonesian men and European women and blame the women for ''uppityness'' in Javanese men. From the many examples in the papers, one must suffice.

It concerned editorial discussion of a letter criticizing European ladies for accompanying their husbands to the rooms of Solo's Habiprojo, a club for Javanese government servants who were, in 1904, all men. One female guest had, on a later occasion, been ''accosted'' by an Indonesian whom she had met at the club and who had offered to escort her, this frightful exchange taking place in the language of the colonial rulers. In concluding remarks, the editor urged that serious thought be given to the question whether the prestige of European ladies was affected by their transgressing the rules of propriety governing the behavior of aristocratic Indonesian women.[20]

This incident is noteworthy for another reason too. Not only does it show an apprehension concerning interracial relations and European "prestige"; it also illustrates the function of the waning Mestizo culture as a middle, mediating arena between European and Indonesian. It will be remembered that at the turn of the century over three-quarters of the Europeans on Java had been born there, and that locally born women with European status still far outnumbered female immigrants. Consequently the wives of many officials were Creoles or part-Indonesians who in their early years had been raised almost exclusively by Indonesians. What this meant for colonial society was that receptions in 1900 were still segregated between the sexes. Ladies sat together in an inner parlor, the men outside in the front gallery. This was the way a proper Eurasian woman was raised and the way she conducted parties as mistress of a household. Thus when upper-class Javanese women became customary guests in the houses of their European counterparts, the break with traditional seclusion was already cushioned. They were not left in a drawing room crowded with men after formal greetings had been exchanged, but rather led to a room with women who sat, as in any kabupaten, according to their husbands' rank. Mestizo codes also allowed for distinct entertainments in different areas for the various groups of guests. For Europeans there would be champagne and a waltz band in a pavilion isolated from the sitting rooms, and elsewhere a gamelan would play and guests would arrange themselves before and behind the screen of the puppet theater according to rank and sex.[21]

Mestizo manners had ceased to dictate public behavior by the second and third decades of this century. By that time immigrants had clustered in cities in sufficient numbers to order their lives as nearly as they could in the Dutch manner. Furthermore, while the number of immigrant men and women remained small in proportion to the total European community in the Indies, yet they dominated the upper levels of government and society and they set the tastes and fashions for the rest.

The Indonesian upper classes were left to reconsider the experience of the preceding few generations. Whilst superficially they appeared most like wealthy Indies Dutch, they too were withdrawing into their own society and concentrating on defining an "Indonesian" identity. For the bupatis like Djajadiningrat, this was accomplished through the Regentenbond and through a campaign to impose adherence to the principle of sons succeeding their fathers in the office of bupati. The debates of the Regentenbond were conducted in Dutch and were predicated on a continuing association with the Netherlands within a commonwealth. By contrast, out of the debates of the youth associations representing the lower ranks of the Javanese aristocracy and young people of Indonesia's other ethnic groups there developed the goal of a state independent of any ties to the Dutch. In 1928 they made the seemingly perverse choice of Malay, pidgin of the VOC and tongue used to degrade, as the language of the new nation they aspired to form. Malay was, at the same time, becoming the language of a new, Indonesian, colonial literature that was as single-mindedly devoted to reform as any Dutch-language Indies novel of our women writers.

Only the problems were different. Where Dutch female authors spoke of abandoned children and concubines, Indonesian authors wrote of the alienating effects of Western education and how to overcome them. They wrote of conflicts between the behavior expected by Indonesian customary law and Islam and the manners acquired from Dutch schools and European friends. There were the evils of polygyny and child marriage to be combatted through the novel, and the sensitive subject of cross-racial marriage as well as of marriage between Indonesians of widely separated social classes and different ethnic groups.[22]

All these issues were debated in the 1920s and '30s. Parallel developments in the political arena can be briefly related. By 1908 an association of distinguished, Western-educated Javanese had been formed. Under the name *Budi Utomo,* which is often translated as "Glorious Endeavor," they sought a revival of Javanese culture, but—and this is an instance of seeming "Mestizoness"—through a society run on European rules with committee chairmen and the rest. Within the next few years, others joined together in similarly organized bodies, taking as the key to their band their common ethnic or religious identity. By 1922, some were ready to merge the local and regional for an association based on an Indonesia-wide identity. Simultaneously there was a movement winning adherents primarily among Eurasians. With several prominent Indonesians, they joined in an "Indies homeland" party. That aspiration was defeated, and the several communities withdrew into parties representing the chief social and political divisions of the colony in the 1930s: Indonesian nationalist parties, aiming for political independence; Eurasian parties, which would give leadership of an independent Indies to the part-European; the parties of immigrant Europeans that in the late 1930s were fascist and based on race supremacy; and organizations for two groups omitted from discussion here, the immigrant Chinese and the Indonesian Chinese. (The latter was another "Mestizo" group that was known under the Indonesian term *peranakan,* or mixed race.)

Membership in all these groups apparently became more fixed and the plural aspects of colonial society more fully developed in the 1930s. In evidence are the separate pay scales, occupation slots, law codes, and education systems. All the same, there was "passing" from one community to the other. In the case of movement into Asian groups there are no figures. The passage across race lines into the European group is, however, open for inspection.

169

It remained exceedingly mixed. The Constitutional Law of 1818 had included in the European category all Christian Indonesians who had joined the European group socially. By 1854, however, a new regulation specifically excluded Christian Indonesians from enjoying privileges reserved for the European community. Henceforth they would be counted among the indigenous Indonesian population.[23] After 1871 individual Asians could apply for European status. This was conferred by administrative decree on those who were Christian, used Dutch as their daily language, dressed as Europeans, and were "Dutch" in manners and occupation.[24] Finally, in 1886, all who lived as "Europeans" and were regarded as such by their associates were confirmed in that status.[25]

The extremely mixed nature of the group with European status, persisting during the period when colonial society was apparently the most plural, is best illustrated by figures collected by A. van Marle. In explaining the increase in the European group over the period 1881 to 1940 from causes other than immigation, he presents the following numbers: legal assimilation (gelijkstelling), 16,500; mixed marriage (for example, counting an Asian bride as European), 16,000; offspring of mixed marriages, 29,000; recognition of illegitimate, part-Asian children, 48,000; and Creoles, 210,000.[26]

The Japanese occupation of the Indonesian archipelago (1942–45) made all that meaningless. Henceforth there were only Indonesians, Asians born outside the archipelago, and Europeans. Europeans were interned for most of the Pacific war, their number including all those Eurasians who remained attached to their special status as Europeans. World war was followed by a national revolution whose outcome, in 1949, was an Indonesian republic independent of political ties to the Netherlands. Once again Mestizos were faced with a choice: to apply for citizenship of Indonesia and accept the Indonesian side of their heritage or to take up a new future overseas. Many persisted in preferring identity as Dutch, and they scattered across the world, principally to Holland and the United States. Another group had made a brief experiment in founding a Eurasian homeland in West New Guinea, one that had ended, for all practical purposes, with the Second World War. It ended as a dream when West New Guinea was incorporated in the Republic of Indonesia in 1963, first as Irian Barat and later under the name Irian Jaya. One other Mestizo society in the archipelago that had been cut off for three centuries from the Dutch through Portuguese rule, and that had developed its own distinctive culture, is now being absorbed into Indonesia as the twenty-seventh province, Timor Timur.

Thus ended Mestizo society. Its special character as a fusion of East and West under the status of European is no more; its legacy remains as one element in the national and regional cultures of Indonesia.

We have now traced the social life of the Dutch, from earliest days in port cities on the coasts of Asia, through development of settled community life in enclaves with a distinctive culture, to a period characterized by direct rule over a territorial empire stretching out to the limits of the Indonesian archipelago. We have watched a condition of isolation and uncertainty be replaced by a network of communities from southern Africa to Japan whose members were linked by marriage and position in the VOC hierarchy and whose daily life was imbued with Asian practices. In turn, we have seen this network dismembered, and a new separation between European and Asian worlds develop in the nineteenth century, based on government policies of plural development and influenced by technological advances and demographic changes in the makeup of the dominant immigrant group.

In the earliest days, the Dutch struggled to establish for themselves a niche in the ports along the Asian trade routes. Their arrival caused no upheaval in the cultural life of the Asian states; they were probably regarded by the royal court of Mataram as one more troublesome and vulgar species of tribute-bearer. Life in the early settlements may be characterized as tumultuous: bachelor communities cut off from their homeland by the vast distances of sea, menaced by tropical diseases whose remedies were not yet known, and vulnerable to attack from Asian states and their European allies who were hostile to Dutch economic aims. Attitudes to Asian peoples in this period were of the coarsest kind. Unions with Asian women, in the absence of a normal proportion of women among the European immigrants and in the absence of the institutions of civic life, were disorderly and exploitative.

The impulse to transform adventurers into citizens very quickly asserted itself, and the development of municipal life took place within walled, fortified cities. Attempts at colonization by sending out batches of families and or-phaned girls or giving permission to those with rank in the merchant hierarchy of the Company to bring out their wives and other female relatives never provided enough women for the growth of colonies of Dutch families. Miscegenation was officially sanctioned by the Company by 1642 and was practised on all social levels but particularly the most senior. By contrast, unions with Asian women formed by the largest component of the European group, the soldiers and sailors, were often irregular and fleeting, despite efforts by the VOC's directors to keep in the settlements those men who had married local women and fathered children there. Children abandoned by the father were usually absorbed by the Asian community to which the mother belonged.

On the other hand, among the elite there developed a peculiar family pattern and system of descent. Characteristically, a man delayed marriage (as opposed to concubinage) until he had risen in the merchant ranks of the civilian hierarchy. His marriage partner was usually the Asia-born daughter of a colleague, a girl barely in her teens if it was her first marriage, the product of a secluded upbringing supervised by Asian slaves, in which styles of dress, personal

171

hygiene, training, entertainment, and language were all Asian and Asia-derived. Such women were themselves part-Asian by descent as well as by upbringing and culture. Their daughters were kept in Asia as brides for new generations of immigrants, while their sons were sent to the Netherlands to make their careers and livelihood. Despite years of residence, then, men did not command patriarchal families nor did the Indies Dutch become landowning gentry attached to property held within the same family over generations. Promotion to positions of power and wealth came to men connected to each other through their wives.

In the VOC centuries many men succumbed to disease, their resistance lowered by their clinging to clothing and hygiene more suitable for northern Europe and by their intemperate use of alcohol. Women, living more nearly according to Asian styles and often being many years junior to their husbands, tended to survive them. In these conditions there was pressure to remarry, especially when the widow was the sole inheritor of marital property. Some women married two and three times, so soon consoling themselves that Batavia's government adopted, for regulation of European behavior, a Koranic law observed by Indonesians that forbade remarriage by women before three months of widowhood had elapsed.

In this, as in many other instances, the Dutch showed themselves profoundly influenced by the Asian context of their lives. The position of women with European status is another example, for the semi-purdah of women showed accommodation to Muslim and Hindu-derived notions of female propriety and stood against the Calvinist model of virtuous housewife and mother in society. The seigneurial style of living of senior Company officials on country estates, where the officials were surrounded by slave retainers and took rights to corvée labor from the local population, owed more to the Javanese nobility than to the style of the respectable classes of eighteenth-century Netherlands society.

It is interesting to note that before the nineteenth century there was little intellectual exchange between Dutch and Indonesian. Senior representatives of the Dutch did not impress the Javanese nobility as bearers of a higher civilization, as they were to do in the late colonial period. The origins and status of the VOC Dutch were regarded with contempt, and this prevented their mixing, in their brief encounters with court members, on terms of equality. During the first two centuries of contact, then, the Dutch were not able to influence Java's nobility, nor were they qualified by their own education to admire the culture of the Indonesian courts.

The greatest contact Dutch people had with Asians was with the subject populations of their settlements, who were themselves also generally members of dispossessed social groups. Intellectual exchange between the two was necessarily limited. Moreover, in considering mutual influence, the intimacy that existed between European men and Asian women in the settlements must

172

be balanced against the inequality of their status and rights. The Asian context was predominant in determining how the immigrant Dutch lived, and in the Asian settlements the cultural forms transmitted by the Dutch were few. Despite directives from successive governors-general, the Asian majorities of Dutch cities never became Dutch speakers or Christians. What was Dutch was the public architecture of the cities and their layout, and the male life of the government office.

Mestizo society took on folkways of its own. It was neither European nor Asian, nor was it static. By the second half of the eighteenth century there appeared a trend towards development of patriarchal families, and a desire to cut remaining ties with Europe. As it turned out, the VOC directors were fairly successful in enforcing the rule that denied senior office to the locally born and so prevented the development of independent colonies, but the impulse towards such a development is discernible. The destruction of these ambitions and of the Mestizo alliance of position and family connection was quick and complete. It sprang, not out of the history of the Dutch in Indonesia, but from the history of Netherlands society in Europe, a society that had been transformed by the French Revolution and Napoleonic Empire. Earlier pressures on Mestizo society—described under the rubrics "Enlightenment," "Interregnum," which are drawn from European history —can best be seen as assaults on Mestizo society that could not succeed because not aimed at the nexus of post and family alliance.

New barriers to cultural comprehension, formed in the nineteenth century, sharpened by a heightened sense of race. The separation was encouraged by the formation in the European community of families on the Dutch model, as women emigrated in increasing numbers. Mestizo culture had always been the medium through which Dutch and Indonesian came to know each other. When it was under attack, new gulfs opened up, for there was no substitution for the old immediacy of contact. The very factors which improved the quality of Dutch life in Indonesia—the links to other communities and to Europe provided by rail, telegraph, newspaper, library, and the like—all combined to foster self-sufficient communities among the immigrants who now dominated the top level of the government hierarchy. These same conditions served to foster new identities among Indonesian groups that were to be drawn in sharp opposition to the colonial regime as the twentieth century opened.

Within the European group in the nineteenth century, the elite were divorced from the mass. The ranks of senior officials ceased to be occupied by men who spent the greatest part of their lives in Asia and who married Asia-born women. Now members of the elite were immigrants and transients. Mestizo culture became more closely associated with lower socioeconomic classes; members became a distinct subgroup within the European, marrying amongst themselves. Absorption into the Indonesian world followed on poverty or a total separation from the European community and its badge of status, white skin color.

Nevertheless, the Dutch in Indonesia remained exceedingly mixed. Members of the new elite boasted of their European identity, yet were not European in the manner of compatriots who did not emigrate. Their lives were passed in a tropical setting where they were a privileged minority ruling a majority who had no say in their governance. In this situation, sexual exploitation and irresponsibility of male immigrants towards Indonesian women servants and their offspring were condoned. European women, as wives, had to deal with that indulgence and the social problems that followed. Because they, in their time, were not yet political members of European society, their views were expressed first through the colonial novel, before the issues of concubinage and deserted children were taken up by the male members of the Netherlands' States-General. In their novels, Dutch women authors revealed an aspect of colonial life that is normally hidden from view.

In the rural areas we see Mestizo society evolving anew in the same conditions of isolation and union of Dutch immigrant men with Indonesian women, but it was different from the society of the VOC days. For one thing, the immigrants were now more likely to be planters and private entrepreneurs, with only a minority representing the Batavian government. For another, a European reference group was now closer at hand, and there was no avenue for political life or the need for secure connections, when men could pursue wealth openly and legally. Assimilation towards the Indonesian side was a greater pull for Eurasian men, and the marriage partners of Eurasian women were more likely to be lower-ranking Dutchmen or men from the Eurasian community.

In the twentieth century events overtook Dutch society of the Indies. No longer the self-contained zone of the VOC centuries, colonial society was split within and subjected to pressures from without—from the Netherlands and increasingly from Indonesian groups that sought to take over the seat of power in Batavia for themselves. Once the ultimate claim to status for the Eurasian was severed, the tie to the European and the prestige of race, Mestizo society as a separate entity could not endure. It disappeared in 1942 to live on only in the sentimental evocations of the *Tempo Doeloe* writers and recorders.

Reference Matter

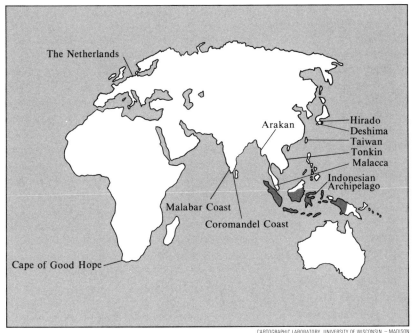

CARTOGRAPHIC LABORATORY, UNIVERSITY OF WISCONSIN – MADISON

1. The Netherlands and VOC Asia

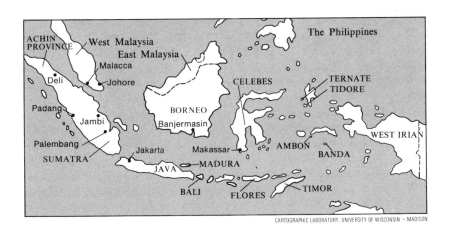

CARTOGRAPHIC LABORATORY, UNIVERSITY OF WISCONSIN – MADISON

2. The Indonesian Archipelago

177

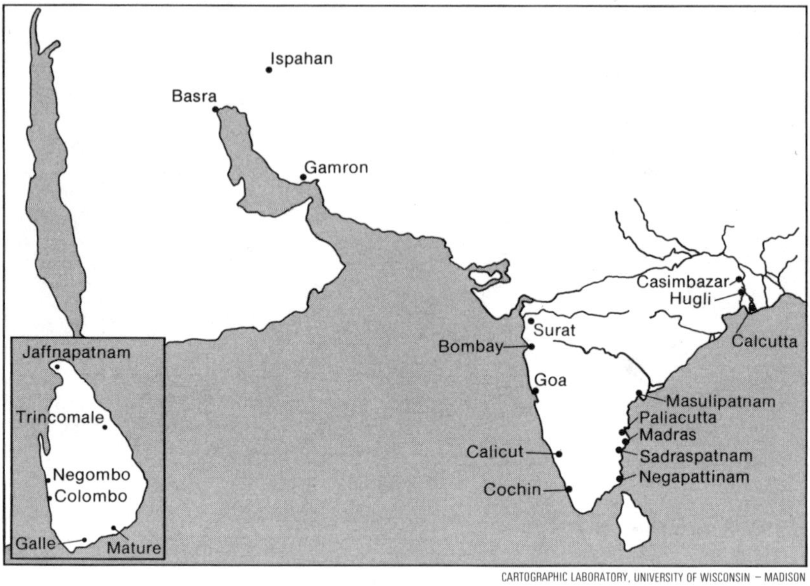
Ispahan
Basra
Gamron
Casimbazar
Hugli
Calcutta
Surat
Bombay
Goa
Masulipatnam
Paliacutta
Madras
Sadraspatnam
Negapattinam
Calicut
Cochin
Jaffnapatnam
Trincomale
Negombo
Colombo
Galle
Mature
CARTOGRAPHIC LABORATORY, UNIVERSITY OF WISCONSIN – MADISON

3. VOC Trading Posts in India and Ceylon. Adapted from end map, W. Wijnaendts van Resandt, *De gezaghebbers der Oost-Indische Compagnie*.

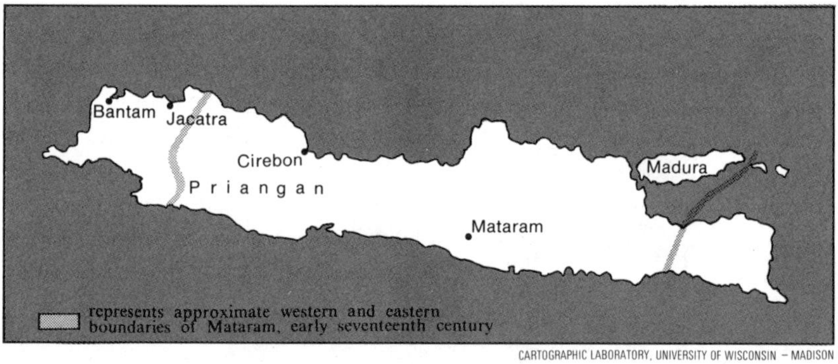
Bantam
Jacatra
Cirebon
Priangan
Madura
Mataram
represents approximate western and eastern boundaries of Mataram, early seventeenth century
CARTOGRAPHIC LABORATORY, UNIVERSITY OF WISCONSIN – MADISON

4. Java, Early Seventeenth Century

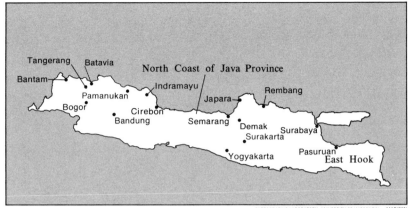

5.   Java, Eighteenth Century

179

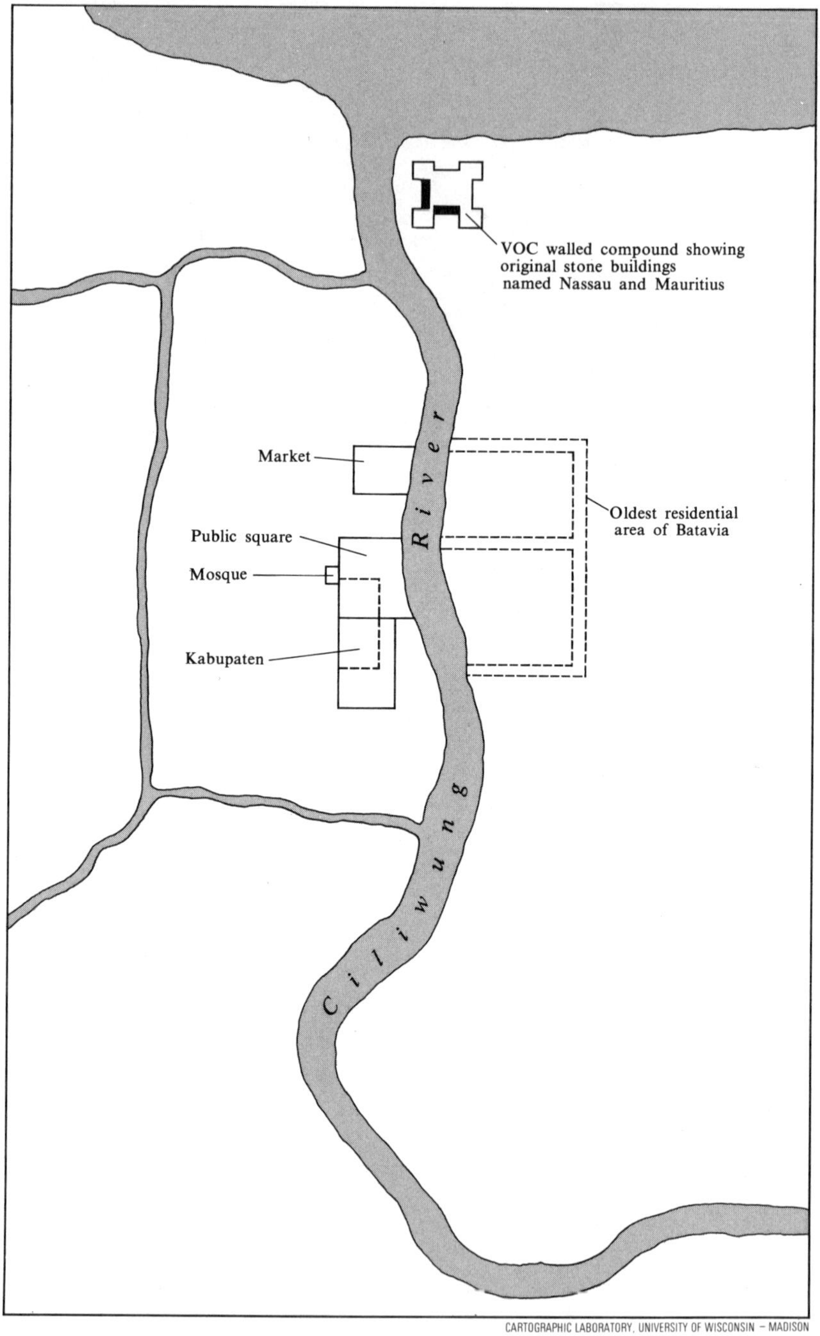
VOC walled compound showing original stone buildings named Nassau and Mauritius
Market
Oldest residential area of Batavia
Public square
Mosque
Kabupaten
Ciliwung River
CARTOGRAPHIC LABORATORY, UNIVERSITY OF WISCONSIN – MADISON

6. Jacatra, 1619. Adapted from H. A. Breuning, *Het voormalige Batavia*, Fig. 1.

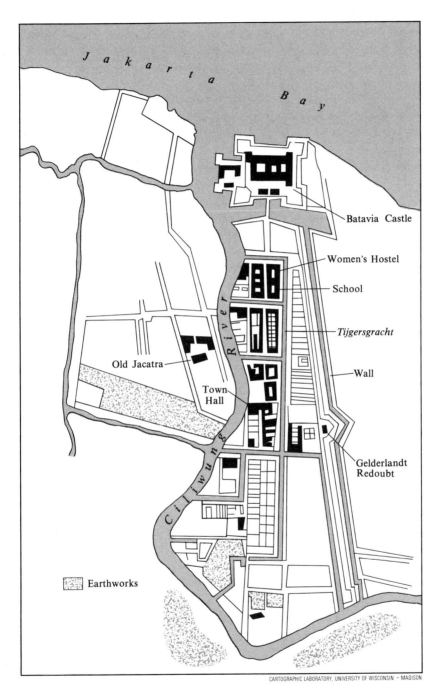

Batavia Castle

Women's Hostel

School

Tijgersgracht

Old Jacatra

Wall

Town
Hall

Gelderlandt
Redoubt

Earthworks

7.   Batavia, 1627. Adapted from H. A. Breuning, *Het voormalige Batavia*, Fig. 5.

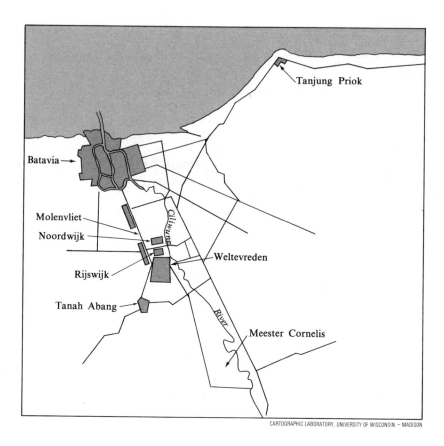

Tanjung Priok

Batavia →

Molenvliet

Noordwijk

Ciliwung

Rijswijk

Tanah Abang

Weltevreden

River

Meester Cornelis

8. Batavia and southern suburbs, early nineteenth century. Adapted from H. A. Breuning, *Het voormalige Batavia*, Fig. 12.

Appendix 1

Family Trees

The genealogical tables in this appendix are not complete, but chart only certain lines that have been selected to show family alliances and descent and marriage patterns. The following are included:

1. Van der Parra Family
2. Alting Family
3. Van Riemsdijk Family, part 1
4. Baud-Senn van Basel Family
5. Huysman-van Imhoff Families
6. Descendants of Sophia Fauconier
7. Cranssen Descendants
8. Coop à Groen Family
9. Van Riemsdijk Family, part 2

Tables 1, 2, 4, 5, 6, and 7 should be read vertically, and tables 3, 8, and 9 horizontally. The abbreviations used are as follows:

b.	born
d.	died
m.	married
–	liaison
betr.	betrothed
T	born in Europe
C	Creole
GG	governor-general

Table 1. VAN DER PARRA FAMILY
Descent in the Male Line

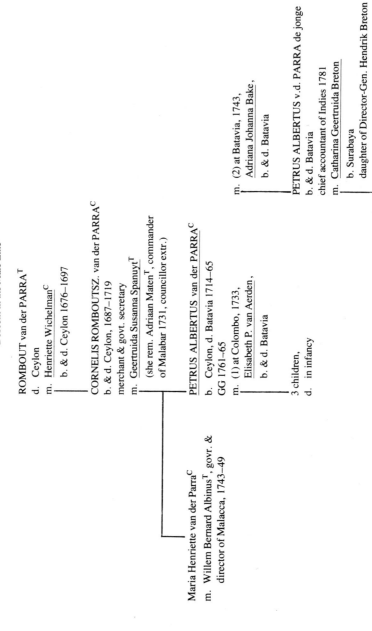

ROMBOUT van der PARRA[T]
d.   Ceylon
m.   Henriette Wichelman[C]
    b. & d. Ceylon 1676–1697

CORNELIS ROMBOUTSZ. van der PARRA[C]
b. & d. Ceylon, 1687–1719
merchant & govt. secretary
m.   Geertruida Susanna Spanuyt[T]
(she rem. Adriaan Maten[T], commander
of Malabar 1731, councillor extr.)

PETRUS ALBERTUS van der PARRA[C]
b.   Ceylon, d. Batavia 1714–65
GG 1761–65
m.   (1) at Colombo, 1733,
Elisabeth P. van Aerden,
b. & d. Batavia

3 children,
d.   in infancy

m.   (2) at Batavia, 1743,
Adriana Johanna Bake,
b. & d. Batavia

PETRUS ALBERTUS v.d. PARRA de jonge
b. & d. Batavia
chief accountant of Indies 1781
m.   Catharina Geertruida Breton
b. Surabaya
daughter of Director-Gen. Hendrik Breton

many descendants in Java

Maria Henriette van der Parra[C]
m.   Willem Bernard Albinus[T], govr. &
director of Malacca, 1743–49

184

Bake Antecedents and Some In-Laws

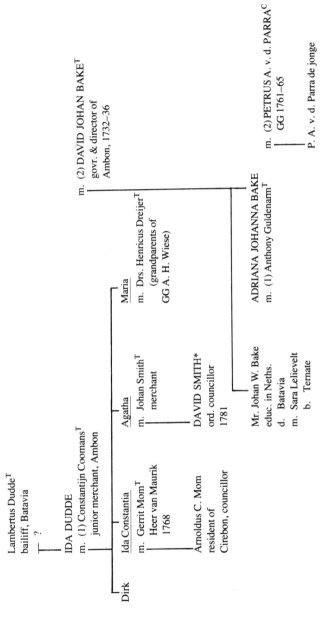

* Smith's first marriage connected the governor-general to Ordinary Councillor Michiel Romp and Councillor Extr. J. R. van der Burgh.

185

Table 2. ALTING FAMILY
Descent and Offices through First Marriage

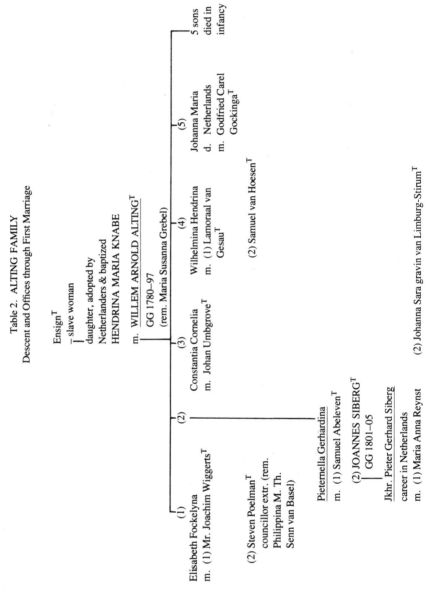

Second Marriage of GG Alting

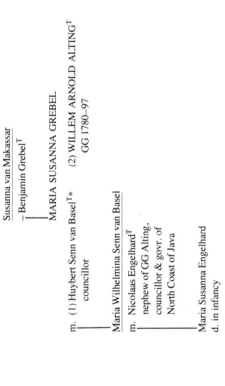

Susanna van Makassar
– Benjamin Grebel[T]

MARIA SUSANNA GREBEL

m. (1) Huybert Senn van Basel[T]*   (2) WILLEM ARNOLD ALTING[T]
        councillor   GG 1780–97

Maria Wilhelmina Senn van Basel

m. Nicolaas Engelhard[T]
    nephew of GG Alting,
    councillor & govr. of
    North Coast of Java

Maria Susanna Engelhard
d. in infancy

* Huybert Senn van Basel's son Willem Adriaan, from his first marriage, brought into the family members of the van Riemsdijk and Wiese clans through his second and third marriages.

Table 3. VAN RIEMSDIJK FAMILY, part 1: Jeremias van Riemsdijk
(for part 2 see table 9)

JEREMIAS v. RIEMSDIJK[T]
1712–77
GG 1775–77

m. 1738 (1) Martina van den Briel 1720–41
1. Helena Johanna, 1741–46

m. 1744 (2) Cornelia van Vianen 1730–47
2. Scipio Cornelis, 1745
3. Cornelia Catharina, 1747
4. Mr. Isebrandus Johannes F. van Riemsdijk (raised in Netherlands, m. & d. there)

m. 1748 (3) Maria Lucretia Wentink ?–1750
5. Johanna Maria, 1750–70
   m. Paulus Godefridus van der Voort[T]

m. 1751 (4) Adriana Louisa Helvetius 1736–72
6. Unnamed, 1751
7. Willem Vincent Helvetius v. Riemsdijk
   m. Catharina Margaretha Craan
8. Egidia Cornelia, 1754–56
9. Adriaan Cornelis, 1755–58
10. Catharina Louysa, 1758–1823
    m. Mr. Arnoldus Constantijn Mom[T]
11. Daniel Frederik, 1760–84
    m. Bartha Johanna Schultz
12. Scipio Cornelis, 1761–81
    m. Laurentia Jacoba Schultz
13. Jeremias Egidius, 1763–68
14. Adriaan Jacob, 1766
15. Unnamed, 1767
16. Johanna Adriana, 1770–80

m. 1774 (5) Theodora Rotgers ?–1777

188

Table 4. BAUD-SENN VAN BASEL FAMILY
Indies Family in the Male Line

<u>JEAN-CHRETIEN BAUD</u>[T]
GG 1833–36

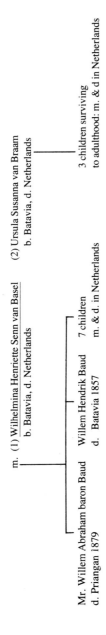

m. (1) Wilhelmina Henriette Senn van Basel   (2) Ursula Susanna van Braam
    b. Batavia, d. Netherlands   b. Batavia, d. Netherlands

Willem Hendrik Baud   7 children   3 children surviving
d. Batavia 1857   m. & d. in Netherlands   to adulthood: m. & d in Netherlands

Mr. Willem Abraham baron Baud
d. Priangan 1879

Table 4, *continued*

Descent through the Female Line

Direct Female Descent	Maternal Line
Margaretha Sophia Ongewassen descended from Eurasian family in Ceylon	?
m. Cornelis Breekpot[T]	soldier[T]
Johanna Henriette Breekpot	daughter baptized as
b. Japara	Johanna Magdalena de Bollan
m. Jacobus Johannes Craan[C], 1753	m. Johannes Maurits van Happel[T]
Catharina Margaretha Craan	Anna Catharina van Happel
m. Willem Vincent Helvetius van Riemsdijk, 1773	m. Mr. Laurens Tolling[T]
	councillor
	Egidia Cornelia Tolling
	m. Mr. Willem Vincent Helvetius[T]
	justice at Batavia
	Adriana Louisa Helvetius
	m. Jeremias van Riemsdijk[T]
	GG 1775–77
Theodora Jacoba van Riemsdijk	Willem Vincent Helvetius van Riemsdijk
m. Willem Adriaan Senn van Basel	councillor
	m. Catharina Margaretha Craan
	Theodora Jacoba van Riemsdijk
	m. Willem Adriaan Senn van Basel
	councillor
Wilhelmina Henriette Senn van Basel	Wilhelmina Henriette Senn van Basel
m. Jean-Chrétien Baud[T]	m. Jean-Chrétien Baud[T]
female descendants m. & d. in Netherlands	7 of 9 descendants m. & d. in Netherlands

Table 5. HUYSMAN-VAN IMHOFF FAMILIES
showing Indies family passing offices to sons in subsidiary settlements

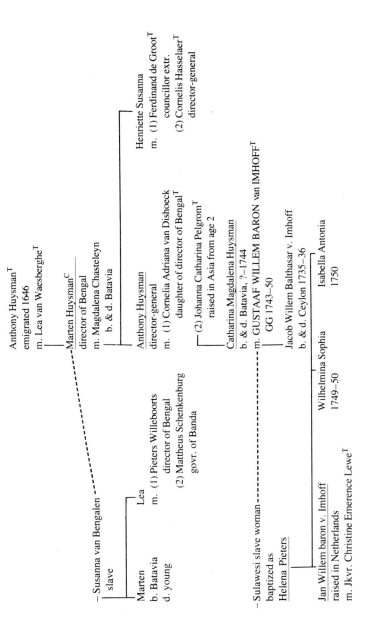

Table 6. DESCENDANTS OF SOPHIA FAUCONIER
showing marriage alliances within ruling class

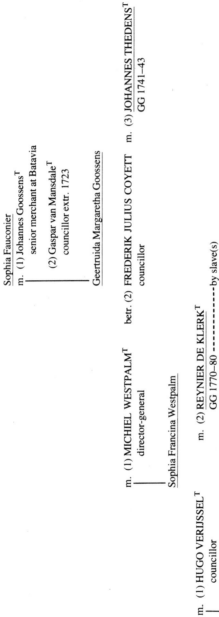

Sophia Fauconier
m. (1) Johannes Goossens[T]
     senior merchant at Batavia

(2) Gaspar van Mansdale[T]
    councillor extr. 1723

Geertruida Margaretha Goossens

betr. (2) FREDERIK JULIUS COYETT   m. (3) JOHANNES THEDENS[T]
    councillor   GG 1741–43

m. (1) MICHIEL WESTPALM[T]   m. (2) REYNIER DE KLERK[T]
    director-general   GG 1770–80 -----------by slave(s)

Sophia Francina Westpalm

Willem Cornelis   Wilhelmina Cornelia
educ. in Neths.

m. (1) HUGO VERIJSSEL[T]
    councillor

Margaretha Sophia Verijssel
m. Jacobus C. M. Radermacher[T]
    (rem. Anna Bosch, stepdaughter of
    Councillor David Smith

Frans Radermacher
sent to Neths. at 12

Table 7. CRANSSEN DESCENDANTS
showing descent through legitimate and illegitimate lines

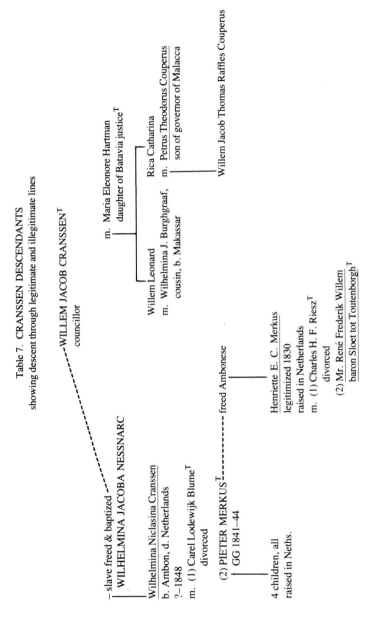

Table 8. COOP A GROEN FAMILY

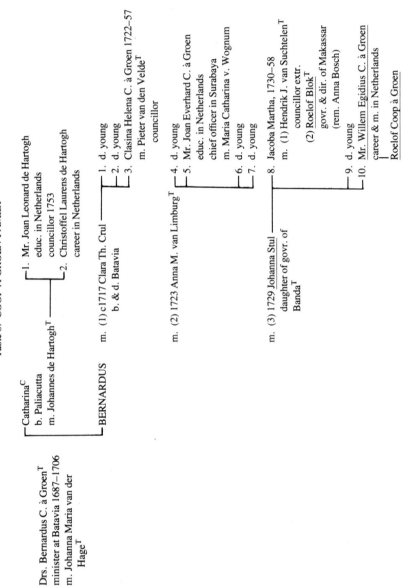

Drs. Bernardus C. à Groen[T]
minister at Batavia 1687–1706
m. Johanna Maria van der
Hage[T]

Catharina[C]
b. Paliacutta
m. Johannes de Hartogh[T]

1. Mr. Joan Leonard de Hartogh
   educ. in Netherlands
   councillor 1753
2. Christoffel Laurens de Hartogh
   career in Netherlands

BERNARDUS   m. (1) c1717 Clara Th. Crul
                     b. & d. Batavia

1. d. young
2. d. young
3. Clasina Helena C. à Groen 1722–57
   m. Pieter van den Velde[T]
   councillor

m. (2) 1723 Anna M. van Limburg[T]

4. d. young
5. Mr. Joan Everhard C. à Groen
   educ. in Netherlands
   chief officer in Surabaya
   m. Maria Catharina v. Wognum
6. d. young
7. d. young

m. (3) 1729 Johanna Stul
       daughter of govr. of
       Banda[T]

8. Jacoba Martha, 1730–58
   m. (1) Hendrik J. van Suchtelen[T]
          councillor extr.
      (2) Roelof Blok[T]
          govr. & dir. of Makassar
          (rem. Anna Bosch)
9. d. young
10. Mr. Willem Egidius C. à Groen
    career & m. in Netherlands
    |
    Roelof Coop à Groen
    Govr. of Banda & Ternate

194

Table 9. VAN RIEMSDIJK FAMILY, part 2: Willem Vincent Helvetius van Riemsdijk
(for part 1 see table 3)

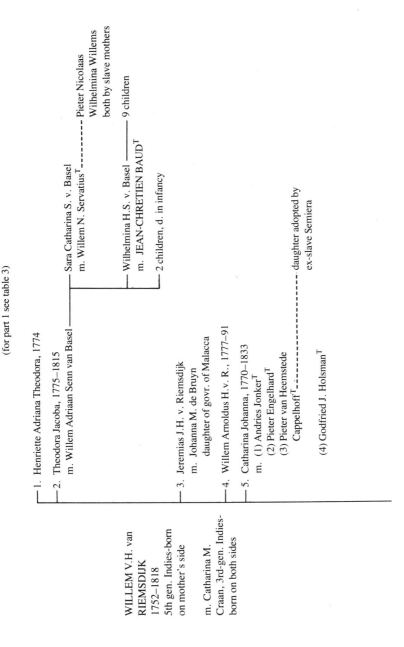

Table 9, *continued*

W.V.H. van
RIEMSDIJK
m. Catharina
Craan

6. Pieter W.H. v. R., 1780–1857
   m. Sophia Cornelia Bangeman
   - 3 children, d. in infancy
   - Willem H.H. v. Riemsdijk
   - Catharina Johanna Reiniera
     m. (1) Folkert J. ten Cate[T] —— 4 children
        (2) Gerrit J. van Capelle —— 1 child
   - Sophia Catharina
     m. Pieter van Swieten[T] —— 13 children

7. Jacobus J.H. v. R., 1782–1854
   m. Johanna M. van Alken

8. Daniel C.H. v. R., 1783–1860
   – Mea
   later baptized Christina
   Simans
   - Dina Cornelia, 1807–77
     m. Tjalling Ament[T] —— 9 children
   - Sophia Wilhelmina
     m. Carel M. Visser[T] —— 9 children
   - Catharina Petronella
     m. Willem Martinus Kijdsmeir —— 8 children
        cousin

9. W.V.H. v. Riemsdijk de jonge
   1784–1847
   m. Wilhelmina M.R. Martens

10. Scipio I.H. v. R.
    – Bamie
    – Manies van Bali
    - Maria Susanna van Riemsdijk
    - Sophia C. Kijdsmeir
      m. Willem J. van de Graaff[T] —— 2 children
    - Willem M. Kijdsmeir
      m. Catharina P. v. Riemsdijk —— 8 children

Table 9, *continued*

W.V.H. van
RIEMSDIJK
m. Catharina
Craan

10. Scipio I.H. v. R.
    – Manies v. Bali (contd.)

Abraham P. Kijdsmeir
– Bibiet - - - - - - - - 1 son, stillborn
– Saiba - - - - - - - - - 1 daughter
Jacoba Mariana, d. young
Theodora M. Kijdsmeir ————— 2 children
m. Gideon M. van de Graaff[T]
Catharina J. Kijdsmeir ————— 4 children
m. Dr. Geerlof Wassink[T]
Scipio I. Kijdsmeir, d. young

11. Adriana Hendriette L. 1787–1878
    m. Jan M. van Beusechem[T]
12. Ignatia Cornelia M. 1789–1816 ————— 1 daughter, d. young
    m. Gerhardus van Rijck
13. Adriaan Frederik, 1791–93
14. Egidius Arnoldus, 1792

– Misschien van Batavia - - - -15. Jan Joseph Kijdsmeir
    adopted 1812
–Ramoena van Soembawa - -16. Jan Sam, 1805–?
    adopted 1814
17. Wilhelmina Rosina, 1807–72
    adopted
    daughter of Klaas Jager & ?
    m. (1) Albert N. Coblyn[T]
       (2) Jkhr. Edward L. Leyssius[T]

Table 9, *continued*

W.V.H. van
RIEMSDIJK

- Dekkan van Mandhaar ----- 18. Lieve Benjamin(s), 1812–65
  - Antje -------------------------------- 1 daughter
    m. Arira, baptized
       Christina Willemse ————————— 12 children

- Oranina van Batavia ----- 19. Oranina Bloemenstiena, 1813–54 ——— 11 children
  m. Friederich N. von Ende[T]

- Dekkan van Mandhaar ----- 20. Wilhelmus D. Benjamins, 1815–58
  m. (1) Frederica W.G. Kemper ——— 9 children
     (2) Petronella J. Coblyn[T] ——— 2 children

- Mietje van Mandhaar ----- 21. Maria Catharina, 1815–88 ——————— 9 children
  m. Frederik H.C. van Motman

198

Appendix 2

Governors-General and Their Wives

1610–14   PIETER BOTH
           wife did not emigrate

1614–15   GERARD REYNST
           Margaretha Nicquet

1616–19   Dr. LAURENS REAEL
           bachelor

1619–23   JAN PIETERSZOON COEN
           bachelor

1623–27   PIETER DE CARPENTIER
           bachelor

1627–29   JAN PIETERSZOON COEN
           Eva Ment

1629–32   JACQUES SPECX
           Jkvr. Maria Odilia Buys

1632–36   HENDRIK BROUWER
           Cecilia van Dorp

1636–45   ANTONIO VAN DIEMEN
           Maria van Aelst, m. in Batavia

1645–50   CORNELIS VAN DER LIJN
           Levijntje Polet, m. in Batavia

1650–53   CAREL REYNIERSZ.
           Judith Bara
           Françoise de Wit, b. India

1653–78   Mr. JOAN MAETSUYKER
           Haasje Berkmans
           Elisabeth Abbema, m. in Batavia

1678–81   RIJCKLOF VAN GOENS
           Jacomina Bartholomeusdr. Rosegaard, m. at Batavia
           Esther de Solemne, b. India
           Johanna van Ommeren, m. in Batavia

1681–84   CORNELIS SPEELMAN
           Petronella Maria Wonderaer, b. Batavia

1684–91   JOANNES CAMPHUYS
           bachelor

1691–1704 Mr. WILLEM VAN OUTHOORN, Creole
           Elisabeth van Heijningen, m. in Batavia

1704–9   JOAN VAN HOORN
           Anna Struijs, b. Batavia
           Susanna Agneta van Outhoorn, b. Batavia
           Johanna Maria van Riebeeck, b. Batavia

1709–13   Mr. ABRAHAM VAN RIEBEECK, Creole
           Elisabeth van Oosten, m. in Batavia

1713–18   CHRISTOFFEL VAN SWOLL
           Geliana van Swoll?

1718–25   HENRICUS ZWAARDECROON
           ?

1725–29   MATTHEUS DE HAAN
           Francina Thivart, m. in Asia
           Catharina Lurelius, m. in Asia

1729–32   Mr. DIEDERIK DURVEN
           Jacoba van Breda, m. in Asia
           Anna Catharina de Roo, b. Asia

1732–35   Mr. DIRK VAN CLOON, Eurasian
           Anthonia Adriana Lengele, b. in Asia

1735–37   ABRAHAM PATRAS
           N. van Brakel, m. in Ambon
           (some sources give wife as Gehasia Cnipping)

1737–41   ADRIAAN VALCKENIER
           Johanna Alida Tolling, b. Batavia
           Susanna Christina Massis, b. Batavia

1741–43   JOHANNES THEDENS
           Anna Susanna Moerbeek, b. Batavia
           Geertruida Margaretha Goossens, b. Batavia

1743–50   GUSTAAF WILLEM baron VAN IMHOFF
           Catharina Magdelena Huysman, b. India

1750–61   JACOB MOSSEL
           Adriana Appels, b. Batavia

1761–75   PETRUS ALBERTUS VAN DER PARRA, b. Ceylon
           Elisabeth van Aerden, b. Batavia
           Adriana Johanna Bake, b. Batavia

1775–77   JEREMIAS VAN RIEMSDIJK
           Martina van den Briel (all wives b. in Asia)

Cornelia Catharina van Vianen
Maria Lucretia Wentink
Adriana Louisa Helvetius
Theodora Rotgers

1777–80 REYNIER DE KLERK
Sophia Francina Westpalm, b. Batavia

1780–97 WILLEM ARNOLD ALTING
Hendrina Maria Knabe, b. Batavia
Susanna Maria Grebel, b. Batavia

1797–1801 Mr. PIETER GERHARDUS VAN OVERSTRATEN
Jacoba Maria Lodisio, b. Batavia

1801–5 JOANNES SIBERG
Pieternella Gerhardina Alting, b. Batavia

1805–8 ALBERTUS HENRICUS WIESE
Christina Elisabeth Marci, b. Batavia
Jacoba Maria Lodisio, b. Batavia

1808–11 HERMAN WILLEM DAENDELS
wife did not emigrate

1811 JAN WILLEM JANSSENS
widower

1816–26 Mr. GODERT A. G. P. baron VAN DER CAPELLEN
Jacoba Elisabeth barones van Tuyll van Serooskerken

1826–30 LEONARD P. J. burggraaf DU BUS DE GISIGNIES
Marie Anne C. B. de Deurwaerder

1830–33 JOHANNES VAN DEN BOSCH
Catharina L. de Sandol Roy, b. Cape of Good Hope
Rudolphine A. E. de Sturler

1833–36 JEAN-CHRETIEN BAUD
Wilhelmina H. Senn van Basel, b. Batavia
Ursula Susanna van Braam, b. Batavia

1836–40 DOMINIQUE JACQUES DE EERENS
Jkvr. Theodora J. H. de Salve de Bruneton

1841–44 Mr. PIETER MERKUS
Wilhelmina Niclasina Cranssen, b. Ambon

1845–51 JAN JACOB ROCHUSSEN
Elisabeth Charlotte Vincent, b. Padang

1851–56 Mr. ALBERTUS J. DUYMAER VAN TWIST
Maria Joanna Beck

1856–61 CHARLES FERDINAND PAHUD
Catharina J. W. Bogaardt, b. Bengal

1861–66 Mr. LUDOLF A. J. W. baron SLOET VAN DE BEELE
Jacoba Maria Visscher

1866–72   Mr. PIETER MIJER, Creole
          Jeannette A. Pietermaat, childhood on Java

1872–75   Mr. JAMES LOUDON
          Jkvr. Louise W. F. F. de Stuers, m. in Indonesia

1875–81   Mr. JOHAN W. VAN LANSBERGE, b. in South America
          Rafaela del Villar

1881–84   FREDERIK s'JACOB
          Jkvr. Leonie S. C. van Hogendorp, m. in Indonesia

1884–88   OTTO VAN REES
          Johanna Henriette Lucassen, b. Java
          Johanna S. W. van Braam Morris, b. Batavia

1888–93   Mr. CORNELIS PIJNACKER HORDIJK
          Theodora E. C. van Bijnkershoek van der Koog

1893–99   Jkhr. CAREL H. A. VAN DER WIJCK, b. Ambon

1899–1904 W. Rooseboom
          All spouses of twentieth-century governors-general were Dutchwomen

1904–9   J. B. VAN HEUTSZ

1909–16   A. W. F. IDENBURG

1916–21   Mr. J. P. graaf VAN LIMBURG STIRUM

1921–26   Mr. D. FOCK

1926–31   Jkhr. Mr. A. C. D. DE GRAEFF

1931–36   Jkhr. Mr. B. C. DE JONGE

1936–41   Jkhr. Mr. A. W. L. TJARDA VAN STARKENBORGH STACHOUWER

Appendix 3

Family and Position in VOC Batavia

Political office and family alliance linked members of the VOC elite. While there was in VOC Batavia no dynastic system along patriarchal lines, candidates for high office came from a pool of men who were connected by marriage to Indies women. Governor-General P. A. van der Parra's Council exemplified this web of office and family relationship. Uncle and nephew, father-in-law and son-in-law sat on his Council in 1775. Such links can be established between twelve of the thirteen members. Only two members were Asia-born, one being the governor-general himself. To van der Parra belongs the further distinction of being the only head of Holland's Asian possessions who never saw Europe. The others conform to the usual pattern as immigrants, marrying locally, keeping daughters in Asia as brides for their colleagues, and sending their sons to Europe.

The Council of the Indies in 1775 consisted of Governor-General Petrus Albertus van der Parra, Reynier de Klerk, Willem Arnold Alting, Hendrik Breton, Johan Vos, Willem Fockens, Thomas Schippers, Jacobus Johannes Craan, David Johan Smith, J. C. M. Radermacher, Hendrik van Stockum, Jan Hendrik Poock (or Pook), and First Councillor and Director-General of Trade Jeremias van Riemsdijk. Links between Council members will be outlined below.

1. PETRUS ALBERTUS van der PARRA (governor-general 1761–75) was born in Ceylon in 1714, the son of Cornelis Romboutsz. van der Parra, secretary of Ceylon's government, and of the Dutch-born Geertruida Susanna Spannijt. His paternal grandfather was Rombout van der Parra, himself a VOC employee on Ceylon and husband of the Ceylonese-born Henriette Wichelman. Her father, Magnus Wichelman, had served the Company in Ceylon and Malabar, and finally as director of Persia.

P. A. van der Parra's mother remarried the Netherlander Adriaan Maten in 1721. Maten was administrator of Colombo by 1729, and served as commander of Malabar during the years 1731–34.

Van der Parra married twice. His second marriage was to Adriana Johanna Bake, widow of the VOC commander Anthonij Guldenarm. Her father was David Johan Bake, who had migrated from Holland in 1718 with the rank of junior merchant. Most of Bake's working life was spent in the Moluccas and included governorship of Ambon (1732–37). He died in Batavia in 1738 with the rank of councillor extraordinary.

Bake's wife and the governor-general's mother-in-law was Ida Dudde, daughter of a Batavian burgher and widow of a low-level VOC employee, Constantijn Coomans. A daughter from her first marriage, Agatha Geertruida Coomans, married the Batavia VOC employee Johan Smith, and their son, DAVID SMITH, sat on van der Parra's Council in 1775. Another daughter, Ida Constantia Coomans, married Gerrit Mom, and their daughter was grandmother to the future governor-general A. H. Wiese (1805–11).

Ida Dudde's son from her second marriage, Willem Jacob Bake, had a daughter christened Ida Wilhelmina. She married Johan Frederik baron van Reede tot de Parkeler, whose first wife had been a daughter of Councillor JOHAN VOS.

The marriage of P. A. van der Parra and Adriana Bake produced only one child, a son born in 1760 and known as Petrus Albertus van der Parra de jonge. He died in 1783, but by that time was already chief fiscal officer of the Indies and husband of Catharina Geertruida Breton, daughter of Councillor HENDRIK BRETON.

2. REYNIER de KLERK sailed to the Indies as a ship's boy in 1710. On his third voyage he reached Batavia in December 1730 and entered civilian service as a book-keeper. His career took him to south Sumatra, Surabaya, Semarang, and Banda. His appointment as councillor extraordinary came in 1754, followed by full councillor in 1762, director-general, and then governor-general from 1777 until his death in office in 1780.

The same year as his appointment as councillor extraordinary, de Klerk married Sophia Francina Westpalm in Batavia. She was the daughter of Michiel Westpalm, who was first councillor and director-general under Governor-General Dirk van Cloon (1732–35), and of Geertruida Margaretha Goossens. Geertruida Goossens was the daughter of the Batavia VOC merchant Johannes Goossens and of Sophia Fauconier. Following Goossens's death, Sophia Fauconier remarried Gaspar van Mansdale, who was nominated councillor extraordinary in 1723. Geertruida Goossens married, in order, Michiel Westpalm and Johannes Thedens, who was acting governor-general from 1741 to 1743. In 1736 she had been betrothed to Frederik Julius Coyett, grandson of the governor of Ceylon and son of the governor of Banda and Ambon. She was, too, godmother to the children of Governor-General Jacob Mossel.

A sister of Sophia Westpalm, Geertruida Johanna Westpalm, married the Dutch lawyer Mr. Johan Hendrik van Panhuys. Their son, Johan Michiel, was head of the Japara residency in the 1780s.

Sophia Westpalm (1722–85) had been married to Councillor Hugo Verijssel. One of the three children from this marriage, Margaretha Sophia Verijssel, was the first wife of the J. C. M. RADERMACHER who sat on the Council in 1775. Radermacher's second wife connected him to DAVID SMITH, as will be outlined below.

De Klerk had no legitimate issue. He was buried in 1780 in the family mausoleum of Hugo Verijssel. His widow recognized Radermacher's son, Frans Reinier, as her heir.

3. WILLEM ARNOLD ALTING went out in 1750 with the rank of junior merchant and climbed the ranks of the VOC hierarchy in Batavia. He was made a councillor extraordinary by 1759 and full councillor in 1772. He was the senior member under Governor-General R. de Klerk and was governor-general from 1780 to 1797, another period of family government marked by alliances, particularly between the Alting, van Riemsdijk, and Senn van Basel families.

Alting had ten children by his first wife. Five survived to adulthood, all girls, and all married native Dutchmen who held posts as senior merchants and residents of Java districts. The most prominent was the second husband of Alting's daughter, Pieternella Gerhardina, who married Mr. Joannes Siberg. Siberg was to follow his father-in-law as governor-general during the years 1801–5.

Alting's second wife was Maria Susanna Grebel, whose first husband was Councillor Huybert van Basel, patriarch of the Senn van Basel clan. Alting's stepdaughter, Maria Wilhelmina Senn van Basel (1770–1821), married his nephew Nicolaas Engelhard, governor of the North Coast of Java and later a councillor. Another relative of Alting's, Pieter Engelhard, was to marry a daughter of Councillor Extraordinary Anthonij Barkeij and later a van Riemsdijk, which brought further links to the Senn van Basel clan also.

4. HENDRIK BRETON was married to Sara Maria van Oordt. During his term as resident of Surabaya a daughter, Catharina Geertruida, was born. She was to marry P. A. van der Parra de jonge in Batavia in 1778. Their descendants were very numerous in the nineteenth century. Breton was first councillor and director-general under GG Alting until his death in office in 1780.

5. JOHAN VOS held among other posts those of senior merchant and governor of Java's North Coast (1765–71), and was appointed full councillor in 1777. His first wife connected him to the governor-general's family, for she was Adriana Agatha Smith, sister of DAVID SMITH. They had married in 1753. She died sometime before 1762, when Vos married Ida Wilhelmina Bake, niece of Governor-General van der PARRA. His daughter, Ida Petronella Jacoba Vos, married F. H. van Reede tot de Parkeler, as noted above.

6. WILLEM FOCKENS served as councillor extraordinary and full councillor during van der Parra's governor-generalship. He died in office in 1780. His wife, Catharina Tobison, was to remarry fellow councillor DAVID SMITH.

7. THOMAS SCHIPPERS went out to the Indies in 1740 as a junior merchant. His career took him to Bantam and Malacca, where he was governor over the years 1764–72. In the latter year he was appointed councillor extraordinary and president of the court in Batavia. He became a full councillor in 1778 and died in Batavia in 1780.

Schippers's third wife was Catharina Cornelia van Mijlendonck, widow of Councillor Hendrik van Ossenbergh and daughter of Johan Elias van Mijlendonck, governor of Ternate 1755–56 and councillor extraordinary. This marriage connected Schippers to the Reynst family, whose members were numerous in the Indies.

8. JACOBUS JOHANNES CRAAN was born in Ambon in 1728, son of the Dutch minister Petrus Craan. He joined the VOC's service as a clerk in 1741 and worked his way up in Malacca and on Java until his appointment as councillor extraordinary. This was followed by full councillor in 1780, the year of his death in Batavia.

Craan was an uncle of HENDRIK BRETON. He married the fifteen-year-old Johanna Henrietta Breekpot in 1753. She was the daughter of Cornelis Breekpot, commander of Malabar during the period 1764–69. From Craan's marriage to Johanna Breekpot was born Catharina Margaretha Craan, who was to marry the son of JEREMIAS van

RIEMSDIJK in 1773 and be the mother of fourteen of his children. The children from the van Riemsdijk-Craan alliance are listed in appendix 1, table 9.

9. DAVID JOHAN SMITH, as noted in section 1, was the son of Governor-General van der PARRA's wife's half-sister, Agatha G. Smith-Coomans. He was sent in 1745 at age five to the Netherlands for schooling on the request of his maternal grandmother, Ida Dudde. He returned in 1762, and profited from his uncle's position as governor-general, being promoted from the rank of junior to senior merchant without the intermediate post of merchant. At thirty-two he was made councillor extraordinary, and full councillor by 1781. By 1789 he was senior councillor and due to be appointed second-in-command as director-general, but withdrew from government service and died on his estate in 1792.

Smith married four times. His first wife (1763) was Hester Petronella Romp, daughter of Ordinary Councillor Michiel Romp and sister of the wife of the future councillor extraordinary Johan van der Burgh. One of their children, Maria Petronella Smith, was to marry Jacobus Theodorus Reynst, which allied the family to the van Mijlendonck and SCHIPPER's clans.

Smith's second wife was Catharina Tobison, widow of WILLEM FOCKENS.

The third wife was Catharina Louisa Gallas, mother, through a previous marriage, of Anna Jacoba Bosch, who was the second wife of J. C. M. RADERMACHER. Catharina died in 1782, and Smith had his stepdaughter Anna placed in van der PARRA's household until her marriage at thirteen to Radermacher.

Smith's fourth marriage lasted longest. It took place in 1782 and was to Johanna Mauritia Mohr, daughter of the well-known Batavia clergyman and astronomer and of Anna Elisabeth van't Hoff.

Finally, Smith was designated guardian of P. A. van der Parra de jonge in the will the governor-general had drawn up in 1773.

10. J. C. M. RADERMACHER has already been recorded as son-in-law of councillor and future governor-general de KLERK. Radermacher had first gone out to the Indies at sixteen as a junior merchant. His marriage to Margaretha Verijssel took place in Batavia in 1761, when de Klerk was already councillor extraordinary. In 1763 Radermacher returned on furlough to the Netherlands. Margaretha accompanied him and probably died in the Netherlands. The only child of the marriage, Frans Reinier Radermacher, was named Sophia de Klerk-Westpalm's heir.

After his return to Batavia in 1767 Radermacher was appointed councillor extraordinary (1776), and full councillor one year later. His second wife, Anna Jacoba Bosch, has already been noted as DAVID SMITH's stepdaughter. She accompanied Radermacher when he repatriated in 1783, but remained at the Cape after his murder at sea, and was to remarry there Christiaan Anthonie Ver Huell, son of the Indies traveler and chronicler. Anna Radermacher-Bosch's sisters were married to men who headed residencies on Java.

11. HENDRIK van STOCKUM went out as ship's boy in 1754 and transferred into the civilian arm of the VOC as a junior assistant in Batavia. By 1768 he was made junior merchant and had climbed the hierarchy to first senior merchant of the Castle by 1771. His appointment as councillor extraordinary came in 1776, followed by that of full

councillor in 1786. Three years later he was senior councillor and director-general, and died in Batavia in 1793.

Van Stockum did not marry until 1779. His bride was Catharina Elisabeth Romswinckel, widow of Otto Frans Nicolaas Marci, who has been in charge of artillery and warehouses for the VOC. A daughter from this first marriage, Christina Elisabeth Marci, was to marry the future governor-general A. H. Wiese. From the van Stockum-Romswinckel marriage was born Catharina Wilhelmina van Stockum, who married Joost Carel Romswinckel at Batavia in 1801. He had been born in the Netherlands, but emigrated and died in Batavia in 1846 after a career culminating in appointment as councillor extraordinary.

As noted above, the Wiese family was connected with the Senn van Basel, van Riemsdijk, and Alting families as well as with the Romswinckel family. Wiese's sister Ida Adriana Helena married Willem Adriaan Senn van Basel, who was half-brother of Maria Wilhelmina Engelhard, step-daughter of Governor-General Alting. W. A. Senn van Basel's second wife was a legitimate daughter of W. V. H. van Riemsdijk, while his sister, Philippina Maria Theodora Senn van Basel, had married Steven Poelman, widow of GG Alting's oldest daughter, Elisabeth Fockleyna Alting.

12. JAN HENDRIK POOCK was the VOC's bailiff in Batavia in 1774 and councillor extraordinary under Governors-General van der Parra, van Riemsdijk, de Klerk, and Alting. I have not established any family connections of this council member yet.

13. JEREMIAS van RIEMSDIJK first went out to the Indies in 1735 as a sergeant in the VOC army. He was the nephew of Governor-General Adriaan Valckenier (1737–41). Valckenier's first wife, Johanna Alida Tolling, was aunt of Jeremias van Riemsdijk's fourth wife, Adriana Louisa Helvetius.

J. van Riemsdijk left the army upon arrival in Batavia and, benefiting from his connections, reached the rank of senior merchant by 1740. He survived Valckenier's disgrace, and was councillor extraordinary by 1753 and full councillor by 1760. He served as van der Parra's director-general from 1764 until his election by unanimous vote of the Council upon van der Parra's death in office in 1775. Van Riemsdijk died in office in 1777.

Van Riemsdijk married five times. His alliances are laid out in appendix 2, table 3. The most important family connections were made on his fourth and fifth marriages. Adriana Helvetius's father was president of Batavia's court, while her maternal grandfather was Councillor Laurens Tolling. One of her uncles was Willem Maurits Bruininck, governor and director of Ceylon from 1740 to 1742. The fifth wife, Theodora Rotgers, had been married previously to a member of Batavia's court and then to Councillor Extraordinary Mr. Maurits Theodorus Hilgers. His brother-in-law Nicolaas Hartingh had married a daughter of Governor-General Jacob Mossel.

Van Riemsdijk's daughter Johanna Maria (by his third wife) married Paulus Godefridus van der Voort in 1765. He rose to be governor and director of Makassar during the decade 1770–80. His son Willem V. H. van Riemsdijk, who was a councillor, married Catharina Craan, daughter of Councillor JACOBUS J. CRAAN. Their daughter Jacoba Dorothea was the second wife of W. A. Senn van Basel and mother of Wilhelmina Henriette Senn van Basel, who married the future governor-general Jean-Chrétien Baud.

Notes

INTRODUCTION

1 J. C. van Leur, *Indonesian Trade and Society: Essays in Asian Social and Economic History* (The Hague, Bandung: W. van Hoeve, 1955); and John R. W. Smail, "On the Possibility of an Autonomous History of Modern Southeast Asia," *Journal of Southeast Asian History* 2 (2):72–102 (July 1961).

2 Holden Furber, *Rival Empires of Trade in the Orient, 1600–1800* (Minneapolis: University of Minnesota Press, 1976), chapter 7, esp. pp. 309–10; M. A. P. Meilink-Roelofsz, "De Europese expansie in Asië: Enkele beschouwingen naar aanleiding van Holden Furbers *Rival Empires of Trade in the Orient, 1600–1800*," *Bijdragen tot de Taal-, Land-, en Volkenkunde* 135 (4):403–42 (1979); and F. Lequin, "A New Approach to the History of the Dutch Expansion in Asia: The Personnel of the Dutch East India Company of the XVIIIth Century," *Journal of European Economic History* 8 (2):431–37 (Fall 1979).

CHAPTER 1: ORIGINS OF THE CITY OF BATAVIA

1 Wijaya Krama is termed the "king of Jacatra" in old Dutch records, and was vassal to the sultan of Bantam. L'Hermite was acting on behalf of Admiral P. Verhoeven, whom the East Indies Company directors had empowered to make contracts with rulers in the archipelago. The text of this contract can be found in app. 1 of Jacobus A. van der Chijs, *De Nederlanders te Jakatra* (Amsterdam: F. Muller, 1860), pp. 201–3.

2 Van der Chijs, *De Nederlanders te Jakatra*, p. 60.

3 C. R. Boxer, *The Dutch Seaborne Empire 1600–1800* (London: Hutchinson, 1965), p. 80.

4 Friderici Bollingii, "Oost-Indisch reisboek, uit het Deensch vertaald door Mej. Joh. Visscher," *Bijdragen tot de Taal-, Land-, en Volkenkunde* 68 (1913):297. Parts of Worms's *Ost-Indianische und Persianische Reisen* (Dresden and Leipzig, 1737) are quoted by J. de Hullu, "De matrozen en soldaten op de schepen der Oost-Indische Compagnie," ibid. 69 (1914):318–65. On the composition of the VOC's employees see also J. R. Bruijn, "De personeelsbehoefte van de VOC overzee en aan boord, bezien in Aziatisch en Nederlands perspectief," *Bijdragen en Mededelingen betreffende de Geschiedenis der Nederlanden* 91 (1):218–48 (1976). His figures show that

non-Dutch nationals represented a large part of the VOC's army and navy throughout the seventeenth and eighteenth centuries.

5 This passage is taken from the narrative of his first journey. J. C. M. Warnsinck, ed., *Reisen van Nicolaus de Graaff gedaan naar alle gewesten des Werelds, beginnende 1639 tot 1687 incluis* ('s-Gravenhage: Martinus Nijhoff, 1930), p. 6.

6 Letter of 3 November 1628 in H. T. Colenbrander, *Jan Pietersz. Coen, bescheiden omtrent zijn bedrijf in Indië* ('s-Gravenhage: M. Nijhoff, 1923), 5:130.

7 See, for example, the letters collected by N. J. Krom in his "Het Leidsche weeshuis en de Oost-Indische Compagnie," *Leidsche jaarboekje 1936* (Leiden, 1936), p. 68.

8 See E. C. Godée Molsbergen, *Geschiedenis van de Nederlandsch Oost-Indische Compagnie en Nederlandsch-Indië in beeld* (Weltevreden: N.O.I. Topografische Inrichting, 1925), no. 67. Seventeenth-century Dutch personal names were often composed of a patronymic, for example, Jacob's son, John's daughter, written as Jacobszoon, Jansdochter and often abbreviated as Jacobsz. and Jansd. The period in the personal names given here reflects the shortened patronymic.

9 Edgar du Perron, *De muze van Jan Compagnie* (Bandung: A. C. Nix, 1948), pp. 190–91. India or Indië was often used by seventeenth-century Dutchmen to refer to the Indonesian archipelago.

10 By resolution of Governor-General A. van Diemen and Council no European married to an Asian woman might repatriate before her death and the death of any children from the marriage. *Realia: Register op de generale resolutiën van het kasteel Batavia 1632–1805* (Leiden, The Hague: Kolff, Nijhoff, 1885–86), 3:127 (23 September 1639).

11 Du Perron, *Muze*, p. 57.

12 Letter of Coen to the VOC directors, 10 December 1616, Colenbrander, *Coen,* 1:245.

13 The text of the first oath is to be found in vol. 1 of the *Nederlandsch-Indisch Plakaatboek 1602–1811,* 16 vols. plus index, ed. J. A. van der Chijs (Batavia, 's-Gravenhage: Landsdrukkerij, M. Nijhoff, 1885–1900), pp. 360–63.

14 Letter written late in December 1649, included in J. K. J. de Jonge, *De opkomst van het Nederlandsch gezag in Oost-Indië,* 13 vols. ('s-Gravenhage: M. Nijhoff, 1862–88), 6:ii.

15 On the development of the Chinese community in and around Batavia and on economic relations between the Chinese and VOC officials, see Leonard Blussé, "Batavia, 1619–1740: The Rise and Fall of a Chinese Colonial Town," *Journal of Southeast Asian Studies* 12 (1):159–78 (March 1981).

16 Part of the text of the burghers' letter is given by de Jonge, *Opkomst,* 6:iii. The directors' response is in 6:xxv. "Moor" was used to describe non-Indonesian Muslim traders. "Heathen" meant non-Muslim Indonesians.

17 Instruction of Governor-General Coen and Council, 19 October 1628, Colenbrander, *Coen,* 5:710. Cunst (or Kunst) had reached the rank of senior merchant and head of the Jambi factory before retiring from the VOC's service. He held many of the honorary posts awarded burghers.

18 Coen, writing to the directors on 31 July 1620: "Counting the burghers, Malays, Klings, women, children, slaves, artisans, and the fort's garrison, we estimate the population at about 2,000." Colenbrander, *Coen,* 1:574. The figure of 8,000 is used

by C. A. L. van Troostenburg de Bruyn, *De Hervormde Kerk in Nederlandsch Oost-Indië* (Arnhem: H. A. Tjeenk Willink, 1884), p. 15. The term *Kling* meant people from continental India trading or settled in the Malay Peninsula or the archipelago, and their descendants.

19 See the section "Statistics," in chap. 4 of Pauline D. Milone, "Queen City of the East: The Metamorphosis of a Colonial Capital" (Ph.D. diss., University of California, Berkeley, 1966), pp. 141–47.

20 Order from the VOC Directors, 16 October 1676, de Jonge, *Opkomst,* 6:163–64.

21 Coen to directors, 11 May 1620, Colenbrander, *Coen,* 1:555.

22 See, for instance, the correspondence of the governors-general with the directors, as edited by W. Ph. Coolhaas in *Generale Missiven van Gouverneurs-Generaal en Raden aan Heeren XVII der Verenigde Oostindische Compagnie,* vol. 1, *1610–1638* ('s-Gravenhage: Martinus Nijhoff, 1960).

23 Coen to directors, 1 January 1614, Colenbrander, *Coen,* 1:9. By "Indians" Coen meant inhabitants of the Indies—that is, of Indonesia.

24 Wages were paid Company employees in cash monthly and in necessities such as firewood, salt, rice, and spices, the amounts being set according to the individual wage-earner's rank. The Batavia government was always nice in its distinctions between ranks. Many of the decrees in the *Plakaatboek* regulated ration allowances.

25 Letter of directors of the Amsterdam chamber to Coen, 7 December 1622, Colenbrander, *Coen,* 4:736–38. The total number of married couples was eight, and there were thirty-one single girls.

26 See, for instance, the letter of Governor-General Both to the directors, 1 January 1614, in P. A. Tiele and J. E. Heeres, *Bouwstoffen voor de geschiedenis der Nederlanders in den Maleischen archipel,* 3 vols. (The Hague: M. Nijhoff, 1886–95), 1:40–41.

27 In Dutch usage a woman legally retains her own surname, that is, her father's name, after marriage. A woman's married name is written giving the husband's surname first, followed by the father's. A hyphenated name such as M. Reynst-Nicquet indicates the person is the wife of Reynst and daughter of Nicquet. In this text women are generally referred to by their maiden names.

28 Coen to directors, 20 June 1623, Colenbrander, *Coen,* 1:975.

29 Governor-General Brouwer to directors, 1 December 1632, de Jonge, *Opkomst,* 5:196.

30 Instructions of directors to Brouwer, 17 March 1632, *Plakaatboek,* 1:271.

31 "Oost-Indise spiegel," in Warnsinck, ed., *Reisen van Nicolaus de Graaff,* p. 21.

32 *Dagh-Register gehouden int Casteel Batavia* (The Hague: Martinus Nijhoff, 1898), 1675 vol., p. 151.

33 Directors to Batavia government, 13 April 1652, de Jonge, *Opkomst,* 6:xxiv. The number of the VOC's directors was set at seventeen and they were often called the "Gentlemen XVII."

34 The author of the journal is not known. De Jonge reproduces it in vol. 4 of *Opkomst.* See esp. pp. 148–54, which cover the period from late March to early April 1619.

35 Both to directors, 1 January 1614, Tiele and Heeres, *Bouwstoffen,* 1:36–41.

36 *Plakaatboek,* 1:82 (11 December 1620).

37 *Plakaatboek,* 1:99–101 (20 July 1622).

211

38 Code for Commissioners of Marriage Affairs in the Statutes of Batavia, 1642, *Plakaatboek*, 1:542: "the above-mentioned commissioners are expressly forbidden from henceforth to grant marriage licenses to Dutch men and Native women unless the latter can understand and speak Dutch well." The test was not applied rigorously; mostly the women were coached in a verse from the Bible in Dutch or in the Ten Commandments.

39 Governor-General P. de Carpentier to directors, 3 January 1624, de Jonge, *Opkomst*, 5:28.

40 Godée Molsbergen, *Geschiedenis*, accompanying note to doc. 68. The woman's full name is given as Magdalena Goossens van Byssaya. The "van" in personal names means "of" or "from." In the seventeenth and eighteenth centuries Asian converts to Christianity were often named by giving them a Christian personal name followed by "van" and place of origin for surname. Van Byssaya suggests that widow Goossens was from Visaya in the central Philippines.

41 *Plakaatboek*, 3:145–46, decree of April–May 1685.

42 Colenbrander, *Coen*, 3:546.

43 Letter of Governor-General Maetsuyker to directors, 17 November 1674, de Jonge, *Opkomst*, 6:125.

44 *Plakaatboek*, 1:27 May 1642, 471.

45 *Plakaatboek*, 1:474–75. This decree was binding on "Heathens and Moors" too, and anyone openly worshipping differently was threatened with confiscation of property, the chain gang, exile, or death, "according to the circumstances."

46 Van Troostenburg de Bruyn, *Hervormde Kerk*, p. 216.

47 Tielen's sentence, dated 26 November 1620, is cited in Colenbrander, *Coen*, 4:240–41. Scotanus was sentenced for an indefinite period of confinement on 28 February 1640 (*Realia*, 3:84).

48 *Plakaatboek*, 1:39.

49 Art. 79 of church regulations, 7 December 1643, *Plakaatboek*, 2:52.

50 See titles for J. d'Outrain and T. Vermeer in J. A. van der Chijs, *Proeve eener Ned.-Indische Bibliographie (1659–1870)* (Batavia: W. Bruining, 1879).

51 Letter dated 19 January 1654, de Jonge, *Opkomst*, 6:42–43. Regulations for the Latin school are to be found in *Plakaatboek*, 2:3–7 (2 December 1642).

52 Directors to Maetsuyker, 7 May 1661, de Jonge, *Opkomst*, 6:1xx.

53 Camphuys's school regulations are dated 4 April 1684, *Plakaatboek*, 3:125–30.

54 Resolution of Governor-General P. de Carpentier and councillors, 1 October 1624, de Jonge, *Opkomst*, 5:56. Instructions for the Orphans' Chancery were issued mid-1625, *Plakaatboek*, 1:173–87.

55 Maetsuyker to directors, 17 November 1674, de Jonge, *Opkomst*, 6:125–26.

56 See, for example, resolutions of 3 January and 10 December 1708, *Realia*, 1:466, and of May 1726, *Realia*, 2:114.

57 Regulations for the orphanage, dated 23 May 1752, *Plakaatboek*, 6:215–16. This list is found in art. 42.

58 All decrees and laws cited below are to be found in the first four volumes of the *Plakaatboek* under such headings as "marriage," "native wives," "repatriation," etc.

59 Susanna Muller was baptized at Malacca in 1666. Her father, Nicolaas, had been born in Hirado, Japan, and was son of a VOC employee there and of a Japanese

woman. He was a Batavia alderman at the time of his death. Susanna married C. van Outhoorn in Batavia in 1683.

60 The figures are taken from Colenbrander, *Coen*, 1:574, and from F. de Haan, *Oud Batavia: Gedenkboek*, 2 vols. (Batavia: G. Kolff, 1922), 2:348, respectively. See also Pauline Milone, "Queen City," pp. 14 ff.

61 Leopold Ludovici, *Lapidarium Zeylandicum, Being a Collection of Monumental Inscriptions of the Dutch Churches and Churchyards of Ceylon* (Colombo: Maitland, 1877). All tombs and headstones are shown in photograph, together with Ludovici's translation of the original Dutch or Latin. This summary of biographical detail in ten inscriptions is taken from pp. 4–91. This evidence from the tombstones both confirms and amplifies deductions made by G. Knaap on the composition of Colombo's population, which he made by analysis of a list of households in the Colombo castle and town in 1694. See G. Knaap, "Europeans, Mestizos and Slaves: The Population of Colombo at the End of the Seventeenth Century," *Itinerario* 5 (2):84–101 (1981).

CHAPTER 2: GROWTH OF SETTLEMENT SOCIETY

1 Acting upon instructions from the VOC's directors, Coen had nominated his successor (his brother-in-law Pieter Vlack) in a letter that was to be opened upon his death. Apparently unaware of these instructions, the councillors who met at Coen's deathbed viewed Coen's action as improper and overturned it, voting Jacques Specx as the succeeding governor-general. See W. Ph. Coolhaas, "Reael, Coen, De Carpentier en Specx," *Bijdragen tot de Taal-, Land-, en Volkenkunde* 129 (1973):269–76.

2 François Valentijn, *Oud en nieuw Oost-Indiën*, 5 vols. (Dordrecht, Amsterdam: Van Braam, Onder de Linden, 1726), 4:295; and J. P. I. du Bois, *Vies des gouverneurs-généraux* (The Hague: de Hondt, 1763), p. 134.

3 *Realia* 1:469 (9 March 1647).

4 Jean-Baptiste Tavernier, *Travels in India*, trans. from the original French ed. of 1676 by V. I. Ball (London: Macmillan, 1889), B.3 pp. 502–4.

5 Maria Scipio was born in Alkmaar. She had been widowed twice before marrying van Riebeeck in 1666. The careers of her husbands took her to Malacca, Batavia, Japan, and the west coast of Sumatra. Her portrait is reproduced as L5 in de Haan's *Platenalbum*, which accompanies his 2-volume *Oud Batavia*, and is painting no. 33 in J. de Loos-Haaxman, *De Landsverzameling schilderijen in Batavia* (vol. 1, text; vol. 2, paintings) (Leiden: Sijthoff, 1941).

6 This painting is L4 of de Haan, *Platenalbum*.

7 Letter to Maria Sweers de Weerd and Johanna Margaretha van Beveren, dated Batavia 14 December 1689, quoted in G. D. J. Schotel and H. C. Rogge, *Het Oud-Hollandsch huisgezin der zeventiende eeuw*, 2d. rev. ed. (Amsterdam: Strengholt and Arnhem, Gijsbers and van Loon, 1968), p. 284.

8 Warnsinck, ed., "Oost-Indise spiegel," pp. 17–18.

9 Jean-Baptiste Tavernier, "Histoire de la conduite des Hollondois en Asie," sec. 5 of *Recueil de plusiers relations et traitez singuliers et curieux* (Paris: n.p., n.d), p. 263.

10 See, for example, M3 of de Haan, *Platenalbum*.

11 Warnsinck, ed., "Oost-Indise spiegel," pp. 13–14. The terms of abuse de Graaff puts into the mouths of his Batavian ladies are forms of Portuguese in the original text. Minute descriptions of the barbarities women inflicted on their slaves are a

constant feature of travelers' narratives. It might be noted that men do not ascribe these barbarous practices to other men when writing of old Batavia. We have no female chronicler with whom to check these accounts.

12 Differences in terminology for individuals of mixed race depending on degree of relationship to a native European are spelled out in the "Oost-Indise spiegel," p. 13. Cornelis de Bruijn gives a similar list in less offensive language in his *Reizen over Moskovië, door Persië en Indië* (Amsterdam: Goerée, 1711), p. 393.

13 The identification was made by J. de Loos-Haaxman, and a copy is reproduced in her *Landsverzameling*, 2, no. 30.

14 Rules of orthography were not yet rigid in the seventeenth century. The father's surname appears in Company records as van Neyenrode and van Nieuwenrode, while a government decision of 22 December 1676 granting Cornelia permission to prosecute her second husband gives the surname as van Nieuwenroode.

15 Warnsinck, ed., "Oost-Indise spiegel," p. 14.

16 These views are expressed in a report on general colonization policy, quoted by de Jonge, *Opkomst*, 6:xviii.

17 Decree of September 1643 cited by W. Wijnaendts van Resandt, *De gezaghebbers der Oost-Indische Compagnie op hare buitencomptoiren in Azië* (Amsterdam: Liebaert, 1944), p. 127; confirmed by an act of legitimation issued 18 December 1646 (*Realia*, 1:3). Caron's application is quoted by C. R. Boxer in the introduction to his edition of *A True Description of the Mighty Kingdoms of Japan and Siam* (1663; London: Argonaut press, 1935), p. lxviii.

18 Wijnaendts van Resandt, *Gezaghebbers*, p. 128, and Boxer, *True Description*, biographical appendix on the Caron family.

19 The decision was recorded on 5 December 1659. See the *Nieuw Nederlandsch biografisch woordenboek*, 10 vols. (Leiden: Sijthoff, 1911–37), vol. 6, entry 1256. The daughter Hadewyna did not survive the voyage. *Amme* is a rendering of the Portuguese *ama*, meaning "nurse." In Southeast Asia and Hong Kong a woman termed *ama(h)* is usually of Chinese origin.

20 *Plakaatboek*, 1:459–60 (June 1641).

21 *Plakaatboek*, 10:149 (10 May 1778). In 1777 the Batavia synod had been ordered to teach all Asian catechizers Dutch and not to engage any more who could not speak it (X, p. 106).

22 De Haan, *Platenalbum*, D14. See also plates showing tombstones of Asian Christians, E13, E14, and E15.

23 Quoted from Haafner's *Lotgevallen en vroegere zeereizen*, in F. de Haan, "De laatste der Mardijkers," *Bijdragen tot de Taal-, Land-, en Volkenkunde* 73 (1917):229.

24 For example, memorial plaques were hung for Elisabeth de Haas-van Riebeeck, wife and sister to councillors of the Indies (d. 1704); Councillor Extraordinary Joan Elias van Meijlendonk (d. 1762); Christina Marci, wife of Director-General A. H. Wiese (d. 1805); and Vrouwe Johanna Louisa van Gotzhuisen (d. 1805), wife of Councillor Extraordinary Pieter Walbeek.

25 One of the set bearing this inscription is included in de Haan's *Platenalbum*, D15.

26 A third was dissolved in 1803. The remaining company was only 31 strong. This

should be compared with figures for 1777, when there were six Mardijker companies totalling 1,200 men. See de Haan, "Laatste der Mardijkers," p. 238.

27 François Valentijn, *Oud en nieuw Oost-Indiën*, 4:366–67.

CHAPTER 3: THE WEB OF COLONIAL SOCIETY:
BATAVIA AND ENVIRONS IN THE EIGHTEENTH CENTURY

1 The lines are quoted by du Perron, *Muze*, pp. 154–55.

2 The direction is taken from her will. See "Testament van Mevrouw Petronella Wonderer," app. 6 of F. W. Stapel, "Cornelis Janszoon Speelman," in *Bijdragen tot de Taal-, Land-, en Volkenkunde* 94 (1936):189. Petronella's maiden name is spelled Wonderaer and Wonderer in VOC texts.

3 Tavernier, *Travels in India*, B.3, p. 509; and Warnsinck, ed., "Oost-Indise spiegel," p. 8.

4 *Dagh-Register*, 1647–48 vol., p. 140, entry for 27 September 1648.

5 Fig. 4, 9, and 12 in H. A. Breuning, *Het voormalige Batavia* (Amsterdam: Allert de Lange, 1954), show how the jungle was steadily pushed back and the extent of the city in 1622, 1632, and 1740, respectively.

6 De Bruijn, *Reizen*, p. 366. The reference to the kitchen not being completed at the same time as the house is explained by the building design adopted from Indonesian architecture. This has the kitchen built apart and at some distance from the main dwelling. Van Riebeeck's wife was the Netherlander Elisabeth van Oosten (1660–1714). She had first married Jan van Heden, chief VOC official on Timor. In 1678 she married van Riebeeck in Batavia.

7 The history of Depok is given by J. W. de Vries, "De Depokkers: Geschiedenis, sociale structuur en taalgebruik van een geisoleerde gemeenschap," in *Bijdragen tot de Taal-, Land-, en Volkenkunde* 132 (1976):228–48. Anthonij Chastelein failed, as executor of his father's will, to register the Depok properties in the names of the twelve families to which the 120 slave beneficiaries belonged before his death in 1715. Anna Chastelein-de Haan's second husband, Councillor Mr. Johan François de Witte, (referred to on p. 76) attempted to overturn the will and get back the lands for his wife's family. It was not until 1850 that the Depok estates were legally declared to belong to the descendants of the original twelve families.

8 A photograph is given in V. I. van de Wall, *Oude Hollandsche buitenplaatsen van Batavia* (Deventer: W. van Hoeve, 1944), p. 28. See also B9 of de Haan, *Platenalbum*. Gunung Sari's floor plan is given in fig. 16 of Breuning, *Voormalige Batavia*, p. 75.

9 Several reproductions of Rach's painting and details of it are in J. de Loos-Haaxman, *Johannes Rach en zijn werk* (Batavia: Kolff, 1928), pp. 37, 39, 59, and 97, and in de Haan, *Platenalbum*, K29.

10 See van de Wall, *Buitenplaatsen*, pp. 81, 82; de Haan, *Platenalbum*, B10; and de Loos-Haaxman, *Rach*, p. 119. The design of the house is discussed in Breuning, *Voormalige Batavia*, pp. 93–95, and its floor plan is drawn in fig. 17, p. 93.

11 *Plakaatboek*, 4:136 (24 June 1719).

12 *Plakaatboek*, 4:240–41 (28 December 1729).

13 J. S. Stavorinus, *Voyage par le Cap de Bonne Espérance à Batavia* (Paris: Jansen, 1798), p. 219. The custom of bowing de Haan attributes to Japanese influence on senior officials, many of whom had worked at the settlement there early in their careers (*Oud Batavia,* 1:176). Three of the seventeenth-century governors-general had been heads of the Japan factory (Specx, Brouwer, Camphuys), and two in the eighteenth century (Thedens and van Imhoff). Twenty councillors and six councillors extraordinary had also been heads of the Japan post in the VOC centuries.

14 du Perron, *Muze,* pp. 122–23.

15 Valentijn, *Oost-Indiën,* 4:340; and du Bois, *Vies,* p. 287, for the story of the donkey train.

16 Examples of VOC furniture such as four-poster beds, chairs, and chests may be seen in Dutch and Indonesian museums. VOC furniture was often carved from Javanese teak, highly polished, and combined European styles with Javanese ornamentation in foliage and fruits. Many chairs bear the VOC crest. See, for instance, V. I. van de Wall, "Het oude koloniale meubel in het land van herkomst," *Cultureel Indië* 4 (1943):51–59.

17 For examples of porcelain, again the museums and de Haan, *Platenalbum,* D22, and D12–15 and D18–21 for examples of silver and glassware. See also articles by C. Steinmetz on medals and trays, "Cultureele gegevens uit familiepapieren," p. iii and iv, in *Cultureel Indië* 5 (1943):31–46 and 128–37, respectively.

18 Large areas of Java had been transferred to VOC suzerainty in the course of the previous century. Following on Speelman's successes against Truna Djaja, Krawang, part of east Priangan, and Semarang had been ceded to Batavia. In 1705 Batavia gained control over the rest of Priangan and Madura, and over the Surabaya area in 1743. Finally, in 1755, the government under Mossel was able to make permanent a division of the old Mataram. Henceforth the sultanates of Solo and Yogyakarta were known to the Dutch as the *Vorstenlanden,* the so-called independently ruled principedoms.

19 The text, translated into Dutch, is given in *de Indische Navorscher* 1(6):42 (September 1934).

20 P. de Roo de la Faille, *Iets over Oud-Batavia* (Batavia: Kolff, 1919), pp. 45–46. The description is quoted from an unknown observer who set down his recollections around 1780.

21 See *de Indische Navorscher* 1(6):42 (September 1934) for the medal and inscription. Petrus A. van der Parra de Jonge married Catharina Breton in 1778. She had been born in Surabaya and was the daughter of Hendrik Breton, director-general under Alting. Both husband and wife spent their entire lives in Asia, as did their many descendants. The van der Parra clan in Asia spans the seventeenth through the nineteenth centuries in the direct male line.

22 *Nieuw Nederlandsch biografisch woordenboek,* 7, entry 941.

23 De Haan, "De laatste der Mardijkers," in *Bijdragen tot de Taal-, Land- en Volkenkunde* 73 (1917):219–54.

24 Agraphina (1792–1875) was the daughter of Michiels's first wife, Maria Wilhelmina de Bruyn (d. 1803). Beijvanck was adjunct-secretary to the exchequer. He had been born in Batavia in 1780. After his death Agraphina married the Netherlander Petrus Henricus Menu. Her daughter Anna Elisabeth Augustijna Beijvanck married into the

patrician van Braam family, which held high offices under the colonial government. Descendants of the Michiels clan with European status were numerous in Batavia and the Netherlands by the twentieth century.

25 See J. B. J. van Doren, *Reis naar Nederlands Oost-Indië*, 2 vols. ('s-Gravenhage: J. and H. van Langenhuysen, 1851), 2:164, for a description of Citrap. Photographs of Citrap may be seen in van de Wall, *Buitenplaatsen*, pp. 121–22. He gives the history of Citrap's owners on pp. 142–53.

26 Ida was the daughter of Lambertus Dudde, burgher and administrator of estates, and later bailiff and president of the aldermen's council in Batavia in 1698. Her first marriage had been to Constantijn Coomans, who was a junior merchant in Ambon. Of the four children from this marriage, one, Ida Constantia (d. 1788), married into the Indies branch of the Mom family. Her husband succeeded to the title "heer van Maurik" in 1768.

27 De Loos-Haaxman, *Rach*, pp. 25, 39.

28 De Haan, *Platenalbum*, K32.

29 Resolution of 23 March 1779, *Realia*, 1:166.

30 An advertisement in the *Java Government Gazette* on 4 December 1813 describes a country house and estate for sale as bordering the property of "juff. Arnolda Schulp."

31 She was probably the wife of a W. Wargaren, a notary at Batavia in 1764.

32 See pp. 238–44 of *Voyage à Batavia*. The account is repeated practically word for word by J. J. Stockdale in his *Sketches, Civil and Military, of the Island of Java* (London: S. Gosnell, 1812), pp. 109–17), without acknowledgment of Stavorinus.

33 Decree of July 1680, *Plakaatboek*, 3:47.

34 Decree of 28 December 1729, *Plakaatboek*, 4:239–42.

35 The code is in *Plakaatboek*, 6:773–95.

36 *Plakaatboek*, 12:137–42 (11 December 1795).

37 The quotation is taken from a letter reproduced in van Troostenburg de Bruyn, *Hervormde Kerk*, pp. 257–58.

38 See decrees of 7 February 1755, *Plakaatboek*, 7:6, 27 September 1768, 8:542–44; and 23 August 1776, 10:47.

39 The 1757 limits were set by decree of 16 August (*Plakaatboek*, 7:232). The ban on importing children was passed in February/March 1757 (7:211).

40 See V. I. van de Wall, *Figuren en feiten uit den Compagniestijd* (Batavia: n.p., 1932), pp. 161–83, for a discussion of the will.

41 Resolution of 31 July 1714, *Realia*, 3:207. After 1758 Indonesian Christians might no longer be sold as slaves in punishment for various offenses but were to work for the government as free labor. *Plakaatboek*, 7:361 (14 December 1758).

42 The 1766 decree is in *Plakaatboek*, 8:109. That protecting the mother was issued on 17 January 1772 (8:734). Normally slaves were sold, with other forms of property, to cover debts of the deceased.

43 It will be noted that Davida formed her surname Augustijns on Michiels's first name, Augustijn. His first wife had been dead sixteen years when their marriage took place.

44 Decree of 21 March 1766, *Plakaatboek*, 8:121.

45 The ban exiling burgher Caspar de Wit is dated 2 October 1742 (*Realia*, 1:63). On 24 February 1808 a decree was passed empowering town courts to supervise and prevent "excesses" against slaves (*Plakaatboek*, 14:610–11).

46 See, for example, letters published in the *Java Government Gazette* in 1816 (4:102); and Dr. Strehler, *Bijzonderheden wegens Batavia*, trans. from the German (Haarlem: Wed. A. Loosjes Pz., 1833), pp. 141–44.

47 See laws on assembly and weapons of 20 August 1762 (*Plakaatboek*, 7:568–71), and 31 March 1778 (10:159–74). The ban on alcohol and opium is in *Realia*, 1:369 (16 January 1798).

48 Elsewhere I demonstrate that important men usually promoted their sons' careers by sending them to Europe. In this case van Hoorn *père*, a failed munitions merchant, was sent to Java with the rank of councillor to recoup his business losses.

49 Valentijn, *Oost-Indiën*, 4:236. Feuding among the various cliques allowed the distant VOC directors a measure of control. What these feuds and the family alliances suggest is the development of a world of interests in Batavia that were quite distinct from those of the VOC in the Netherlands.

50 The quotations are taken from a letter J. van Riemsdijk sent one of his children. It is cited by Breuning, *Voormalige Batavia*, p. 68.

51 F. W. Stapel, *Geschiedenis van Nederlandsch-Indië* (Amsterdam: J. M. Meulenhoff, 1930), pp. 182–83.

52 Decision of 1 June 1729 (*Realia*, 1:473). Versluys and de Witte were brothers-in-law as husbands to two daughters of Governor-General Mattheus de Haan. Versluys's first wife had been Adriana (d. 1727); de Witte married Anna, widow of Anthonij Chastelein, who was one of the heirs to the Depok properties (see n. 7 above and related text).

CHAPTER 4: THE ASSAULT ON INDIES CULTURE

1 On van Imhoff as governor of Ceylon and in particular his attention to reforming the schooling provided by the Company to local boys of European, Tamil, and Singhalese origin, see Jurrien van Goor, *Jan Kompenie as Schoolmaster: Dutch Education in Ceylon 1690–1795* (Groningen: Wolters-Noordhoff, 1978), chap. 4. The VOC played a far greater role in promoting Western education in Ceylon than in its other settlements, including its capital, and sent numbers of seminarians for theological studies in the Netherlands. Some were later to serve in parishes in Dutch Asia, including Batavia.

2 The *Consideratien over den tegenwoordigen staat van Nederlandsche Oost-Indische Maatschappij* were presented to the Directors on 24 November 1741. They are discussed by N. J. Krom in his *Gouverneur-Generaal Gustaaf Willem van Imhoff* (Amsterdam: van Kampen en Zoon, 1941), pp. 84–97.

3 Constitution of the theological seminary at Batavia, 25 June 1745, *Plakaatboek*, 5:241–47.

4 *Plakaatboek*, 7:147–48 (11 November 1755). The figures for pupils are given in de Haan, *Oud Batavia*, 2:271–72.

5 Directors to van Imhoff, 6 September 1745, *Plakaatboek*, 5:87. The regulations for the academy, issued on 25 August 1743, are in pp. 78–86 of that volume. The program of study was spelled out on 17 October 1745 (5:309–13).

6 Article 12 of marine academy regulations, *Plakaatboek*, 5:81–82.

7 Article 19, *Plakaatboek*, 5:82.

8 The charter was issued on 9 February 1745 (*Plakaatboek*, 5:189). The first page of issue 10 is reproduced in de Haan, *Platenalbum*, H8.

9 *Plakaatboek*, 5:335–36.

10 Under van Imhoff's regime Lutherans were permitted to worship publicly, and in 1745 they were allowed to build a church.

11 The order to close the convalescent home was dated 30 June 1761, when mineral springs were declared useless for restoring health (*Plakaatboek*, 7:500 ff.).

12 Request dated 25 October 1777, *Realia*, 1:345.

13 The prize list is given in *de Indische Navorscher* 1 (19):157–58 (October 1935).

14 Decree on "native teachers" is dated 25 November 1777 (*Plakaatboek*, 10:106). Instructions to Vermeer and Reinking are in the school regulations of 19 December 1777 (10:124–25).

15 5 February 1780, supplement to school regulations, *Plakaatboek*, 10:425–27.

16 Twenty-one girls with European status attended Boterkoper's school in 1778, along with 48 boys, 13 Chinese, 13 Muslims (i.e., free Asians), and slaves (de Haan, *Oud Batavia*, 2:261). The Rua Malacca or Malacca Street ran north-south on the west side of the Ciliwung. It was so named for the many Portuguese Asians who settled there round the inner Portuguese church in the 1640s, after the Dutch victory over the Portuguese in 1641 at Malacca.

17 Permission for Portuguese and Malay to be used in schools is contained in decision of 28 July 1786 (*Plakaatboek*, 10:849–50). Permission for classes in the poorhouse school to be taught in Portuguese is in decree of 12 August 1788 (11:35). Decision on catechism classes is dated 9 September 1788 (11:54).

18 *Plakaatboek* 10:343–45 (December 1788).

19 Titles of the *Transactions* are listed in Lian The and Paul W. Van der Veur, *The Verhandelingen van het Bataviaasch Genootschap* (Athens: Ohio University Center for International Studies, 1973), by author, with a brief description of contents, and by volume, pp. 27–128. Pages 1–26 give a brief history of the Academy.

20 The and Van der Veur, *Verhandelingen*, p. 3.

21 D. de Visser Smits, "Naamlijst van vrijmetselaren in Ned. Oost Indië van 1760 tot 1860," in his *Vrijmetselarij: Geschiedenis, maatschappelijke beteekenis en doel*, pp. 298–309. The membership list was sent me by Dr. Paul W. Van der Veur.

22 De Roo de la Faille, *Iets over Oud-Batavia*, p. 27.

23 Cantervisscher was the son of Tammerus Cantervisscher, junior merchant on Coromandel in 1751, and of Carolina Susanna Simons. Under the Company, C. A. Cantervisscher rose to be a councillor. He married a Petronella Hartingh from Semarang in 1790, founding a large Indies clan that was very mixed racially. Cantervisscher was initiated as a mason in 1790, Beijvanck in 1809.

24 De Haan, *Oud Batavia*, 2:280.

25 Smith married four times. In order, his wives were (1763) Hester Petronella Romp, daughter of Councillor Michiel Romp; (1780) Catharina Tobison, widow of Councillor Willem Fockens; (1781) Catharina Louisa Galles; and (1782) Johanna Mauritia Mohr.

26 Decree of 25 August 1808, *Plakaatboek*, 15:145–46.

27 Thomas Stamford Raffles, *The History of Java*, 2d ed., 2 vols. (London: John Murray, 1830), 2:270.

28 These figures are given by William Thorn, *Memoir of the Conquest of Java* (London: T. Egerton, 1815), p. 8. In addition to the Europeans, the invading force included 5,777 soldiers who were sepoys of the Madras, Bengal, and Bombay armies.

29 Lord Minto to his wife, in *Lord Minto in India* (London: Longmans, Green, 1880), pp. 304–5, 306.

30 See, for example, the *Java Government Gazette* 4 (1815), no. 195.

31 Unsigned letter to the editor, printed in the *Gazette* 2, no. 53 (27 February 1813).

32 See letters to the editor, *Gazette* 4, nos. 198, 199 (1815).

33 See, for example, the *Gazette* 3, nos. 139, 143, 147 (1814).

34 Thorn, *Conquest of Java*, p. 248.

35 *Gazette* 4, esp. nos. 175, 184 (1815).

36 Thorn, *Conquest of Java*, p. 249.

37 F. de Haan, *Priangan* (Batavia, 's-Gravenhage: Kolff, Nijhoff, 1910), vol. 1, pt. 2 ("Personalia"), p. 80.

38 Thomas Otto Travers, *The Journal of Thomas Otto Travers 1813–1820*, ed. John Bastin (Singapore: Government Printer, 1960), p. 57.

39 *Gazette* 2, no. 95 (18 December 1813).

40 According to the *Java Annual Directory and Almanac for 1816* (Batavia: Government Press, 1816), 112 males in the Solo region had European status. Women were not counted in the Almanac as residents or in any other statistics.

41 The visit to Yogyakarta, 8–12 December 1813, is recounted in the *Gazette* 2, no. 98 (8 January 1814).

42 Thorn, *Conquest*, p. 290.

43 See Thorn, *Conquest*, p. 239, and John Crawfurd, *History of the Indian Archipelago* (Edinburgh: Archibald Constable, 1820), 2:268, for remarks on the Javanese and alcohol.

44 Raffles, *History of Java*, 1:347. The "last Javan war" refers to the dynastic wars of the mid-eighteenth century in which the Company played a role and eventually enforced a division of Mataram into the sultanates of Solo and Yogyakarta.

45 Ibid.

46 Travers, *Journal*, entry for January 1816, p. 65.

47 Cornelis de Bruijn, *Reizen over Moskovië*, pp. 379–80.

48 See *Gazette* 2, no. 60 (17 April 1813); 4, no. 170 (27 May 1815); and 3, no. 124 (16 July 1814). This trio was all of one family: Dorothea van Riemsdijk was the mother of Sara Senn van Basel and aunt of Catharina Mom.

49 See, for instance, edicts of 8 August 1810 (*Plakaatboek*, 16:296–97), and 22 July 1811 (16:718).

50 *Gazette* 1, no. 7 (April 1812). Barrett, a commissioner of the court of requests, died in Batavia in September 1814. His widow, who was the daughter of a former senior merchant of the VOC, married J. I. van Sevenhoven after the death of his first wife, Catharina Mom.

51 Jan Samuel Timmerman Thyssen was head of the firm Timmerman Thyssen and Westerman in Batavia during the British period, and a member of the Bible Society and Harmonie Club. He succeeded his father-in-law, Abraham Couperus, as governor of Malacca from 1818 until his death there in 1823. Gesina Couperus (1785–1812) was his second wife.

52 *Gazette* 2, no. 84 (2 October 1813).

53 See entry for July 1815 in Travers's *Journal*, p. 53.

54 David Divine, *The Daughter of the Pangaran* (Boston, Toronto: Little, Brown, 1963). The novel centers on the relationship between Hare and the title character.

55 Williams was the administrator of a private estate west of Batavia and later a member of a trading company in the capital. A Dutch-language version of *Njai Dasima* was written and published by Alvares Theodorus Manusama at Batavia in 1926. It has been republished by Tong-Tong International at San Francisco in 1962. Komedie Stamboel was a Malay language theater putting Western and Middle Eastern stories into dramatic form with Indonesian and part-European actors. The name is formed from a contraction of "Istanbul" to Stamboel."

CHAPTER 5: THE DESTRUCTION OF VOC SOCIETY
AND THE CREATION OF THE NEW COLONIAL

1 The *Bataviasche Courant* (*Batavian Journal*) was published by the government press in the capital. Its first issue appeared on 20 August 1816. In time its name was changed to *Javasche Courant* in recognition of the island-wide community it served, and it became a daily paper.

2 Q. M. R. Ver Huell, *Herinneringen van eene reis naar de Oost-Indië*, 2 vols. (Amsterdam: Zweesardt, 1835), 1:32.

3 J. B. J. van Doren, *Reis naar Nederlands Oost-Indië*, 2 vols. ('s-Gravenhage: J. and H. van Langenhuysen, 1851), 2:43.

4 *Staatsblad van Nederlandsch-Indië* ('s-Gravenhage: A. D. Schinkel, 1839–86), 1818 vol., no. 87, art. 7, p. 217.

5 *Staatsblad*, 1836, no. 48, art. 2, p. 115.

6 *Staatsblad*, 1825, no. 32, pp. 110–14.

7 *Staatsblad*, 1836, no. 35, pp. 103–5.

8 *Staatsblad*, 1849, no. 19, 8 April. Page numberings in this and later volumes are for individual laws only rather than being continuous. For these volumes, therefore, laws are identified by number and date only.

9 On the "May movement" of 1848 see J. Th. Petrus Blumberger, *De Indo-Europeesche beweging in Nederlandsch-Indië* (Haarlem: H. D. Tjeenk Willink en Zoon, 1939), pp. 13 ff.

10 *Staatsblad*, 1864, no. 194, 10 September. See also W. M. F. Mansvelt, "De positie der Indo-Europeanen," in *Koloniale Studien* 16 (1):298 (1932). The Dutch terms stand for senior and junior officials' examinations, respectively.

11 The many branches of the family, numbering around 2,000 persons in the 1920s, were traced in accordance with provisions of W. V. H. van Riemsdijk's will concerning divisions of property in land, and the findings were published by P. R. Feith and P. C. Bloys van Treslong Prins in *De bekende landheer van Tjampea c.a. Willem Vincent Helvetius van Riemsdijk* (Batavia: Kolff, 1933).

12 Ament was a Netherlander who settled permanently in Java. He had nine children by Dina van Riemsdijk. Their descendants were still living in Batavia in the 1920s.

13 *Staatsblad*, 1818, no. 8, art. 113, p. 234; and 1855, Government Law no. 2, 4 January 1855. Article 115 declared that slavery would be abolished throughout the Indies on 1 January 1860 (though not debt-slavery) (pp. 27–28).

221

14 *Javasche Courant* 24, 21 March 1840. This van Riemsdijk was a granddaughter of W. V. H. van Riemsdijk in the legitimate line. She had four children by ten Cate, who was a native Netherlander and husband number one, and a fifth by her second husband, Gerrit Jacobus van Capelle, who stemmed from Ambon.

15 Ver Huell, *Herinneringen,* 1:197–98.

16 The generations descending on Wilhelmina's mother's side were (1) Johanna Henriette Breekpot, 1738–80; (2) Catharina Margaretha Craan, 1754–92; and (3) Theodora Jacoba van Riemsdijk, 1775–1815.

17 The generations descending on Anthoinette's mother's side were (1) Catharina Hermina Regel, born Madras; and (2) Catharina Johanna Wilhelmina Bogaardt, born Bengal.

18 This was Johanna Sara Wilhelmina van Braam Morris, Batavia-born wife of Governor-General Otto van Rees (1884–88).

19 The Agriculture Law permitted Indonesians to lease their land to private planters on short-term contracts, and also allowed planters to obtain government-owned, uncultivated land on Java and Madura on heritable lease for periods of up to seventy-five years.

20 The figures cited above are taken from two sources: John S. Furnivall, *Netherlands India: A Study in Plural Economy* (Cambridge: Cambridge University Press, 1944), p. 212; and B. H. M. Vlekke, *Nusantara: A History of Indonesia,* rev. ed. (The Hague and Bandung: W. van Hoeve, 1959), p. 314. The last census in which an attempt was made to distinguish groups within the European category was 1854. Of the 18,000 Europeans, 9,360, or half, were counted as being "visibly" part-Asian, and another large portion of the remainder were regarded as Eurasian. See A. van Marle, "De groep der Europeanen in Nederlands Indië," *Indonesië* 5 (5):487 (1955).

21 Advertisements placed by women seeking employment as governesses, midwives, and in retailing start appearing in Indies newspapers around 1840. Their activities can be traced through the private, regional newspapers that date on Java from the 1860s as well.

22 R. Nieuwenhuys, "Over de Europese samenleving van 'tempo doeloe' 1870–1900," *de Fakkel* 1 (1940/41):777, 782.

23 For a detailed survey of Indies clubs, see Hein Buitenweg [pseud. for H. C. Meijer], *Soos en samenleving in tempo doeloe* (The Hague: Servire, 1965). The book is richly illustrated with photographs of the years from about 1870 to the 1930s.

24 A different style of Mestizo culture evolved in Sumatra, influenced by the model of nearby British Malaya. A picture of colonial society in Deli before World War II has been drawn by Lily Clerkx in *Mensen in Deli* (Amsterdam: Amsterdam University Press, 1961).

25 van Doren, *Reis,* 2:229.

26 G. W. Skinner, "Change and Persistence in Chinese Culture Overseas: A Comparison of Thailand and Java," *Journal of the South Seas Society* 16 (1960):86–100. Quotation from p. 95.

27 W. F. Wertheim, *Het sociologisch karakter van de Indo-Maatschappij* (Amsterdam: Vrij Nederland, 1947), p. 5.

CHAPTER 6: THE INNER LIFE OF LATE COLONIAL SOCIETY

1 This summary of critiques of colonial life is based on: J. Hennus, *Eene stem uit Oost-Indië in gemeenzame brieven aan zijnen vader* (Utrecht: van der Post Jr., 1847);

A. W. P. Weitzel, *Batavia in 1858* (Gorinchem: Noorduijn, 1860); "Oudgast," *Onze Oost* (Amsterdam: J. A. Sleeswijk, 1897); B. Veth, *Het leven in Nederlandsch-Indië* 4th ed. (Amsterdam: P. N. van Kampen en Zoon, [c. 1900]); J. Chailly-Bert, *Java et ses habitants* (Paris: Armand Colin, 1900); Hendrik P. N. Muller, "De Europeesche samenleving," in H. Colijn, ed., *Neerlands Indië* (Amsterdam: Elsevier, 1912), 2:371–84; and E. Stark, *Uit Indië, Egypte en het Heilige Land*, 2d ed. (Amersfoort: Veen, 1913).

2 See the following works: Augusta de Wit, *Java, Facts and Fancies* (London: Chapman and Hall, 1905); Marie van Zeggelen, *De Hollandsche vrouw in Indië*, 2d ed. (Amsterdam: Groesbeek and Nijhoff, [c. 1910]); and the exponents of "tempo doeloe" (the good old days): Victor Ido [Hans van de Wall], *Indië in de goede oude tijd* (The Hague: van Hoeve, 1966); E. Breton de Nijs [Rob Nieuwenhuys], *Tempo Doeloe* (Amsterdam: Querido, 1961); and Hein Buitenweg [H. C. Meijer], *Kind in tempo doeloe* (Wassenaer: Servire, 1964), and *Wat wij in ons hart sloten* (The Hague: Servire, 1962), this last with Willem Krols. See also *Het meisje uit Indië*, published by *Tong-Tong*, the magazine of Eurasians in Holland (The Hague: Uitgeverij Tong-Tong, 1966).

3 See the collection of essays *Zoo leven wij in Indië*, 3d ed., ed. C. W. Wormser (Deventer: van Hoeve, 1943). The "wij" (we) and "ons" (our) in the titles of chapters and texts refer only to immigrant Europeans, and there is considerable discussion of avoiding "Indianization." On this subject see also Rob Nieuwenhuys's quotations from the Indies journalist Ritman in *Tussen twee vaderlanden* (Amsterdam: G. A. van Oorschot, 1959), p. 16.

4 See, for example, pp. 58, 88, and 116 of R. Nieuwenhuys, *Tempo Doeloe*; also the photograph of Mevrouw Junghuhn, guests, and servants in C. Steinmetz, "Cultureele gegevens uit familiepapieren II: Dr. Franz Wilhelm Junghuhn (1809–1864)," *Cultureel Indië* 4 (1942):175.

5 Augusta de Wit, *Java, Facts and Fancies*, pp. 250–54. The Western-educated bupati of Serang and later of Batavia, Achmad Djajadiningrat, comments on behavior expected of Indonesians by their Dutch superiors in the administration in his *Kenang-Kenangan* (Batavia: Kolff-Buning–Balai Poestaka, 1936), p. 154. This is the Indonesian translation of his memoirs, which appeared in 1936 as *Herinneringen van Pangeran Aria Achmad Djajadiningrat* (Amsterdam, Batavia: Kolff).

6 See esp. H. P. N. Muller, "De Europeesche samenleving," in *Neerlands Indië*, 2:371–84, for a good example of omission. See also D. M. G. Koch, *Verantwoording* (The Hague: Bandung: van Hoeve, 1956). In this book, the term European always means that minority born in Holland, although this is never explicitly stated.

7 *De Locomotief, Samarangsch Handels en Advertentie-Blad* 14, no. 8 (27 January 1865), and 34, no. 17 (21 January 1885).

8 *Locomotief* 34, no. 204 (26 August 1885).

9 *Locomotief* 34, no. 7 (9 January 1885), and 13, no. 97 (5 December 1864), respectively.

10 *Locomotief* 34, no. 68 (18 March 1885). The "four languages" were Dutch, German, French, and English.

11 *Locomotief* 34, no. 17 (21 January 1885).

12 Examples of this kind of advertisement may be found in *Locomotief* 14, nos. 26 and 34 (31 March and 28 April 1865).

13 See, for example, *Locomotief* 14, no. 36 (5 May 1865), and 35, no. 147 (26 June 1866).

14 *Locomotief* 34, nos. 9 and 41 (12 January and 16 February 1885), respectively. "Indische" means Eurasian or Creole, in this context.

15 *Locomotief* 34, no. 207 (29 August 1885).

16 *Locomotief* 34 (1885), nos. 206 (28 August), 246 (12 October), 27 (31 January), 130 (1 June), and 144 (17 June), respectively.

17 *Locomotief* 80 (1904), nos. 14 (11 January), 205 (3 September), and 181 (5 August), respectively.

18 *Javasche Courant*, 1850, nos. 39 and 83 (15 May and 16 October), respectively.

19 *Locomotief* 80, no. 286 (7 December 1904).

20 *Locomotief* 14, no. 17 (27 February 1865), signed "P. R."

21 *Locomotief* 14, no. 20 (10 March 1865), signed "K." "K" seems to be using "European" in two distinct ways in his argument, meaning in the first use children of parents classified as European, and in the second, immigrants.

22 I. J. Brugmans, *Geschiedenis van het onderwijs in Nederlandsch-Indië* (Groningen, Batavia: J. B. Wolters, 1938), p. 295.

23 E. F. E. Douwes Dekker is the author of the most famous novel of colonial life, *Max Havelaar* (8th ed., Rotterdam: A. D. Donker, 1967). It was first published in 1860 under the pseudonym Multatuli. P. A. Daum's Indies novels appeared first in serial form in the *Bataviaasch Nieuwsblad* above the name Maurits. The editions used are: *Goena-Goena, een geschiedenis van stille kracht* (Amsterdam: Querido, 1964), first published in 1887 (1889 in book form); *Hoe hij Raad van Indië werd* (Semarang, Dorp, 1888); *Uit de suiker in de tabak* (Amsterdam: Salamander, 1962); and *"Ups" en "Downs" in het Indische leven* (5th ed., Amsterdam: Contact, 1946), first published 1890 (book form 1892). Louis Couperus's Indies novel *De stille kracht*, 1900, was first published in English in 1922 as *The Hidden Force: A Story of Modern Java*, trans. A. Teixeira de Mattos (London: Jonathon Cape, 1922). Two other Indies novels by male authors which have been used as sources for the social history of the Indies are Jan ten Brink's *Oost-Indische dames en heeren* (Arnhem: D. A. Thieme, 1866), and G. Valette's *Baren en oudgasten* ('s-Gravenhage: H. J. Stemberg, 1880).

24 See Rob Nieuwenhuys, *Oost-Indische spiegel* (Amsterdam: Querido, 1972), sect. 9, "Romantiek in sarong kabaja"; and J. M. van der Kroef, "The Colonial Novel in Indonesia," *Comparative Literature* 10 (2): 215–31 (Summer 1958).

25 Madelon Lulofs, *Coolie*, trans. G. J. Renier and Irene Cléphane (New York: Viking, 1936); and *White Money*, same trans. (New York, London: Century, 1933).

26 The titles and editions used are: Katja-Mata [Marie Frank], *Een natuurlijk kind en andere Nederlandsch-Indische verhalen* (Leiden: Noothaven van Goor, 1875); Annie Foore [Françoise IJzerman-Junius], *Indische huwelijken*, 2nd ed. (Rotterdam: 1895), *De van Sons, een verhaal uit Indië* (The Hague: Stemberg, 1881), and *Bogoriana*, 3d ed. (Haarlem: Tjeenk Willink en Zoon, 1908); Mina Kruseman, *Een huwelijk in Indië* (The Hague: Martinus Nijhoff, 1873); Thérèse Hoven, *In sarong en kabaai* (Amsterdam: Veen, 1892), *Vervreemd*, (Amersfoort: Valkhoff, n.d.), and *Nonnie en andere verhalen* (Tiel: Campagne en Zoon, n.d.); and Melati van Java [Marie Sloot], *De familie van den Resident*, 3d ed. (Schiedam: H. A. M. Roelants, n.d.).

27 Marie Sloot, *Soerapati*, 3d ed. 2 vols. (Schiedam: H. A. M. Roelants, 1928).

28 Marie van Zeggelen, *Kartini, een baanbreekster voor haar volk*, 3d ed. (Amsterdam: J. M. Meulenhoff, 1947).

29 Françoise Junius, *Bogoriana*, p. 39.

30 Marie Frank, "In een sterfhuis," eighth in the collection *Een natuurlijk kind*, p. 271.

31 See G. Valette, *Baren en oudgasten*, pp. 41–53; Oudgast, *Onze Oost*, pp. 42, 90 (Oudgast is a pen name and means "old-timer"); and Rob Nieuwenhuys, "Over de Europese samenleving van 'tempo doeloe' 1870–1900," *de Fakkel* 1 (1940/41):778.

32 Françoise Junius, "Geketend," the final story in the collection *Indische huwelijken*, pp. 104–207.

33 Quoted by W. F. Wertheim, *Indonesian Society in Transition*, 2d rev. ed. (The Hague, Bandung: van Hoeve, 1959), p. 138, n. 1.

34 "De vergissing van den Engelschman," no. 6 in Frank's collection *Een natuurlijk kind*, pp. 202–34.

35 Thérèse Hoven, " 't was maar een baboe," last story in *In sarong en kabaai*, pp. 201–23. The quotation is from p. 215.

36 Mina Kruseman, *Een huwelijk in Indië*.

37 Marie Frank, "Een natuurlijk kind," title story of the collection, pp. 1–73.

38 Ibid., p. 21.

39 Françoise Junius, "Willie's Mama," *Indische huwelijken*, pp. 39–103.

40 Mr. Conrad Theodor van Deventer published "A Debt of Honor" in *de Gids* of August 1899. Brooshoeft was for many years the editor of the *Locomotief*. His famous pamphlet "The Ethical Course in Colonial Policy" was first published in 1901. Those accepting his and van Deventer's convictions about colonial reform were called Ethici.

41 Marie Sloot, *De familie van den Resident*, p. 104.

42 Sloot, *Familie*, p. 122.

43 Thérèse Hoven, *Vervreemd*, pp. 98–99. *Sinjo* (new spelling *sinyo*) is derived from the Portuguese *senhor*, and was used in colonial times as a pejorative term for Eurasian men. *Indo* is the common abbreviation of the Dutch *Indo-Europeaan* meaning Eurasian.

44 See J. Th. Petrus Blumberger, *De Indo-Europeesche beweging*, and P. W. Van der Veur, "E. F. E. Douwes Dekker, Evangelist for Indonesian Political Nationalism," *Journal of Asian Studies* 18 (4): 551–66 (August 1958).

45 Sloot, *Soerapati*, p. 23. Surapati is the modern Indonesian spelling.

46 Junius, *De van Sons*, p. 118.

47 Ibid., p. 120.

48 Ibid., p. 145.

49 Ibid., p. 209.

50 J. S. Furnivall, *Netherlands India* (Cambridge: Cambridge University Press, 1944), p. 446.

51 E. Breton de Nijs [Rob Nieuwenhuys], *Vergeelde portretten uit een Indisch familiealbum*, 5th ed. (Amsterdam: Salamandar, 1963); Maria Dermoût, *De tienduizend dingen*, trans. into English by Hans Koningsberger as *The Ten Thousand Things* (New York: Simon and Schuster, 1958), and *Nog pas gisteren*, trans. by Hans Koningsberger as *Yesterday* (New York: Simon and Schuster, 1959).

EPILOGUE

1 A. W. P. Weitzel, *Batavia in 1858* (Gorinchem: Noorduijn, 1860), pp. 157–58. He says that the Dutch spoke Indonesian languages so badly that they always offended Indonesians of good family.

2 A small sampling might include Thérèse Hoven's "Een inlandsch feest" and "Bij onze gestaarte broeders op visite," both in the collection *In sarong en kabaai*, pp. 147–53 and 111–21, respectively. For photos, see Rob Nieuwenhuys, *Tempo Doeloe*, pp. 101, 102, 106; and H. C. Meijer, *De laatste tempo doeloe*, pp. 66, 136, 146.

3 For articles on Raden Saleh, see Tamar Djaja, *Pusaka Indonesia*, 4th ed. (Djakarta: Bulan Bintang, 1966), 2:470–76 (no. 44); J. de Loos-Haaxman, *Verlaat rapport Indië* (The Hague: Mouton, 1968), chs. 14, 15, and paintings 58–66; and V. I. van de Wall, "Beschrijving van eenige werken van Raden Saleh," in *Cultureel Indië* 4 (1942):159–67. The seven paintings under discussion are reproduced in the article.

4 Q. M. R. Ver Huell, *Herinneringen*, 2:61–62.

5 Ver Huell, *Herinneringen* 2:82–84. "Regent" was the term used by the Dutch for the Javanese official, the bupati, who headed an administrative unit immediately below the residency, in turn headed by a European official with the title resident. The regent or bupati reported to the resident.

6 *Locomotief* 15, no. 41 (22 May 1866), and 53, no. 107 (7 May 1904), respectively.

7 *Locomotief* 14, no. 65 (14 August 1865).

8 *Locomotief* 14, no. 90 (supp. to the issue for 10 November 1865).

9 *Locomotief* 15, no. 18 (2 March 1866).

10 *Locomotief* 34, no. 119 (18 May 1885). Much of the *Locomotief* obituary was reprinted from the *Tegalsch Advertentieblad*.

11 See, for instance, R. A. Kartini, "Het huwelijk bij de Kodjas," in *Bijdragen tot de Taal-, Land- en Volkenkunde*, 1899, fasc. 6, pt. 6, pp. 695–702. Excerpts from her essays are quoted by Hendrik Bouman, *Meer Licht over Kartini* (Amsterdam: H. J. Paris, 1954). Her memorial to the Dutch government entitled "Geef den Javaan opvoeding!" has been translated into English by Jean Taylor as "Educate the Javanese!" and printed in *Indonesia* 17:86–98 (April 1974).

12 Her collected letters to Dutch acquaintances were edited by J. H. Abendanon as *Door duisternis tot licht*, 4th ed. ('s-Gravenhage: "Luctor et Emergo," 1923).

13 W. F. Wertheim, *Indonesian Society in Transition*, 2d rev. ed. (The Hague, Bandung: van Hoeve, 1959), pp. 292–93.

14 The *Java Bode* article was reprinted in *Locomotief* 53, no. 18 (22 January 1904).

15 *Herinneringen van Pangeran Aria Achmad Djajadiningrat*, (Amsterdam, Batavia: G. Kolff, 1936). They were published in Indonesian translation that same year under the title *Kenang-Kenangan*.

16 See letters to Stella Zeehandelaar of 12 January 1900 and to R. M. Abendanon-Mantri of 27 October 1902, in *Duisternis*.

17 These advertisements are taken from the *Locomotief* as follows: 15, no. 38 (11 May 1866); 34, no. 76 (26 March 1885); 53, no. 27 (2 February 1904), for death notice on the mother; 53, no. 154 (4 July 1904); 53, no. 178 (1 August 1904), for marriage announcement for R. A. Patemah; and 53, no. 271 (19 November 1904).

18 Photographs of reception rooms of Javanese aristocrats may be seen in Rob Nieuwenhuys, *Tempo Doeloe*, pp. 105, 106, 111.

19 *Locomotief* 53, no. 179 (3 August 1904).

20 *Locomotief* 53, no. 180 (4 August 1904).

21 The colonial novels are a major source of information on party manners. The works
of J. ten Brink, Daum, and Couperus all reveal the persistent Mestizo custom of
segregation. This, of course, had deep roots in colonial history.

22 As examples see Merari Siregar, *Azab dan Sengsara* (Torment and Trouble) 4th ed.
(Jakarta: Balai Pustaka, 1965); Marah Rusli, *Siti Nurbaya* (Miss Nurbaya) 2d ed.
(Kuala Lumpur: Pustaka Melayu Baru, 1966); Abdul Muis, *Salah Asoehan* (A Wrong
Upbringing) (Weltevreden: Balai Pustaka, 1928), and *Pertemuan Djodoh* (The Cou-
ple's Meeting) (Bukittinggi, Jakarta: Nusantara, 1964 ed.); Takdir Alisjahbana, *La-
jar Terkembang* (With Sails Unfurled) (Jakarta: Balai Pustaka, 1928); and Hamidah,
Kehilangan Mestika (Loss of the Jewel) (Jakarta: Balai Pustaka, n.d.).

23 *Staatsblad*, 1855, no. 2 (4 January), publication of Constitutional Law No. 129 in the
Nederlandsch Staatsblad, 2 September 1854. See chap. 6, art. 109, pp. 26–27.

24 A. van Marle, ''De groep der Europeanen,'' *Indonesië* 5 (2):99.

25 Ibid., p. 109.

26 Ibid. (5):500.

Glossary

The terms listed below are from Indonesian languages *(I)* or from Dutch *(D)*.

adat (I)	custom, tradition, law, and lore
bupati (I)	head of an administrative district on Java lower than a province
gamelan (I)	Javanese orchestra
kabupaten (I)	administrative district headed by a bupati residence of the bupati
kampung (I)	village Indonesian residential quarter in city
kebaya (I)	overblouse, woman's blouse
mardijker (D)	free(d) person, usually a Christian of non-Indonesian Asian origins
nyai (I)	term used by the Dutch to denote a concubine to a European; a housekeeper
raden (I)	title of a senior Javanese official
raden ajeng (I)	title of an unmarried daughter of a senior Javanese official
raden ayu (I)	title of a consort of a senior Javanese official
ronggeng (I)	dancing girl
susuhunan (I)	title of the ruler of Solo
wayang (I)	shadow puppet theater type of theater using human actors in puppet styles

Selected Bibliography

Note: The authorities on which this study is founded are generally acknowledged in footnotes to the text. The sources for the family histories are not usually cited, however, since the relationships described have been determined by drawing on various studies of several authors. The following note outlines the nature of the material used to establish family trees.

The principal sources used to establish Indies clans are the Dutch scholars P. C. Bloys van Treslong Prins, P. R. Feith, F. de Haan, M. A. van Rhede van der Kloot, and W. Wijnaendts van Resandt. Bloys van Treslong Prins collected texts from tombstones of the European community on Java and began publishing them in 1934. The epitaphs are grouped by geographic region, but there is an index of surnames. In collaboration with P. R. Feith, the same author published the complete genealogical table for the van Riemsdijken down to the 1920s, a task commissioned for testamentary purposes. Wijnaendts van Resandt published summaries of the careers of all heads of settlements subsidiary to Batavia, in which he gave the names of spouses and children, and appended a register of family names. The posts of senior merchant and governor were common stepping stones to higher office, so that his work ties in with similar compilations by F. de Haan for officials in Priangan and by van Rhede van der Kloot for the governors-general.

Additional sources were L. Ludovici's collection of Dutch tombstone inscriptions from Ceylon, Steinmetz's notes on the texts on china and memorial trays that summarize family alliances, and notes in Dutch genealogical journals.

The sources I have used dictated that the family histories discovered be those of local elites. The same reasons of worldly distinction made the senior officials and their families the subjects of paintings, odes, descriptions by travelers, and legal regulations, and again more accessible for study than the soldier and sailor.

The bibliography that follows is divided into seven sections for ease of reference. All titles in foreign languages are also given in English in my translation. Authors' names are listed according to Dutch practice.

DICTIONARIES, BIBLIOGRAPHIES, ENCYCLOPEDIAS

Bruggencate, K. ten. *Nederlands-Engels woordenboek* (Dutch-English dictionary). 6th ed. Groningen: J. B. Wolters, 1963.

Buur, Dorothée. *Persoonlijke documenten Nederlands-Indië/Indonesië* (Personal documents from Netherlands India/Indonesia). Leiden: Koninklijk Instituut voor Taal-, Land- en Volkenkunde, 1973.

Chijs, J. A. van der. *Proeve eener Ned. Indische bibliographie (1659–1870): Vermeerderde en verbeterde herdruk voor de jaren 1659–1720, supplement en verbeteringen voor de jaren 1721–1870* (Sampling of a Netherlands Indies bibliography, 1659–1870: Enlarged and improved reprint for the years 1659–1720, supplement and revisions for 1721–1870). Batavia: W. Bruining & Co., 1879.

Coolhaas, W. Ph. *A Critical Survey of Studies in Dutch Colonial History*. Koninklijk Instituut voor Taal-, Land- en Volkenkunde Bibliographic Series, no. 4. 's-Gravenhage: M. Nijhoff, 1960.

Echols, John M., and Hassan Shadily. *An Indonesian-English Dictionary*. 2d ed. Ithaca: Cornell University Press, 1963.

Encyclopaedië van Nederlandsch-Indië (Encyclopedia of the Netherlands Indies). 's-Gravenhage, Leiden: M. Nijhoff and E. J. Brill, n.d.

Meilink-Roelofsz, M. A. P. "Sources in the General State Archives in The Hague Relating to the History of East Asia between c. 1600 and c. 1800." In *Felicitation Volumes of Southeast-Asian Studies* presented to His Highness Dhaninivat Kromamun Bidyalbh Bridhyakorn on the occasion of his 80th birthday, 1:167–84. Bangkok, The Siam Society, 1965.

Middelnederlandsch woordenboek (Middle Dutch dictionary). Compiled by E. Verwijs and J. Verdam, completed by F. A. Stoett. 11 vols. 's-Gravenhage: M. Nijhoff, 1885–1941.

Pluvier, J. M. "Recent Dutch Contributions to Modern Indonesian History." *Journal of Southeast Asian History* 8 (2):201–25 (September 1967).

Santa Maria, Luigi. *I Prestiti Portoghesi nel Malese-Indonesiano* (Portuguese loan words in Malay-Indonesian). Naples: Seminario de Indianistica, 1967.

The, Lian, and Paul W. Van der Veur. *The Verhandelingen van het Bataviaasch Genootschap: An Annotated Content Analysis*. Athens: Ohio University Center for International Studies, 1973.

Yule, Henry, and A. C. Burnell. *Hobson-Jobson: A Glossary of Colloquial Anglo-Indian Words and Phrases, and of Kindred Terms, Etymological, Historical, Geographical and Discursive*. 2d ed. London: John Murray, 1903.

ARCHIVAL MATERIALS

Collectie Kartini (Kartini Collection). Leiden. Koninklijk Instituut voor Taal-, Land- en Volkenkunde. No. 897.

Leiden. Koninklijk Instituut voor Taal-, Land- en Volkenkunde, H853. B. van den Ende-van Huffel, "Jeugdherinneringen uit tempo doeloe" (Memories of youth in the olden days).

Leiden. Koninklijk Instituut voor Taal-, Land- en Volkenkunde, H1007. E. Houtman-Mesman and A. Bouman-Houtman, "Uit tempo doeloe" (In Olden Times).

VOLUMES COMPILING PRIMARY DOCUMENTS, LAWS, LETTERS, PAINTINGS, AND PHOTOGRAPHS; NEWSPAPERS

Bastin, John, and Bea Brommer, eds. *Nineteenth-Century Prints and Illustrated Books of Indonesia, with particular reference to the print collection of the Tropenmuseum,*

Amsterdam: A Descriptive Bibliography. Utrecht, Antwerp: Het Spectrum, 1979.

Bataviasche Courant (Batavian journal), 1816, nos 1–20 (20 August–28 December).

Bland, Robert Norman. *Historical Tombstones of Malacca, mostly of Portuguese Origin, with the inscriptions in detail and illustrated by numerous photographs.* London: Stock, 1905.

Buitenweg, Hein. See Meijer, H. Chr.

Chijs, J. A. van der. *De Nederlanders te Jakatra. Uit de bronnen, zoo uitgegevene als niet uitgegevene* (The Dutch in Jakatra. From both published and unpublished sources). Amsterdam: F. Muller, 1860.

Chijs, J. A. van der, ed. *Nederlandsch-Indisch Plakaatboek 1602–1811* (Collection of Netherlands Indies edicts 1602–1811). 16 vols. and index. Batavia, 's-Gravenhage: Landsdrukkerij, M. Nijhoff, 1885–1900.

Colenbrander, Herman Theodoor. *Jan Pietersz. Coen: Bescheiden omtrent zijn bedrijf in Indië* (Jan Pietersz. Coen: Documents on his undertakings in the Indies). 5 vols. 's-Gravenhage: M. Nijhoff, 1919–23.

Coolhaas, W. Ph. *Generale Missiven van Gouverneurs-Generaal en Raden aan Heeren XVII der Verenigde Oostindische Compagnie* (General correspondence from governors-general and councillors to the Gentlemen XVII of the United East Indies Company). Vol. 1, *1610–1638.* 's-Gravenhage: M. Nijhoff, 1960.

Dagh-Register gehouden int Casteel Batavia vant passerende daer ter plaetse also over geheel Nederlandts-India (Daily Register kept in Batavia Citadel on events there and in all Netherlands India). 28 vols. 's-Gravenhage: M. Nijhoff, 1896–1912.

Elliott, Gilbert. *Lord Minto in India: Life and Letters of Gilbert Elliot, First Earl of Minto from 1807 to 1814 while Governor-General of India.* London: Longmans, Green & Co., 1880.

Godée Molsbergen, Everhardus C. *Geschiedenis van de Nederlandsch Oost-Indische Compagnie en Nederlandsch-Indië in beeld* (History of the Netherlands East Indies Company and of Netherlands India in pictures). Weltevreden: Topografische Inrichting, 1925.

Haan, F. de. *Oud Batavia Gedenkboek Platenalbum* (Album of plates, Old Batavia commemorative volume). Batavia: C. Kolff & Co., 1923.

Henige, David P. ed. and comp., *Colonial Governors from the Fifteenth Century to the Present.* Madison: University of Wisconsin Press, 1970.

Hennus, Johannes. *Eene stem uit Oost-Indië in gemeenzame brieven van Johannes Hennus aan zijnen vader* (A voice out of the East Indies in private letters from Johannes Hennus to his father). Utrecht: van der Post, 1847.

Hoynck van Papendrecht, P. C. "Some Old Private Letters from the Cape, Batavia and Malacca (1778–1788)." *Journal of the Malayan Branch of the Royal Asiatic Society* 2, pt. 1 (June 1924):9–24.

The Java Annual Directory and Almanac for 1816. Batavia: A. H. Hubbard, Government Press, 1816.

Java Government Gazette 1, no. 45, through 5, no. 234 (2 January 1813–17 August 1816), plus Extraordinary Issue of 19 August 1816.

Javasche Courant (Java journal), 1830, nos. 1–154 (5 January–30 December); 1840, nos. 1–105 (1 January–30 December); and 1850, nos. 1–104 (2 January–28 December).

Jonge, J. K. J. de. *De opkomst van het Nederlandsch gezag in Oost-Indië: Verzameling van onuitgegeven stukken uit het oud-koloniaal archief* (The origins of Dutch rule in the East Indies: Collection of unpublished documents from old colonial archives). 13 vols. 's-Gravenhage: M. Nijhoff, 1862–88.

Kartini, Raden Adjeng. *Door duisternis tot licht: Gedachten over en voor het Javaansche volk* (From darkness into light: reflections on and for the Javanese people). 4th ed., introduced by J. H. Abendanon. 's-Gravenhage: "Luctor et Emergo," 1923.

De Locomotief: Samarangsch Handels en Advertentieblad (The Locomotive: Semarang trade and advertising paper) 13 (1864), nos. 69–104 (29 August–30 December); 14 (1865), nos. 1–104 (2 January–29 December); 15 (1866), nos. 1–52 (2 January–29 June); 34 (1885), nos. 1–315 (2 January–31 December); and 53 (1904), nos. 1–305 (2 January–31 December).

Loos-Haaxman, J. de. *Dagwerk in Indië: Hommage aan een verstild verleden* (Daily work in the Indies: Hommage to times past). Franeker: T. Wever, 1972.

Loos-Haaxman, J. de. *Johannes Rach en zijn werk* (Johannes Rach and his work). Batavia: Kolff, 1928.

Loos-Haaxman, J. de. *De landsverzameling schilderijen in Batavia: Landvoogdsportretten en compagnieschilders* (The state collection of paintings in Batavia: Portraits of governors-general and Company painters). Vol. 1, text; vol. 2, paintings. Leiden: Sijthoff, 1941.

Loos-Haaxman, J. de. *Verlaat rapport Indië: Drie eeuwen westerse schilders, tekenaars, grafici, zilversmeden en kunstnijveren in Nederlands-Indië* (Record of the Indies: Three centuries of Western painters, sketchers, graphicists, silver-smiths and craftsmen in Netherlands India). 's-Gravenhage: Mouton & Co., 1968.

Ludovici, Leopold. *Lapidarium Zeylandicum, being a Collection of Monumental Inscriptions of the Dutch Churches and Churchyards of Ceylon.* Colombo: Maitland & Co., 1877.

Meijer, H. Chr. *De laatste tempo doeloe* (The Last Bygone Days). The Hague: Servire, 1964.

Meijer, H. Chr. *Soos en samenleving in tempo doeloe* (Club and society in the good old days). The Hague: Servire, 1965.

Nieuwenhuys, Rob. *Batavia, koningin van het oosten* (Batavia, Queen of the East). 2d ed. 's-Gravenhage: Thomas & Evas, 1977.

Nieuwenhuys, Rob. *Tempo Doeloe: Fotografische documenten uit het oude Indië 1870–1914* (Times past: Photographic documents from the Old Indies 1870–1914). Amsterdam: E. M. Querido, 1961.

Nijs, E. Breton de. See Nieuwenhuys, Rob.

Perron, Edgar du. *De muze van Jan Compagnie: Overzichtelijke verzameling van Nederlands-Oostindiese belletrie uit de Companjiestijd (1600–1780)* (John Company's muse: General sampling of Netherlands East Indies belles lettres from the Company times 1600–1780). Bandung: A. C. Nix & Co., 1948.

Realia: Register op de generale resolutien van het kasteel Batavia 1632–1805 (Realities: Register of general resolutions from Batavia Citadel 1632–1805). Vol. 1, *A–H.* Leiden: Kolff, 1882. Vol. 2, *I–O.* The Hague: Nijhoff, 1885. Vol. 3, *P–Z.* The Hague: Nijhoff, 1886.

Staatsblad van Nederlandsch-Indië (Statute book of the Netherlands Indies). Vols. for

1816, 1817, 1818, 1825, 1836, 1849, 1855, 1864, and 1885. 's-Gravenhage: A. D. Schinkel, 1839–86.

Tiele, P. A., and J. E. Heeres. *Bouwstoffen voor de geschiedenis der Nederlanders in den Maleischen Archipel* (Materials for the history of the Dutch in the Malay archipelago). 3 vols. The Hague: Nijhoff, 1886, 1890, 1895.

JOURNALS, MEMOIRS, AND TRAVELERS' NARRATIVES

Bollingii, Friderici. "Oost-Indisch reisboek, uit het Deensch vertaald door Mej. Joh. Visscher" (East Indian travel book, translated from the Danish by Miss. Joh. Visscher). *Bijdragen tot de Taal-, Land- en Volkenkunde* 68 (1913):291–381.

Bruijn, Cornelis de. *Reizen over Moskovië, door Persië en Indië* (Travels through Muscovy, Persia and the Indies). Amsterdam: Goerée, 1711.

Chailly-Bert, J. *Java et ses habitants* (Java and its people). Paris: A. Colin & Cie., 1900.

Coolsma, S. *Terugblik op mijn levensweg (1840–1924)* (Retrospect on my life, 1840–1924). Rotterdam: Bredée, 1924.

Djajadiningrat, P. A. A. *Kenang-Kenangan.* (Memoirs) Batavia: Kolff-Buning–Balai Poestaka, 1936.

Doren, J. B. J. van. *Reis naar Nederlands Oost-Indië of Land- en zeetogten gedurende de twee eerste jaren mijns verblijfs op Java* (Journey to Netherlands East India, or land and sea travels during the first two years of my sojourn on Java). 2 vols. 's-Gravenhage: J. & H. van Langenhuysen, 1851.

Haafner, Jacob. *Travels on Foot through the Island of Ceylon.* Translated from the Dutch. London: Sir Richard Phillips & Co., 1821.

Huysers, Ary. *Beknopte beschrijving der Oostindische établissementen* (Brief description of the East Indian settlements). 2d enl. ed. Amsterdam: Roos, 1792.

Koch, D. M. G. *Verantwoording: Een halve eeuw in Indonesië* (Rendering account: Half a century in Indonesia). 's-Gravenhage, Bandung: W. van Hoeve, 1956.

Maurik, Justus van. *Indrukken van een "Totok": Indische typen en schetsen* (Impressions of a newcomer: Indies types and sketches). Amsterdam: van Holkema & Warendorff, 1897.

Meijer, H. Chr. *Kind in tempo doeloe* (The child in bygone times). Wassenaar: Servire, 1969.

Meijer, H. Chr., and Willem Krols. *Wat wij in ons hart sloten* (What we locked up in our hearts). The Hague: Servire, 1962.

Money, J. W. B. *Java; or How to Manage a Colony, showing a Practical Solution of the Questions Now Affecting British India.* 2 vols. London: Hurst & Blackett, 1861.

Naber, Johanna W. A. *Onbetreden paden van ons koloniaal verleden 1816–1873. Naar nog onuitgegeven familiepapieren* (Untrod paths of our colonial past 1816–1873. Based upon unpublished family papers). Amsterdam: van Kampen & Zoon, 1938.

"Oudgast." *Onze Oost* (Our East). Amsterdam: J. A. Sleeswijk, 1897.

Stark, E. *Uit Indië, Egypte en het Heilige Land* (From the Indies, Egypt and the Holy Land). 2d ed. Amersfoort: Veen, 1913.

Stavorinus, J. S. *Voyage par le Cap de Bonne-Espérance à Batavia, à Bantam et au Bengale, en 1768, 69, 70 et 71* (Journey via the Cape of Good Hope to Batavia, Bantam and Bengal, in 1768, 69, 70 and 71). Translated from the Dutch by H. J. Jansen. Paris: Jansen, 1798.

Stockdale, John Joseph. *Sketches, Civil and Military, of the Island of Java.* London: S. Gosnell, 1812.

Strehler, Dr. *Bijzonderheden wegens Batavia en deszelfs omstreken: Uit het dagboek, gedurende twee reizen derwaarts in 1828–1830* (Particulars on Batavia and its environs: From the diary during two journeys there in 1828–1830). Translated from the German. Haarlem: Wed. A. Loosjes Pz., 1833.

Tavernier, Jean-Baptiste. *Recueil de plusieurs relations et traitez singuliers et curieux de J. B. Tavernier, qui n'ont point esté mis dans ses six premiers voyages* (Anthology of several accounts and treatises both singular and curious by J. B. Tavernier not included in his first six voyages). Paris: n.p., n.d.

Tavernier, Jean-Baptiste. *Travels in India.* Translated from the original French edition of 1767 by V. I. Ball. London: Macmillan, 1889.

Thorn, William. *Memoir of the Conquest of Java, with the Subsequent Operations of the British Forces in the Oriental Archipelago.* London: T. Egerton, 1815.

Thunberg, Charles Peter. *Travels in Europe, Africa and Asia Made between the Years 1770 and 1779.* Vol. 2. London: F. & C. Rivington, 1795.

Travers, Thomas Otto. *The Journal of Thomas Otto Travers 1813–1820.* Edited by John Bastin. Singapore: Government Printer, 1960.

Valentijn, François. *Oud en nieuw Oost-Indiën* (Old and New East Indies). Vols. 4, 5. Amsterdam: Dordrecht, 1726.

Ver Huell, Q. M. R. *Herinneringen van eene reis naar de Oost-Indiën* (Memoirs of a journey to the East Indies). 2 vols. Amsterdam: Zweesaardt, 1835.

Veth, B. *Het leven in Nederlandsch-Indië* (Life in the Netherlands Indies). 4th ed. Amsterdam: van Kampen & Zoon, n.d.

Warnsinck, J. C. M., ed. *Reisen van Nicolaus de Graaff gedaan naar alle gewesten des werelds, beginnende 1639 tot 1687 incluis* (Journeys of Nicolaus de Graaff to all quarters of the world, beginning in 1639 up until 1687 inclusive). 's-Gravenhage: M. Nijhoff, 1930.

Weitzel, A. W. P. *Batavia in 1858 of schetsen en beelden uit de hoofdstad* (Batavia in 1858, or sketches and pictures of the capital city). Gorinchem: Noorduijn, 1860.

Wit, Augusta de. *Java, Facts and Fancies.* London: Chapman & Hall, 1905.

Wormser, Carel Willem, ed. *Zoo leven wij in Indië* (How we live in the Indies). 3d ed. Deventer: van Hoeve, 1943.

Zeggelen, Marie van. *De Hollandsche vrouw in Indië* (The Dutchwoman in the Indies). 2d ed. Amsterdam: K. Groesbeek & Paul Nijhoff, n.d.

NOVELS AND SHORT STORIES

Brink, Jan ten. *Oost-Indische dames en heeren: Vier bijdragen tot de kennis van de zeden en usantiën der Europeesche maatschappij in Nederlandsch-Indië* (East Indian ladies and gentlemen: Four contributions to knowledge of the morals and manners of the European community in Netherlands India). Arnhem: D. A. Thieme, 1886.

Couperus, Louis. *The Hidden Force: A Story of Modern Java.* Translated by Alexander Teixeira de Mattos. London: Jonathon Cape, 1922.

Daum, P. A. *Goena-Goena, een geschiedenis van stille kracht* (Guna-Guna: A story of black magic). Amsterdam: Querido, 1964.

Daum, P. A. *Hoe hij Raad van Indië werd* (How he became councillor of the Indies). Samarang: Dorp and Co., 1888.

Daum, P. A. *Uit de suiker in de tabak* (From sugar to tobacco). Amsterdam: Salamander, 1962.

Daum, P. A. *"Ups" en "Downs" in het Indische leven* (Ups and downs in Indies life). 5th ed. Amsterdam: Contact, 1946.

Dermoût, Maria. *The Ten Thousand Things.* Translated by Hans Koningsberger. New York: Simon and Schuster, 1958.

Dermoût, Maria. *Yesterday.* Translated by Hans Koningsberger. New York: Simon and Schuster, 1959.

Divine, David. *The Daughter of the Pangaran.* Boston, Toronto: Little, Brown and Company, 1963.

Douwes Dekker, Eduard F. E. *Max Havelaar, of de koffieveilingen der Nederlandsche Handel-Maatschappij* (Max Havelaar, or the coffee auctions of the Netherlands Trading Company). 8th ed. Rotterdam: A. D. Donker, 1967.

Fabricius, Johan. *Halfbloed* (Half-Caste). 's-Gravenhage: H. P. Leopold, 1946.

Foore, Annie. See IJzerman-Junius, Françoise.

Hertog, A. den. *Vrouwen naar Jacatra* (Women bound for Jakarta). Leiden: Sijthoff, 1934.

Hoven, Thérèse. *In sarong en kabaai* (In Sarong and Kebaya). Amsterdam: L. J. Veen, 1892.

Hoven, Thérèse. *Nonnie en andere verhalen* (Nonnie and other tales). Tiel: Campagne en Zoon, n.d.

Hoven, Thérèse. *Vervreemd: Indische roman* (Estranged: Indies novel). Amersfoort: Valkhoff en Co., n.d.

IJzerman-Junius, Françoise. *Bogoriana* (World of Bogor). 3d ed. Haarlem: H. D. Tjeenk Willink en Zoon, 1908.

IJzerman-Junius, Françoise. *Indische huwelijken* (Indies marriages). 2d ed. Rotterdam: D. Bolle, 1895.

IJzerman-Junius, Françoise. *De van Sons, een verhaal uit Indië* (The van Sons, a story from the Indies). The Hague: Stemberg, 1881.

Katja-Mata. See Vanger-Frank, Marie C.

Kruseman, Mina. *Een huwelijk in Indië* (A marriage in the Indies). 's-Gravenhage: Nijhoff, 1873.

Maurits. See Daum, P. A.

Het meisje uit Indië: Een eerste keuze uit de duizend-en-een bijdragen voor Tong-Tong van "Sheherazaden uit oud-Indië" (The young Indies girl: a preliminary choice from the thousand and one contributions for Tong-Tong's "Sheherazades from the Indies of Olden Days"). The Hague: Uitgeverij Tong-Tong, 1966.

Melati van Java. See Sloot, N. Marie C.

Multatuli. See under Douwes Dekker, Eduard F. E.

Nieuwenhuys, Rob. *Vergeelde portretten uit een Indisch familiealbum* (Yellowed portraits from an Indies family album). 5th ed. Amsterdam: Salamander, 1963.

Nijs, E. Breton de. See Nieuwenhuys, Rob.

Norel, K. *Janmaats en sinjeuren* (John Tars and lords). Leiden: Sijthoff, 1941.

235

Robinson, Tjalie. *Piekerans van een straatslijper* (Reflections of a loafer). 4th ed. Bandung: N. V. Masa Baru, n.d.

Sloot, N. Marie C. *De familie van den Resident* (The resident's family). 3d ed. Schiedam: H. A. M. Roelants, n.d.

Sloot, N. Marie C. *Soerapati: historisch romantische schets uit de geschiedenis van Java* (Surapati: historical romance from the history of Java). 3d ed., 2 vols. Schiedam: Roelants, 1928.

Valette, G. *Baren en oudgasten: Indische schetsen* (Newcomers and oldtimers: Indies sketches). 's-Gravenhage: Stemberg, 1880.

Vanger-Frank, Marie C. *Een natuurlijk kind en andere Nederlandsch-Indische verhalen* (A natural child and other Netherlands Indies tales). Leiden: Noothaven van Goor, 1875.

Vrankrijker, A. C. J. de. *François Caron: Een carrière in het verre Oosten* (François Caron: A career in the Far East). Amsterdam: Elsevier, 1943.

Walraven, Willem. "De Clan" (The clan). *Orientatie,* Special Walraven Issue, no. 23–24 (August–September 1949): 30–41.

Walraven, Willem. "Op de grens" (On the borderlines). *Orientatie,* Special Walraven Issue, no. 23–24 (August–September 1949): 18–29.

PERSONAL AND FAMILY HISTORIES

Bloys van Treslong Prins, P. C. "Aanvullingen of 'De Gouverneurs-Generaal en Commissarissen-Generaal van Nederlandsch-Indië (1610–1888) door M. A. van Rhede van der Kloot" (Supplement, or "The governors-general and commissioners-general of the Netherlands Indies, 1610–1888, by M. A. van Rhede van der Kloot"). *De Nederlandsch Leeuw* 47(11):343–46 (November 1929).

Bloys van Treslong Prins, P. C. "Bio-genealogische studien III: Gerrit Willem Casimir van Motman en zijn nazaten" (Bio-genealogical studies III: G. W. C. van Motman and his descendants). *Ons Nageslacht* 6 (1):5–17 (April 1933).

Bloys van Treslong Prins, P. C. "Die Deutschen in Niederlandisch-Indien" (Germans in Netherlands India). *Mitteilungen der Deutschen Gesellschaft für Natur- und Völkerkunde Ostasiens* 39, D, 1937.

Bloys van Treslong Prins, P. C. *Genealogische en heraldische gedenkwaardigheden betreffende Europeanen op Java* (Genealogical and heraldic memorabilia on Europeans in Java). Vol. 1. Batavia: Albrecht, 1934.

Feith, P. R. and P. C. Bloys van Treslong Prins. *De bekende landheer van Tjampea, c.a. Willem Vincent Helvetius van Riemsdijk: Zijn naaste familie en zijne afstammelingen* (The well-known owner of Tjampea property W. V. H. van Riemsdijk: His closest relations and descendants). Batavia: Kolff, 1933.

Godée Molsbergen, E. C. *Jan van Riebeeck en zijn tijd: Een stuk zeventiende-eeuws Oost-Indië* (Jan van Riebeeck and his times: A piece of seventeenth-century East Indies). Amsterdam: van Kampen en Zoon, 1937.

Haan, F. de. "De laatste der Mardijkers" (The last of the Mardijkers). *Bijdragen tot de Taal-, Land- en Volkenkunde* 73 (1917):219–54.

Haan, F. de. "Personalia der periode van het Engelsch bestuur over Java 1811–1816" (Staff during the period of English rule on Java 1811–1816). *Bijdragen tot de Taal-, Land- en Volkenkunde* 92 (1935):477–669.

Haan, F. de. *Priangan: De Preanger-Regentschappen onder het Nederlandsch bestuur tot 1811* (Priangan: The Preanger regencies under Netherlands rule until 1811). Vol. 1, pt. 2, "Personalia" ("Staff"). Batavia: 's-Gravenhage, Kolff, Nijhoff, 1910.
De Indische Navorscher (The Indies inquirer) 1, no. 1, through 6, no. 3 (April 1934– March 1940).
Maignien, Edmond. *Abraham Patras, gouverneur-général des Indes Néerlandaises et sa famille* (Abraham Patras, governor-general of the Netherlands Indies and his family). Grenoble: Joseph Baratier, 1892.
De Nederlandsche Leeuw (The Netherlands Lion) 48 (1930): nos. 6, 9, 10.
Nieuw Nederlandsch biografisch woordenboek (New Netherlands biographical dictionary). 10 vols. Leiden: Sijthoff, 1911–37.
Rhede van der Kloot, M. A. van. *De Gouverneurs-Generaal en Commissarissen-Generaal van Nederlandsch-Indië 1610–1888* (The governors-general and commissioners-general of Netherlands India 1610–1888). 's-Gravenhage: Stockum en Zoon, 1891.
Stapel, Frederik Willem. *De Gouverneurs-Generaal van Nederlandsch-Indië in beeld en woord* (The governors-general of Netherlands India in pictures and text). The Hague: Stockum en Zoon, 1941.
Troostenburg de Bruijn, C. A. L. van. *Biographisch woordenboek van Oost-Indische predikanten* (Biographical dictionary of East Indies clergymen). Nijmegen: Milborn, 1893.
Wijnaendts van Resandt, Willem. *De gezaghebbers der Oost-Indische Compagnie op hare buitencomptoiren in Azië* (The administrators of the East Indies Company in the outer offices in Asia). Amsterdam: Liebaart, 1944.

OTHER BOOKS AND ARTICLES

Barnard, Lady Anne. *South Africa a Century Ago: Letters Written from the Cape of Good Hope (1797–1801)*. London: Smith, Elder and Co., 1901; reprinted by the Scholarly Press, St. Clair Shores, Michigan, 1972.
Barnouw, Adriaan J. *The Pageant of Netherlands' History*. London: Longmans, Green and Co., 1952.
Berg, N. P. van den. "Het toneel te Batavia in vroegeren tijd" (Theater in Batavia in earlier times). In *Uit de dagen der Compagnie, geschiedkundige schetsen* (From Company days: historical sketches), pp. 97–191. Haarlem: Tjeenk Willink en Zoon, 1904.
Blussé, Leonard. "Batavia, 1619–1740: The Rise and Fall of a Chinese Colonial Town." *Journal of Southeast Asian Studies* 12 (1):159–78 (March 1981).
Bois, J. P. I. du. *Vies des gouverneurs-généraux, avec l'abrégé de l'histoire des établissements hollandois aux Indes Orientales* (Lives of the governors-general, with a short history of the Dutch settlements in the East Indies). The Hague: de Hondt, 1763.
Bouman, Hendrik. *Meer licht over Kartini* (More Light on Kartini). Amsterdam: H. J. Paris, 1954.
Boxer, C. R. *The Dutch Seaborne Empire 1600–1800*. London: Hutchinson, 1965.
Boxer, C. R. "Ledger and Sword: Cornelis Speelman and the Growth of Dutch Power in Indonesia 1666–1684." *History Today* 8 (1958), no. 3.
Boxer, C. R. *The Portuguese Seaborne Empire 1415–1825*. New York: Alfred Knopf, 1969.

Boxer, C. R. *Race Relations in the Portuguese Colonial Empire 1415–1825*. Oxford: Clarendon Press, 1963.

Boxer, C. R., ed. *A True Description of the Mighty Kingdoms of Japan and Siam by François Caron and Joost Schouten*. Reprinted from the English edition of 1663. London: Argonaut Press, 1935.

Breuning, H. A. *Het voormalige Batavia: Een Hollandse stedestichting in de tropen, anno 1619* (Batavia of old: A Dutch town founded in the tropics, 1619). Amsterdam: Allert de Lange, 1954.

Brugmans, I. J. *Geschiedenis van het onderwijs in Nederlandsch-Indië* (History of education in Netherlands India). Groningen: J. B. Wolters, 1938.

Bruijn, Jaap R. "Between Batavia and the Cape: Shipping Patterns of the Dutch East Indies Company." *Journal of Southeast Asian Studies* 11 (21):251–65 (September 1980).

Bruijn, J. R. "De personeelsbehoefte van de VOC overzee en aan boord, bezien in Aziatisch en Nederlands perspectief" (Personnel requirements of the VOC overseas and on board ship, viewed from Asian and Dutch perspective). *Bijdragen en mededelingen betreffende de geschiedenis der Nederlanden* 91 (1): 218–48 (1976).

Butcher, John G. *The British in Malaya, 1880–1941: The Social History of a European Community in Colonial South-East Asia*. Oxford: Oxford University Press, 1979.

Castles, Lance. "The Ethnic Profile of Djakarta," *Indonesia* 3:153–204 (April 1967).

Clerkx, Lily. *Mensen in Deli: Een maatschappijbeeld uit de bellettrie* (Society in Deli: Portrait of a community from the belles lettres). Amsterdam: Amsterdam University Press, 1961.

Coolhaas, W. Ph. "Reael, Coen, De Carpentier en Specx." *Bijdragen tot de Taal-, Land- en Volkenkunde* 129 (2 & 3):269–76 (1973).

Coolhaas, W. Ph. "Zijn de Gouverneurs-Generaal van Imhoff en Mossel juist beoordeeld?" (Are governors-general van Imhoff and Mossel judged correctly?). *Bijdragen tot de Taal-, Land- en Volkenkunde* 114 (1) (1958):29–54.

Collis, Maurice. *Raffles*. London: Faber and Faber, 1966.

Crawfurd, John. *History of the Indian Archipelago*. Vol. 2. Edinburgh: Archibald Constable and Co., 1820.

Day, Clive. *The Policy and Administration of the Dutch in Java*. New York, London: Macmillan, 1904.

Deventer, Marinus L. van. *Geschiedenis der Nederlanders op Java* (History of the Dutch on Java). Vol. 2. Haarlem: Tjeenk Willink, 1887

Edwardes, Michael. *Bound to Exile: The Victorians in India*. London: Sidgwick and Jackson, 1969.

Furber, Holden. *Rival Empires of Trade in the Orient, 1600–1800*. Minneapolis: University of Minnesota Press, 1976.

Furnivall, John S. *Netherlands India: A Study of Plural Economy*. Cambridge: Cambridge University Press, 1944.

Graaff, E. A. van de. *De statistiek in Indonesië* (Statistics in Indonesia). 's-Gravenhage, Bandung: van Hoeve, 1955.

Graaf, J. H. de. *Geschiedenis van Indonesië* (History of Indonesia). 's-Gravenhage, Bandung: van Hoeve, 1949.

Goor, Jurrien van. *Jan Kompenie as Schoolmaster. Dutch Education in Ceylon 1690–1795*. Groningen: Wolters-Noordhoff, 1978.

Haan, F. de. *Oud Batavia: Gedenkboek* (Old Batavia: Commemorative volume). 2 vols. Batavia: Kolff, 1922.

Haan, J. C. de, ed. *Nederlanders over de zeeën: 350 jaar Nederlandsche koloniale geschiedenis* (Netherlanders overseas: 350 years of colonial history). 2d ed. Utrecht: W. de Haan, 1942.

Klaveren, J. J. van. *The Dutch Colonial System in the East Indies*. 2 vols. Rotterdam: Benedictus, 1953.

Klerck, E. S. de. *History of the Netherlands East Indies*. 2 vols. Rotterdam: W. L. and J. Brusse, 1938.

Knaap, G. "Europeans, Mestizos and Slaves: The Population of Colombo at the End of the Seventeenth Century." *Itinerario* 5 (2):84–101 (1981).

Koop, John Clement. *The Eurasian Population in Burma*. Cultural Report Series, no. 6. New Haven: Yale University Press, 1960.

Koopman-Smit, M. *Het paradijs der vrouwen: Tegenschrift op Veth's "Leven in Indië"* (The women's paradise: Rebuttal of Veth's "Life in the Indies"). 's-Gravenhage: Veenstra, 1900.

Kroef, Justus M. van der. "The Colonial Novel in Indonesia," *Comparative Literature* 10 (3):215–31 (Summer 1958).

Kroef, Justus M. van der. "The Indonesian City: Its Culture and Evolution," *Asia* 2 (8):563–79 (March 1953).

Kroef, Justus M. van der. "The Indonesian Eurasian and His Culture," *Phylon* 16 (4):448–62 (1955).

Krom, N. J. *Gouverneur-Generaal Gustaaf Willem van Imhoff* (Governor-General Gustaaf Willem van Imhoff). Amsterdam: van Kampen en Zoon, 1941.

Krom, N. J. "Het Leidsche weeshuis en de Oost-Indische Compagnie" (The Leiden orphanage and the East Indies Company). In *Leidsche jaarboekje 1936* (Leiden year book for 1936). Leiden: n.p., 1936.

Ledyard, Gari. *The Dutch Come to Korea*. Seoul: Royal Asiatic Society, 1971.

Lequin, F. "A New Approach to the History of the Dutch Expansion in Asia: The Personnel of the Dutch East India Company in the XVIIIth Century." *Journal of European Economic History* 8 (2):431–37 (Fall 1979).

Leur, J. C. van. *Indonesian Trade and Society: Essays in Asian Social and Economic History*. The Hague, Bandung: van Hoeve, 1955.

Loos-Haaxman, J. de. "Een portret van de landvoogd Adriaan Valckenier" (A portrait of Governor-General Adriaan Valckenier). *Bijdragen tot de Taal-, Land- en Volkenkunde* 112 (1956):267–70 and reproduction of the portrait.

Lubberhuizen-van Gelder, A. M. "Hendrik Veeckens, een ambtenaar van den ouden stempel" (Hendrik Veeckens, an official of the old school). *Cultureel Indië* 7 (1945): 89–106.

Lubberhuizen-van Gelder, A. M. "Onze voorouders op de Coromandelkust" (Our forefathers on the Coromandel coast). *Cultureel Indië* 3 (1941):201–16.

Lubberhuizen-van Gelder, A. M. "Een oude Indische inventaris" (An Old Indies inventory). *Cultureel Indië* 8 (1946): 211–20.

239

Mansvelt, W. M. F. "De positie der Indo-Europeanen" (The position of Indo-Europeans). *Koloniale Studien* 16 (1):290–311 (1932).

Marle, A. van. "De groep der Europeanen in Nederlands-Indië: Iets over ontstaan en groei" (The European group in the Netherlands Indies: Remarks on origins and growth). *Indonesië* 5 (2):77–121; (3):314–41; and (5):481–507 (1955).

Marsden, Peter. *The Wreck of the "Amsterdam."* New York: Stein and Day, 1975.

Masselman, George. *The Cradle of Colonialism.* New Haven: Yale University Press, 1963.

Meilink-Roelofsz, M. A. P. "De Europese expansie in Azië: Enkele beschouwingen naar annleiding van Holden Furbers *Rival Empires of Trade in the Orient, 1600–1800*" (European expansion in Asia: some introductory remarks to Holden Furber's *rival empires of trade in the orient, 1600–1800*). *Bijdragen tot de Taal-, Land- en Volkenkunde* 135 (1979):403–42.

Milone, Pauline D. "Indische Culture and Its Relationship to Urban Life." *Comparative Studies in Society and History* 9:407–26 (July 1967).

Milone, Pauline D. "Queen City of the East: The Metamorphosis of a Colonial Capital." Ph.D. dissertation, University of California, Berkeley, 1966.

Muller, Hendrik P. N. "De Europeesche samenleving" (The European community). In *Neerlands Indië*, edited by H. Colijn. 2:371–84. Amsterdam: Elsevier, 1912.

Nieuwenhuys, Rob. "Drie vertellers van het Indische leven" (Three raconteurs of Indies life). *Orientatie* 22:20–33 (July 1949).

Nieuwenhuys, Rob. *Oost-Indische spiegel: Wat Nederlandse schrijvers en dichters over Indonesië hebben geschreven vanaf de eerste jaren der Compagnie tot op heden* (East Indies mirror: What Dutch writers and poets have written about Indonesia from the first years of the Company until the present). Amsterdam: Querido, 1972.

Nieuwenhuys, Rob. "Over de Europese samenleving van 'tempo doeloe' 1870–1900" (On European society in 'the olden days' 1870–1900). *de Fakkel* 1 (1940/41):773–803.

Nieuwenhuys, Rob. *Tussen twee vaderlanden* (Between two fatherlands). Amsterdam: G. A. van Oorschot, 1959.

Petrus Blumberger, J. Th. *De Indo-Europeesche beweging in Nederlandsch-Indië* (The Indo-European movement in Netherlands India). Haarlem: Tjeenk Willink en Zoon, 1939.

Raffles, Thomas Stamford. *The History of Java.* 2d. ed. 2 vols. London: John Murray, 1830.

Reksonegoro, Kardinah. "Kartini—de feiten" (Kartini—the facts). *Bijdragen tot de Taal-, Land- en Volkenkunde* 122 (1966):283–87.

Resink, G. J. *Indonesia's History between the Myths: Essays in Legal History and Historical Theory.* The Hague: van Hoeve, 1968.

Ricklefs, M. C. *A History of Modern Indonesia, c. 1300 to the Present.* Bloomington: Indiana University Press, 1981.

Roo de la Faille, P. de. *Iets over Oud-Batavia* (On Old Batavia). Batavia: Kolff, 1919.

Skinner, G. W. "Change and Persistence in Chinese Culture Overseas: A Comparison of Thailand and Java," Parts 1 and 2. *Journal of the South Seas Society* 16 (1960):86–100.

Smail, John R. W. "On the Possibility of an Autonomous History of Modern Southeast Asia," *Journal of Southeast Asian History* 2 (2):72–102 (July 1961).

Soewondo-Soerasno, Nani. *Kedudukan wanita Indonesia dalam hukum dan masjarakat* (The position of Indonesian women in law and society). Djakarta: Timun Mas, 1955.

Spear, Percival. *The Nabobs: A Study of the Social Life of the English in Eighteenth-Century India.* London: Oxford University Press, 1963.

Stapel, F. W. "Cornelis Janszoon Speelman," *Cultureel Indië* 2 (1940):235–42.

Stapel, F. W. *Geschiedenis van Nederlandsch-Indië* (History of the Netherlands Indies). Amsterdam: J. M. Meulenhoff, 1930.

Steinmetz, C. "Culturele gegevens uit familiepapieren II: Dr. Franz Wilhelm Junghuhn (1809–1864)" (Cultural data from family papers II: Dr. Franz Wilhelm Junghuhn (1809–1864). *Cultureel Indië* 4 (1942):60–72, 173–82.

Steinmetz, C. "Culturele gegevens uit familiepapieren III: Van trouwen en sterven onder de Compagnie" (Cultural data from family papers III: On marrying and dying in company times). *Cultureel Indië* 4 (1942): 274–83, and 5 (1943):31–46.

Steinmetz, C. "Culturele gegevens uit familiepapieren IV: Zilvere gedenkborden" (Cultural data from family papers IV: Silver memorial trays). *Cultureel Indië* 5 (1943): 128–37.

Swaan-Koopman, C. *Vrouwen in Indië* (Women in the Indies). Amsterdam: H. J. Paris, 1932.

Taylor, Jean. "Educate the Javanese!" Translation from the Dutch of a memorial by Raden Adjeng Kartini. *Indonesia* 17:83–98 (May 1974).

Taylor, Jean. "Raden Adjeng Kartini." *Signs: Journal of Women in Culture and Society* 1 (3):639–61 (Spring 1976).

Terpstra, H. "Anthonij van Diemen." *Cultureel Indië* 2 (1940):163–68.

Terpstra, H. "Tropische levenskunst in de XVIIe eeuw" (Way of life in the tropics in the seventeenth century). *Cultureel Indië* 8 (1946):199–210.

Thomassen à Theussink van der Hoop, A. N. J. "Vergeelde portretten" (Yellowed portraits). *Bijdragen tot de Taal-, Land- en Volkenkunde* 114 (1958):121–32.

Toussaint, J. R. "Dutch Ladies Who Lived in Ceylon," *Journal of the Dutch Burgher Union of Ceylon* 29 (2):31–43 (October 1939).

Troostenburg de Bruijn, C. A. L. van. *De Hervormde Kerk in Nederlandsch Oost-Indië onder de Oost-Indische Compagnie (1602–1795)* (The Reformed Church in the Netherlands East Indies under the East Indian Company, 1602–1795). Arnhem: Tjeenk Willink, 1884.

Van der Veur, Paul W. "Cultural Aspects of the Eurasian in Indonesian Colonial Society," *Indonesia* 6:38–53 (October 1968).

Van der Veur, Paul W. *Education and Social Change in Colonial Indonesia.* Athens: Ohio University Century for International Studies, 1969.

Van der Veur, Paul W. "The Eurasians of Indonesia: A Problem and Challenge in Colonial History," *Journal of Southeast Asian History* 9 (2):191–207 (September 1968).

Vlekke, Bernard H. M. *Nusantara: A History of Indonesia.* rev. ed. The Hague, Bandung: van Hoeve, 1959.

Vreede-de Stuers, Cora. "Kartini: Feiten en ficties" (Kartini: Facts and Fancies). *Bijdragen tot de Taal-, Land- en Volkenkunde* 121 (1965):233–44.

Vries, J. W. de. "De Depokkers: Geschiedenis, sociale structuur en taalgebruik van een geisoleerde gemeenschap" (The Depok people: history, social structure and language usage of an isolated community). *Bijdragen tot de Taal-, Land- en Volkenkunde* 132 (1976):228–48.

Wall, V. I. van de. "Beschrijving van eenige werken van Raden Saleh" (Description of several works of Raden Saleh). *Cultureel Indië* 4 (1942):159–67.

Wall, V. I. van de. *Figuren en feiten uit den Compagniestijd* (People and facts from the Company period). Batavia: n.p., 1932).

Wall, V. I. van de. "Het oude koloniale meubel in het land van herkomst" (Old colonial furniture in its country of origin). *Cultureel Indië* 4 (1943):51–59.

Wall, V. I. van de. *Oude Hollandsche buitenplaatsen van Batavia* (Old Dutch country villas of Batavia). Deventer: van Hoeve, 1944).

Wall, V. I. van de. *Vrouwen uit den Compagnie's tijd* (Women in the Company period). Weltevreden, Amersfoort: Visser, 1928.

Wertheim, W. P. *Indonesian Society in Transition: A Study of Cultural Change*. 2d rev. ed. The Hague, Bandung: van Hoeve, 1959.

Wertheim, W. P. *Het sociologisch karakter van de Indo-Maatschappij* (The sociological character of the Eurasian community). Amsterdam: Vrij Nederland, 1947.

Zadoks-Josephus Jitta, Annie N. "Medische pioniers der V.O.C." (Medical pioneers of the VOC). *Cultureel Indië* 8 (1946):55–59.

Zeggelen, Marie van. *Kartini, een baanbreekster voor haar volk* (Kartini, a pioneer for her people). 3d ed. Amsterdam: J. M. Meulenhoff, 1947.

Index

Achin (variant of Indonesian Aceh), 177

Aelst, Maria van: as first lady, 35–36, mentioned, 66

Alting, Willem Arnold: appoints son-in-law as director-general, 34; family connections, 62, 63, 67, 83–84, 92, 186–87, 204; portrait of, 63, fig. 4; revokes Mossel's sumptuary laws, 68; revokes de Klerk's education reforms, 84–85; on van der Parra's Council, 93–94, 203

Asian women: soldiers' views on, 8, 15–17; in Jacatra compound, 15; marriage with Europeans, 16–17; banned from the Netherlands, 16, 30; status as brides, 17, 29, 122, 148; nationality of, 42, 156, 170; influence on segregation of elite women, 59, 168; status as mothers, 70, 122, 148; changing relations with Europeans, 108–9. *See also* Slaves

Bake, Adriana Johanna: family connections, 59–60, 62, 184

Bantam (variant of Indonesian Banten), 179

Baptism, 16; baptismal name, 17, 17*n40*

Batavia: established by Coen, 3, 10, 19; size, seventeenth century, 10, eighteenth century, 30, 30*n60*, 50, 52, 75–76, nineteenth century, 97, 102, 129–130; emergence of the Batavian, 19, 48–50; women forbidden to leave, 20; move to southern suburbs, 20, 52, 95; in poem of circumstance, 52

Batavia Castle, 5, 6; as seat of VOC power, 10, 19; worship in, 20; numbers of slaves in, 70; razed by Daendels, 95; mentioned, 22, 36

Batavia Church: records of, 7, 14; organization of, 20–24; as arena for display of status, 41; promotes Dutch language, 46–

47, 84. *See also* Clergy; Dutch Reformed Faith

Batavia elite: style of, 36–42; female costume, 37–42, 67, 97–99, 116; Cornelia van Beveren on, 39, 59, 102, 168, 172; childrearing practices, 45; country villas of, 52–56; Asian influence on, 54, 58, 60, 76, 168; at mid-eighteenth century, 78–79; viewed by British, 97–102; and by nineteenth century Dutch, 115–116; displaced from political power, 117–19, 120, 123

Batavia Town Hall: worship in, 20; second building, 64

Batavian Academy of Arts and Sciences: 85–87, 88, 90; renamed Batavia Literary Society, 105; during British interregnum, 106; mentioned, 161. *See also* Enlightenment

Bataviasche Courant (renamed *Javasche Courant*), 116, 125

Bataviasche Nouvelles, 81–82, 138

Baud, Jean-Chrétien: founds Delft Academy, 118; family connections, 126–27, 195

Benevolent Institution, 101, 105

Betel: adopted by Europeans, 41; as civility, 69; opposed by Olivia Raffles, 99; used by Johanna van IJsseldijk-Oland, 116

Betel box: as status symbol, 41, 139; in paintings, 40, fig. 2, 42, 62, 63, fig. 4; in sumptuary laws, 67

Beveren, Cornelia Johanna van: describes her wedding, 39; mentioned, 45

Blijver: defined, 134

Borneo (variant of Indonesian Kalimantan), 177

Both, Pieter: composition of his fleet, 11, 12; on women settlers, 12, 13*n26;* on concubinage, 15; mentioned, 13, 119

243

Brandes Girls' School, 83–84, 85

British interregnum: ruling caste compared with VOC elite, 96–97; attitudes toward Batavian European community, 97–98; attacks on Mestizo culture, 98–102; revival of Batavian Academy, 105, 106; scholarly interest in Indonesia, 106; impact on Javanese elite, 107–9; judgments of, 110; Dutch reactions to, 112; British as Indiesmen, 112–13

Brouwer, Hendrik: favors Eurasian colony, 14; in Japan, 57n13

Bruijn, Cornelis de: visits Batavia, 53–54; visits Bantam court, 110

Bupatis: at van der Parra's installation, 58–59; response to Dutch, 159–67; and *Regentenbond*, 163, 168

Burghers (also called Free Townsmen): 9–12; van der Lijn on, 9; as orphanage trustees, 26–27; repatriation rights limited, 29; in subsidiary settlements, 31. *See also* Private trade

Camphuys, Johannes: on education, 26; as patron of Portuguese church, 48; retires in Indies, 51; in Japan, 57n13; mentioned, 72

Caron, François: family history, 43–45; recalled for private trade, 44; mentioned, 54

Celebes, the (variant of Indonesian Sulawesi), 177

Ceylon (renamed Sri Langka), 178

Chastelein, Cornelis: country villa of, 53–54; family connections, 53–54; and descendants, 54n7, 76n52

Christian Asians: forbidden sexual relations with non-Christians, 16; in VOC schools, 24; obligation to learn Dutch, 24, 84; status of, 49, 76, 170; community of Depok, 54; prohibition of sale as slaves, 70n41; excluded from marine academy, 81; mentioned, 8, 19, 24

Clergy: 21–24; subordinate to VOC, 21; promote Malay language, 23; views of Asian lay workers, 46; sumptuary laws on, 69. *See also* Batavia Church; Dutch Reformed Faith

Cloon, Dirk van: as Eurasian governor-general, 5; mentioned, 72

Clubs, 129–30

Coen, Jan Pieterszoon: colonization policies of, 3, 9, 11; on soldiers, 7; and burghers, 9; attacks Jacatra, 10, 19; on Dutchwomen, 12; on Asian women, 12; husband of Eva Ment, 14, 35; Brouwer on, 14; on concubines, 15–16; succession to governor-generalship, 33, 33n1; promotes brother-in-law, 35–36; mentioned, 79

Colonization policies: of VOC directors, 3, 11, 12, 14–15, 24, 25–26, 28–30, 33–34, 45; of Coen, 3, 9, 11; of Brouwer, 14; of de Carpentier, 16; of Matelief, 24; on employment of locally born men, 25, 31, 85, 118–19; laws, 28–30; of van Imhoff, 79

Concubinage: practised by Dutch, 4; banned, 15–16; opposed by Candidius, 21; status of concubines, 70–71; status of concubine mothers, 70, 141–42, 147; concubines' sons excluded from marine academy, 81; and British, 112–13; viewed as cause of degeneracy, 135; as cultural mediators, 136, 147; costume, 147; in nineteenth century, 147–48; in Indies novel, 145–47 *passim*

Contract: VOC contracts for civilians, 6; for soldiers, 7, 9; for Dutchwomen, 12, 15; for clergy and lay workers, 22, 23; extension required on marriage, 29

Coop à Groen family, 104, 194

Costume: of Dutchwomen, 37–42, 62–64, 65, 97–98, 99, 101, 138, 142, 143, fig. 11; of Mardijker men, 47–48; of Augustijn Michiels, 61; of Adriana Bake, 62; and Alting's wife, 62, 63, fig. 4; of Mestizas, 66; in sumptuary laws, 67–68; European style promoted by British, 99, 101; and by Mevrouw de Eerens, 116; of mistresses, 147

Country villas: described, 52–56, 55, fig. 3, 61; as center of Mestizo culture, 75–76; mentioned, 20, 22, 51

Couperus family: Abraham, 95, 112n51; Petrus Theodorus, 103, 112, 193; Louis (novelist), 145, 147, 152

Coyett, Frederik Julius: owner of Gunung Sari, 54; family connections, 54, 56, 192

Craan family: Jacobus Johannes, 93–94, 120, 190, 205–6; Catharina Margaretha, 95, 120, 188, 190, 195

Cranssen, Willem Jacob: family connections, 103, 112, 193; member of Benevolent Institution, 105; mentioned, 104, 112

COMPOSED BY PIED TYPER, LINCOLN, NEBRASKA
MANUFACTURED BY THOMSON-SHORE, INC., DEXTER, MICHIGAN
TEXT IS SET IN TIMES ROMAN, DISPLAY LINES IN WEISS

Library of Congress Cataloging in Publication Data
Taylor, Jean Gelman, 1944–
The social world of Batavia.
Bibliography: pp. 229–242.
Includes index.
1. Jakarta (Indonesia)—Social conditions. 2. Elite
(Social sciences)—Indonesia—Jakarta—History.
3. Netherlands—Colonies—Asia, Southeastern—History.
I. Title.
HN710.J23T39   1983   306'.09598'2   83–47772
ISBN 0–299–09470–7